T0331013

PROJECT SCOPE MANAGEMENT

A Practical Guide to Requirements
for Engineering, Product, Construction,
IT and Enterprise Projects

Best Practices and Advances in Program Management Series

Series Editor
Ginger Levin

PROJECT SCOPE MANAGEMENT

A Practical Guide to Requirements
for Engineering, Product, Construction,
IT and Enterprise Projects

Jamal Moustafaev, MBA, PMP

CRC Press
Taylor & Francis Group
Boca Raton   London   New York

CRC Press is an imprint of the
Taylor & Francis Group, an **Informa** business
AN AUERBACH BOOK

CRC Press
Taylor & Francis Group
6000 Broken Sound Parkway NW, Suite 300
Boca Raton, FL 33487-2742

Printed on acid-free paper
Version Date: 20141006

International Standard Book Number-13: 978-1-4822-5948-3 (Hardback)

Library of Congress Cataloging-in-Publication Data

Moustafaev, Jamal, 1973-
   Project scope management : a practical guide to requirements for engineering, product, construction, IT and enterprise projects / Jamal Moustafaev.
      pages cm. -- (Best practices and advances in program management series)
   Includes bibliographical references and index.
   ISBN 978-1-4822-5948-3 (hardcover : alk. paper) 1. Project management. 2. Planning.
   I. Title.

   HD69.P75M693 2015
   658.4'04--dc23   2014039472

Visit the Taylor & Francis Web site at
http://www.taylorandfrancis.com

and the CRC Press Web site at
http://www.crcpress.com

To my son Shamil, whose arrival in this world midway through the creation of this book has changed my perspective on so many things…

Contents

Foreword

One of my favorite quotes attributed to Yogi Berra, but adopted and modified by many other authors, reads as follows:

"If you don't know where you are going, you'll probably end up some place else."

This is the essential challenge of every project. Let me repeat that: *every project,* no matter the project type or domain. In short, for any type of project to have any realistic chance of success at arriving at a desired outcome, there must be a generally accepted set of goals and objectives. The goals will be represented by broad statements of aims or results that are sought by the sponsoring organization, statements that are more specific than mission or purpose,* but less specific than objectives. Objectives, on the other hand, are represented by predetermined results toward which the project's effort will be directed.[†]

But herein lies the difficulty. Just exactly what are the results that are expected? The project management theorists will have it that the answer is a thorough examination, almost prosecution of the project's stakeholders to elicit their exact requirements, before even starting the project. This would be followed by, or at least implied by, "Speak

---

* Wideman, *Comparative Glossary of Terms,* vol. 5.5.
[†] Ibid.

now or forever hold your peace!" The practical reality, of course, is entirely different. A woman does not go into a clothing store and give the salesperson an exact set of "requirements" to achieve the general impression she wishes to accomplish. Rather, she will search a number of racks, even search in a number of stores, before alighting on what appears to fit her expectations most nearly. And even then, there is the question of whether the chosen garment actually achieves the desired effect.

And so it is with projects, and certainly for first-time projects. You cannot expect project sponsors and associated stakeholders to spell out their exact requirements to the level of detail necessary to be able to produce the final product. Back to the woman in the clothing store: Her approach is, "I'll know it when I see it!" And so it is with real projects, any sort of projects, including large engineering projects of any kind. There has to be a period of development in which ideas are tested in real-time and the necessary decisions are taken to proceed with the next steps. In fact, projects are all about progressive decision making in the development and production of the desired end product. Or in simpler words: "Uncover the details as the work progresses!"

Perhaps because this reality flies in the face of idealistic theory, there has been a dearth of books on the market dedicated to product scope management and the art of gathering requirements. This includes for all types of projects and converting them to practical *and desired* reality.

Hence, Jamal's latest book is designed to tackle this essential area of managing a project. "Hot" topics include such items as

- How to find stakeholders, customers, and users who can provide you with requirements in the first place
- How to draw forth high-level scope requirements on multidisciplinary, engineering, product development, and IT projects
- How to define detailed requirements on such multidisciplinary projects
- Best practices of documenting requirements on software development and IT projects
- Similarly, on engineering and product development projects and multidisciplinary projects

- How to write project charters and what their role is in the scope management process
- How to control project scope, especially in the end game, and how to troubleshoot scope problems

In this book, author Jamal Moustafaev illustrates his thoughts and experiences with a large number of high-profile, well-documented projects, citing a multitude of fascinating historical facts and examples analyzed from the point of view of project scope management. The book unites the best practices of scope management from the fields of traditional project management, information technology, software development, engineering, product development, architecture, construction, and multidisciplinary projects. It is based on the most advanced and popular works by prominent authors and contains the latest advances in project scope management. It also concentrates on the hands-on practicality of tools and techniques rather than focusing on their academic prominence.

Best of all, Jamal's book is easy to read and uses an informal, non-academic language to explain all the key points.

R. Max Wideman, P. Eng.
FCSCE, FEIC, FICE, FPMI
Vancouver, British Columbia

Preface

Why a Book on Scope Management?

The readers of my previous book, *Delivering Exceptional Project Results: A Practical Guide to Project Selection, Scoping, Estimation and Management*, know that I have already tried to highlight and, it is hoped, managed to shed some light on some of the problems of scope definition and management. I am referring to the fact that business requirements elicitation (i.e., the initial phase of product scope definition) is underdeveloped in today's project management science with the exception of the IT and software development sectors, where scope definition (aka business analysis) is relatively advanced but excluded from the project manager's domain of responsibilities.

As a result, most industries have a very prominent knowledge gap in project scope planning, a gap that starts sometime after the Project Charter has been completed and approved and ends somewhere around the point when the work commences based on the detailed blueprints, technical drawings, and bills of materials.

And yet, scope definition remains the key ingredient in the success of any project. After all, as one of my clients used to say, "If one does not understand completely what he or she is going to build, what is the point of engaging in scheduling or budgeting?" Later in this book, we show that a big portion of our project failures are rooted in our inability to elicit, analyze, and properly document project requirements.

Key Features of This Book

Contents

We have decided not to reinvent the wheel and attempt the creation of a brand-new scope management process, especially considering the fact that all of the said processes have already been defined by the traditional school of project management. Having said that, if any readers prefer to adhere to some other methodology, I am still convinced that the book will be of significant value to them, but they will probably have to read the chapters in some other sequence, different from the one presented in this book.

In this book, we start by discussing how to collect project requirements and then move to defining scope, followed by the creation of the work breakdown structures. Finally, we examine the verification and control of the scope. However, most of the book—approximately 70%—is dedicated to collecting requirements and defining product and project scope inasmuch as they represent the bulk of the project scope management work undertaken on any project regardless of the industry or nature of the work involved. Furthermore, the focus is exclusively on practical and sensible tools and techniques rather than academic theories that work great on paper but unfortunately cannot be applied in real life.

Real-Life Project Case Studies

What is attempted in this book is taking five completely different projects, including

- "CRM System Implementation" at a financial institution (multidisciplinary)
- "Mobile Number Portability" at a wireless provider (multidisciplinary)
- "Port Upgrade" container terminal upgrade by a port authority (engineering/construction/multidisciplinary)
- "Energy Efficient House" design and construction (engineering/product/construction) by a product company
- "Airport Check-In Kiosk Software" design and development (software development) by a software product company

and tracing their development from a project scope management perspective from the very initiation of the project to the end of the execution and control phases. In the course of this book, we create project charters, high-level scope, detailed requirements specifications, requirements management plans, traceability matrices, and a work breakdown structure for the projects selected.

Why These Case Studies Specifically?

One of the major reasons for this particular selection is the inherent differences between the ways the requirements are captured in different industries; even the process itself has different names in different domains. In IT and software development it is called "business analysis," whereas in engineering and product development we refer to it as "conceptual design." But most important, with the increase in the size and complexity of the projects in modern organizations, especially the functional siloed ones, we are now encountering a completely new breed of ventures: projects that cannot be classified as purely technical or purely engineering. These are the ventures that involve multiple departments of the company and include marketing, sales, product, engineering, training, IT, customer relations, public relations, and many other groups of requirements.

Let us consider several examples. Into what category of projects does the deployment of an ERP system fall? Is it just an information technology initiative that should be handled exclusively by IT department employees? Many companies made that mistake only to discover later that because this project involves pretty much every division in the organization, all the requirements of each department need to be captured and properly implemented for the project to succeed.

Here is another example that we discuss in detail later in the book: the "Port Upgrade," the construction of a container terminal for a port authority. Is it "just" a construction project that can be outsourced to a construction vendor? And what is the value of a fully built container terminal without proper marketing, without roads and railroads leading to it, and without proper security systems and procedures, just to name a few scope components?

This group of projects presents the most experienced project managers with a multitude of questions that are impossible to answer quickly and easily. Here are some of them:

- How should the requirements be captured?
- What methodology should be used in capturing, analyzing, and documenting these requirements?
- As a project manager, am I responsible just for my part of the scope (e.g., install the ERP system or build the terminal) or for the success of the overall project?
- Should the project manager employ the engineering or architectural standards of scope definition?
- How should the inappropriateness of the above-mentioned approaches be addressed for documenting IT or marketing requirements and vice versa?
- Should each department write its own separate scope document, or is the project manager responsible for capturing all the requirements in one place?
- In that case, is there a chance of dependencies between different scope elements that will most likely be overlooked if the requirements are captured in different documents written in different technical "languages"?

Answers to these difficult questions are discussed in depth in this book. And to reflect the real-world project diversity properly, the selection of the project case studies for this book is supposed to reflect the variety of project categories that we encounter in the world today.

Please note that all these case studies are based on real-life projects, albeit somewhat altered either to protect the identities of the clients or to eliminate unnecessary complexity or detail, where I acted either as a hands-on project manager or a process improvement consultant. Thus, please keep in mind that none of the documents included in this book is completely perfect from the project management point of view. And although some of them have undergone technical team inspections, customer walk-throughs, and peer reviews, it is very likely that experienced project managers, especially the ones who worked on similar projects in the past, will discover certain discrepancies, irregularities, mistakes, and missing requirements.

The purpose behind this book is not to demonstrate perfect and completely faultless artifacts of scope documentation but to fill that apparent void in the tools, techniques, and methodologies in the field of project scope management and to try to come up with a universal approach to scope definition by attempting to pick the best practices of software development, engineering, construction, and several other fields by blending them and making them available to all industries.

Also, as it became quite popular with the readers of my previous book, each chapter starts with a fascinating historical case study where we analyze either interesting historical facts or very famous inventions, such as the Viking ship, the katana sword, the composite bow, the Burj Al Arab, and so on, from the project scope management perspective.

Who Is This Book For?

This book is designed for several groups of people. First, this book is for the project managers, either officially designated or just those who have been tapped on the shoulder by management and told to "handle this little project" in addition to their day-to-day duties, working at large multidepartmental organizations who need to handle complex projects involving marketing, IT, product development, human resources, training, and other divisions, to name just a few.

The second group that I had in mind is the engineers, architects, and product managers who all had scope definition expertise for at least several centuries but may benefit from (1) familiarizing themselves with the project management perspective on scope management and (2) learning some fresh new ideas from other fields, especially from software development.

It is hoped that functional managers and technical specialists from all areas—marketing, human resources, information technology, engineering, finance, accounting, and so on—will also find this book useful inasmuch as they are getting more and more involved in larger multidisciplinary interdepartmental projects.

Last but definitely not least, it is for the people in the IT sector. Despite the fact that they already have the luxury of having access to the business and systems analysis domains, they are encountering the issue of managing what is being perceived as an IT project but in reality has multiple impacts on several or even all departments of the organization. If one thinks about this topic a bit, one may realize that there is no such thing as a pure information technology project anymore. Even a replacement of a server may and probably will affect several groups of users outside the information technology division whose needs will have to be considered during the project implementation.

Book Overview

The book keeps to the traditional approach to project management with the following phases:

- Collect requirements
- Define scope
- Create work breakdown structures
- Verify scope
- Control scope

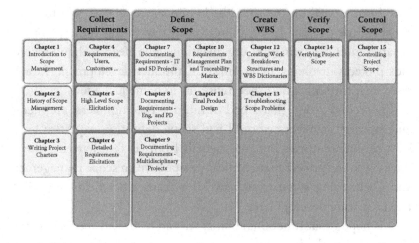

Collect Requirements		Define Scope		Create WBS	Verify Scope	Control Scope
Chapter 1 Introduction to Scope Management	Chapter 4 Requirements, Users, Customers ...	Chapter 7 Documenting Requirements - IT and SD Projects	Chapter 10 Requirements Management Plan and Traceability Matrix	Chapter 12 Creating Work Breakdown Structures and WBS Dictionaries	Chapter 14 Verifying Project Scope	Chapter 15 Controlling Project Scope
Chapter 2 History of Scope Management	Chapter 5 High Level Scope Elicitation	Chapter 8 Documenting Requirements - Eng, and PD Projects	Chapter 11 Final Product Design	Chapter 13 Troubleshooting Scope Problems		
Chapter 3 Writing Project Charters	Chapter 6 Detailed Requirements Elicitation	Chapter 9 Documenting Requirements - Multidisciplinary Projects				

Chapter 1 describes the current challenges faced by project managers in various industries with respect to the scope definition. It also provides the reader with the assessment of the current state of the projects, the root causes of our failures, and the significant impact of the requirements on overall project success.

Before we delve into the detailed analysis of project scope management, in Chapter 2 we talk about the history of design throughout the ages by examining the Egyptian pyramids, the Colosseum, composite bow, Viking longship, and several other key milestones in the course of human history.

Later, in Chapter 3 we examine the creation of the project charters, as they are the main input into the first stages of the project scope management process. It should be noted, however, that the first high-level scope of the project should be outlined in the business case document that is supposed to justify the project idea to the executives of the company. But because writing the business cases belongs to the project portfolio management domain, it is omitted from the scope of this book.

Moreover, the chapter is supported by five complete project charter samples, including the "CRM System Implementation" at a financial company, "Mobile Number Portability" at a wireless provider, "Port Upgrade" at port authority terminal, "Energy Efficient House" design and construction, and the "Airport Check-In Kiosk Software" design and development.

Chapter 4 discusses different requirements types and taxonomies as well as various categories of users, customers, and ways of identifying them. Chapter 5 delves into high-level requirements elicitation by discussing various requirements gathering techniques, including interviews, problem reports, and brainstorming, to name a few.

Chapter 6 continues the scope elicitation theme by going deeper into detailed scope definition. Chapters 7 through 9 discuss the best practices of requirements documentation in IT and software development, engineering, and multidisciplinary projects, respectively. Chapters 7 to 9 also have requirements specifications documents for each of the five projects mentioned earlier (see Taylor & Francis Group/CRC Press website http://www.crcpress.com/product/isbn/9781482259483 for all the supplementary documents for the book).

Chapter 10 focuses on writing the requirements management plan (RMP) and traceability matrix (RTM); once more, this chapter includes five sample documents for each of the projects mentioned earlier (see Taylor & Francis Group/CRC Press website http://www.crcpress.com/product/isbn/9781482259483 for all the supplementary documents for the book).

Chapter 11 discusses several final product design techniques that are borrowed mainly from the engineering and product design domains. Chapter 12 analyzes the art and science of creating the work breakdown structures and ventures into the estimation domain of project management by demonstrating several useful and practical techniques of assessing project resource requirements and schedules. Chapter 12 has one sample WBS developed for the "Mobile Number Portability" project (see Taylor & Francis Group/CRC Press website http://www.crcpress.com/product/isbn/9781482259483 for all the supplementary documents for the book).

Chapter 13 is dedicated to the topic of troubleshooting scope-related problems and how to deal with them in an efficient and practical way. Chapter 14 discusses various scope verification topics, including customer walk-through, technical team inspections, and peer reviews. Finally, Chapter 15 deals with scope control and management in the Execution stage of the project.

Good luck on your projects and enjoy the book!

Jamal Moustafaev
Burnaby, British Columbia

About the Author

Jamal Moustafaev, MBA, PMP, president and founder of Thinktank Consulting, is an internationally acclaimed expert in the areas of project/portfolio management, project scoping, process improvement, and corporate training. He has completed projects for private sector companies and government organizations in the United States, Canada, Europe, Asia, and the Middle East, including the US Department of Defense (USA), Siemens (Germany), Petronas Oil (Malaysia), and TeliaSonera (Sweden), to name a few.

Moustafaev is a certified Project Management Professional (PMP®). He holds an MBA in finance and a BBA (finance and management science) from Simon Fraser University. In addition to teaching a highly acclaimed Project Management Essentials course at the British Columbia Institute of Technology (Vancouver, Canada), Moustafaev also offers several project and portfolio management corporate seminars through his company:

- Practical Portfolio Management—Selecting and Managing the Right Projects
- Successful Hands-On Management of IT and Software Projects

- Successful Hands-On Management of Modern-Day Projects
- Project Scope Management

Jamal Moustafaev may be contacted at
Thinktank Consulting Inc.
E-mail – info@thinktankconsulting.ca
Website – www.thinktankconsulting.ca

1

INTRODUCTION TO
SCOPE MANAGEMENT

Who? What? Why?

Historical Perspective: The Rusted Staple Story

Abwehr, the German military intelligence organization was created in 1921 as a part of the Ministry of Defense. It remained a small and consequently not very important part of the Wehrmacht until January 1, 1935 when it was taken over by the soon-to-be Admiral Wilhelm Canaris (see Figure 1.1).

In a fairly short period of time Canaris was able to reorganize his agency into one of the most efficient intelligence-gathering organizations in the world. Abwehr's activities spanned the entire world including the United States, Canada, Africa, and Europe as well as England and Russia.

With the opening of the Eastern Front, Abwehr was tasked with establishing Abwehr schools in the occupied territories of Poland, the Baltic states, and the western parts of the Soviet Union. These organizations were responsible for recruitment, training, and deployment of commando-style agents whose primary purpose was reconnaissance and sabotage behind enemy lines.

The aforementioned recruits were typically handpicked by the Abwehr officers from among millions of Soviet POWs who were captured in the first several months of the invasion. Some of them were convinced to enlist in the intelligence schools because they could no longer bear the horrible living conditions in the German POW camps, whereas others did this for ideological reasons, not the least of which was hatred of Stalin's tyrannical regime in Russia.

Figure 1.1   Admiral Wilhelm Canaris.

All the "students" went through an extensive training that included hand-to-hand combat, target practice, interrogation and intelligence-gathering techniques, as well as radio operations, to name a few. Afterward, the graduates were supplied with absolutely the best documentation provided by Abwehr's Department 1-G responsible for false documents, photos, inks, passports, and chemicals. It is important to note that German technology in producing counterfeit documents was probably the best in the world at the time. After all, they mastered the production of British pounds and US dollars that perplexed the most experienced experts on either side of the Atlantic.

Yet, despite the first several months of successful infiltrations, the agents dropped behind the enemy lines started failing one after another; some were shot while resisting arrest, some were jailed, and a certain percentage of them were recruited to work as double agents, thus supplying the Abwehr headquarters with false information.

It took the Germans several years to discover the root cause of their problem. It turned out that the documentation itself, as far as images, stamps, and fonts, was perfect. The problem lay in a couple of simple staples that were used to fasten the pages of the document together! German industry was producing these staples from stainless steel. Thus, they were very resistant to the rusting process, whereas the Soviets manufactured their staples from the cheapest iron wires available, thus causing them to be covered in rust in a matter of weeks if not days!

Therefore, even the most uneducated Soviet recruits, who sometimes couldn't even read, were able to determine whether the man standing in front of them was a spy or a genuine soldier of the Red Army. The algorithm was pretty simple: If you can see rust stains on the pages of the document, it is the real deal, and if the staples are clean and shiny, you have an enemy agent standing in front of you.

Examined through a project management lens, this story highlights one of the most interesting and enigmatic areas of project delivery: project scope management, or to be even more accurate, the scope definition domain. The product scope for the counterfeit documentation produced by the technical experts at Abwehr consisted of several features, including, but not limited to, proper paper with correct watermarks, appropriate photos, and correct fonts and inks; however, it failed to incorporate a feature requiring the staples to be made from low-grade steel that would rust in a matter of days.

Just as in many other software development, IT, architecture, or engineering endeavors, a simple omission of just one of these scope components led to the failure of the entire project.

Why Write a Book about Project Scope Management?

Current State of Project Scope Management

The field of project scope management seems to be one of the most neglected domains in project management. Until recently, most of the project management textbooks stated something to the effect of, "Once the project manager gets the product scope definition from the technical experts, she can embark on the creation of the project work breakdown structure (WBS) with the assistance of her team."

How exactly this product scope definition is arrived at and what steps should be undertaken to get from the point when the customer walks into the room and states that she needs a custom desk for her office to the point in time where both the blueprints and the bill of materials for said desk are finalized remained unclear.

Interestingly enough, the information technology and software development industries do have a framework called business analysis, or systems analysis, or requirements engineering that was specifically designed to fill this void in the field of project management. In the IT field, the tasks of gathering business requirements and breaking them down into high-level features and functional and nonfunctional requirements typically fall under the responsibility of the business analysts.

In architecture, engineering, and product development, the tasks of eliciting product scope fell into the laps of engineers, architects, and designers who later supplied the project manager with the product scope so that he could build a work breakdown structure, network diagram, and the like.

Key Problems with Scope

An observation of project management practices in various industries confirms that in many instances scope management in general and scope definition in particular tend to be viewed as exclusive technical areas, which leads to several very legitimate questions frequently asked by many of my colleagues:

- If the project manager is to lead the project, should he also lead the product definition stage?
- If scope size and complexity have a direct impact on project timing and budget, shouldn't the project manager be aware— at least at a high level—of how the technical team arrived at the current scope in order to be able to make trade-off decisions?
- Our engineers (designers, developers, architects, etc.) are very good at design but not very skilled at interacting with customers and extracting the requirements from them. What should we do in this scenario?

Finally, and most importantly, what about enterprise or multidisciplinary projects? With the size and complexity of projects growing, it is not unusual now that the project scope encompasses the entire organization. Let us look at a couple of examples from different industries.

Note: These are the two of the five projects we analyze in detail and create project scope management documentation for throughout this book.

Port Upgrade: Container Terminal Construction Project The first one is, as it was initially labeled by the senior executives, the "construction of the new container terminal" project. The logic at the top of the port authority literally was, "Because this is a construction project, there is no need to worry on our end; we will just outsource the construction part to the contractor."

But a very quick analysis discovered the following situation (see Figure 1.2). The organization consisted of multiple departments, including real estate, public relations, legal, marketing, planning, engineering, IT, logistics, and security divisions, to name just a few. It turned out that each one of these departments had its own portion to contribute to the overall larger scope of the project. In other words, the real estate department had to purchase the land required for construction. They had to perform this task in close collaboration with the legal department that made sure no local laws or bylaws were broken. The PR department was responsible for working with federal, state, and municipal governments to communicate the plans and the progress of the project and to ensure that their interests were considered in the project.

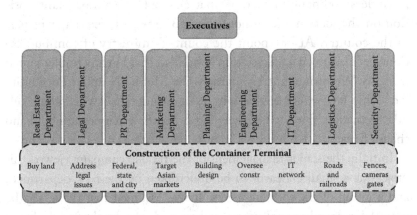

Figure 1.2 Port upgrade project.

Furthermore, the marketing department representatives had to start their "cheerleading" dances for their Asian partners in order to promote the yet-to-be-built port facility. In the meantime, the planning division had to oversee the design of the new facility and pass it over to the engineering department, which would be responsible for finding the contractor and monitoring him during the execution stage. At some later point, the IT specialists were supposed to set up the entire network in the new building including hardware and software. And finally, the security people had to ensure that the new facility conformed to the federal government's security standards.

So, here is the key question: Is this really just a construction project? And inasmuch as it obviously is not, what techniques, standards, and methodologies should be used in capturing the scope? Should the project manager utilize the engineering or architectural standards? But they are not very suitable for documenting the IT or marketing requirements. Or should each department write its own separate scope document? But in that case is there a chance of dependencies between different scope elements that will most likely be overlooked if the requirements are captured in different documents and are written in different "languages"? For example, is it possible (let us consider the most primitive example for simplicity's sake) that the server room designed by the architects will be of inadequate size or design for the needs of the information technology people?

Wireless Company: Mobile Number Portability Project   This story involves a wireless company in Europe that enjoyed a very dominant position on the local market (more than 53%) with three major players in the country. At one point the country's ministry of communications decided to enact legislation similar to that already implemented in many Western countries, namely the Mobile Number Portability Act. This law would enable wireless customers to switch their cellular providers freely while keeping both their phone numbers and the prefixes.

Initially the senior management of the mobile company viewed this project as a small endeavor to be undertaken by their IT department and a group of network engineers. It was assumed that there may be a need for an additional server or two and some tinkering with the call-processing software. However, a quick guided brainstorming of the project scope produced a multitude of questions. Here are some of them:

- With this new law, switching mobile providers will become very easy. Should our marketing team prepare for the "marketing war" that would most surely start as soon as this law goes into effect?
- There probably will be a significant increase in the number of calls to the customer service centers. Should we increase the number of attendants in these centers?
- Will there be any impacts on the value-added services our company provides?
- Should we create new curriculum and conduct training for sales, marketing, and call-center people, to name just a few departments?
- Should our legal agreements with customers be revised?

The scope of the project suddenly "exploded" (see Figure 1.3) with the appreciation of the fact that, from that point on, the entire company had to be involved in the project.

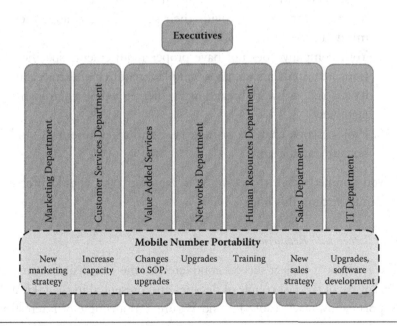

Figure 1.3 Mobile number portability project.

Does This Sound Like Your Life?

Let us start this section of the chapter with a simple quiz. Examine the 10 signs that the organization has poor project scope management techniques and try to determine how many of them are applicable to the organization for which you are currently working:

1. Even the high-level project goals are never clearly defined.
2. Customers are too busy to participate in the process of requirements elicitation.
3. A lot of people who are not actual customers or users speak and provide requirements on the customers'/users' behalf.
4. Product scope exists in the heads of "experts" (business or technical) and is never written down.
5. All the product features are, according to customers—whether real or surrogate—equally important.
6. Technical team members discover missing or ambiguous information in the documents and they have to guess.
7. Technical team members and customers frequently focus on what the product should look like, and its functionality is ignored.
8. Customers either do not sign off on the requirements or design documents or provide their sign-off and change their minds all the time.
9. Your company does not have proper requirements specifications, requirements management plan, requirements traceability matrix, and work breakdown structure templates, to name just a few.
10. Project scope changes or increases, and time, resources, and budget stay the same.

If you counted more than five "Yes" answers, you should probably continue reading this book.

Why Bother with Requirements?

The analysis of project success conducted by the Standish Group over the course of the last couple of decades and presented in the CHAOS Reports* shows (see Table 1.1 and Figure 1.4) a couple of interesting

---

* Standish Group. *CHAOS Reports* 1994–2009.

Table 1.1   CHAOS Report 1994–2009

	1994 (%)	1996 (%)	1998 (%)	2000 (%)	2002 (%)	2004 (%)	2006 (%)	2009 (%)
Successful	16	27	26	28	34	29	35	32
Challenged	53	33	46	49	51	53	46	44
Failed	31	40	28	23	15	18	19	24

trends. Before we examine these trends, it is worthwhile to note in the context of these studies that project success/failure has been defined in the following manner:

- Successful project: project that was delivered on time and on budget and met all of the customer requirements
- Challenged project: a project that was significantly late or overbudget:
  - Cost overruns of less than 20%—on 46% of the projects
  - Cost overruns of more than 20%—on 54% of the projects
- Failed project: project was cancelled due to severe budget overruns, lateness, or failure to deliver expected results

The examination of the table suggests several interesting observations:

- The rate of successful projects has been increasing almost steadily over the past 15 years, save for a disappointing dip in 2009.
- Failed projects have been decreasing in proportion (again a bit erratically) with a couple of discouraging upticks in 2006 and 2009 (the most recent measurements).

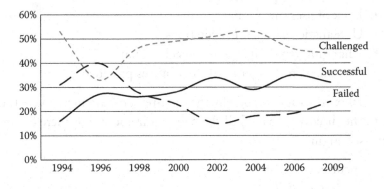

Figure 1.4   CHAOS Report 1994–2009.

- Challenged projects on the other hand have been all over the place between the years of 1994 and 2009, with the highest reading being at 53% in 1994 and 2004 and the lowest at 33% in 1996.

What conclusions can we draw from these statistics? Well, for one, we are still a long way from perfection. Project performance has been decreasing lately and has not improved significantly over the past decades. If this were a final exam and a student managed to provide full answers to 32% of the questions, failed to answer 24% of the problems, and finished only half of each of the remaining 44%, his mark might be calculated as follows:

Final mark in 2009 = 1 × 32% + 0 × 24% + 0.5 × 44% = 54

For comparison his final mark in 1994 would have been:

Final mark in 1994 = 1 × 16% + 0 × 31% + 0.5 × 53% = 42.5

In other words we managed to improve from a failing mark of F to probably D−. Considering the vast efforts invested in the development and the spread of the project management methodologies, these are very disappointing results, especially once we learn that these dry "failure" and "challenge" percentages amount to approximately $55 billion in wasted resources!

If we drill into the root cause of such poor performance, we quickly determine that according to the Standish Group five of the eight top reasons why projects fail are related to requirements. These are

- Incomplete requirements
- Lack of user involvement
- Unrealistic customer expectations
- Changing requirements and specifications
- Customers no longer need the features provided

Further investigation of why the requirements are incomplete leads us to the discovery that of all the bad requirements out there on projects (see Figure 1.5):

- Incorrect fact: 49%
- Omission: 29%

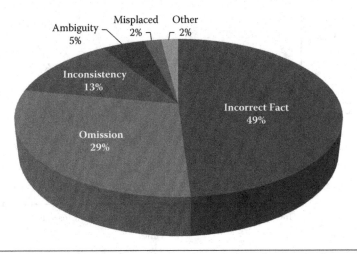

Figure 1.5 Sources of bad requirements.

- Inconsistent requirements: 13%
- Ambiguous requirements: 5%
- Misplaced requirements: 2%
- Other reasons: 2%

Here are some additional and very fascinating facts about the scope definition process. Of all the features requested by customers, only 52% made it into the final product. The conclusion one can draw from this fact is that project managers and project teams are not very effective with their estimates, either because they are not skilled in the unbiased assessment of the efforts required to deliver the full scope requested by the customers or because the budgets and the deadlines are being arbitrarily imposed from above.

Furthermore, the rework needed to correct the requirements errors, whether they were made early in the project lifecycle (50%–60%) or during the later stages (40%–50%), can account for as much as 50% of the total project cost. This implies that if an organization really wants to improve efficiency and cut costs, it should focus its improvement efforts squarely on scope management. In other words, in a perfect world where all the requirements mistakes are eliminated, all the project budgets can be cut by 50%!

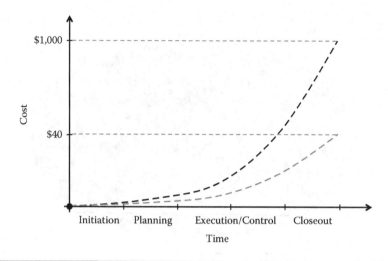

Figure 1.6   Cost of mistakes.

A study* conducted by Barry Boehm (one of the thought leaders in the field of software development) involved an analysis of 63 software development projects in companies such as IBM, GTE, and TRW in an attempt to investigate the relative costs of fixing an error at various stages of a project. The results from this investigation demonstrated an extraordinary escalation in the average cost of a mistake, from $1 at the initiation stage of the project to a $40–$1,000 range at the closeout (see Figure 1.6). One can argue that although this information is based on the information technology industry, this trend, to a certain extent, holds true for most other domains as well.

Interestingly enough, the problems mentioned in the study above are not rooted in the inability of the technical people to produce detailed designs, blueprints, bills of materials, or architecture documents. The main challenge is usually encountered in the initial stages of the projects, when there is a need to extract a high-level initial set of customer problems, issues, and needs in order to propose potential solutions.

Finally, the obvious question: Do the investments in product scope definition pay off? A study conducted by Werner M. Gruehl at NASA and reported by Ivy Hooks† revealed the following interesting facts

---

* Boehm, B. (1981). *Software Engineering Economics*. Englewood Cliffs, NJ: Prentice-Hall.
† Hooks, I. (1995). *Managing Requirements*, pp. 1–2.

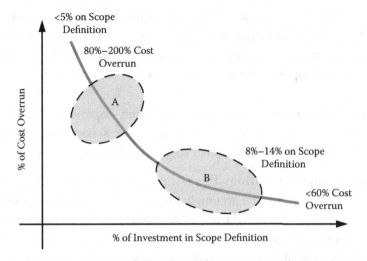

Figure 1.7   Why invest in scope definition?

(see Figure 1.7). The companies that spent less than 5% of the total project costs on requirements elicitation experienced cost overruns of between 80% and 200%. On the other hand, organizations that invested between 8% and 14% of total project cost on scope elicitation had cost overruns of less than 60%.

Developing a Shared Platform

Glossary

A lot of confusion exists regarding various terms in project scope management, especially considering the variations in terminology from industry to industry, so let us try to predefine all the key terms and agree on the taxonomy of requirements before proceeding further.

Project Scope Management: Project scope management is primarily concerned with defining and controlling what is and is not included in the project. It encompasses the processes needed to ensure that the project includes all the work required, and only the work required, to complete the project successfully.

Product Scope Definition: This is a process of elicitation and documentation of all the features and functions that characterize a product or a service.

Note: Very frequently when "product scope definition" is mentioned in the conversation or literature, people (including even certified project managers) mistakenly relate the term exclusively to the domain of product development, which is obviously not the case.

Note: Terms such as *requirements gathering, requirements elicitation, requirements extraction,* and *scope elicitation* are synonymous with one another and are used interchangeably throughout this book.

Project Scope Definition: This is a process of defining all the work that needs to be accomplished to deliver a product or service with the specified features and functions. In the project management domain, the work breakdown structure is the final output of the project scope definition process.

Business Requirement: The requirement is an opportunity to be seized, a problem to be solved, or a need that requires an answer.

Feature: This is a distinctive high-level component of the product scope.

Requirement: A more granular component of the product scope, it usually has a child–parent relationship with a product feature.

Function: This is what a designed device must do in order to be successful. It usually consists of an action verb and an object or a noun and implies transportation or transfer of energy, materials, or information. Functions are typically used in the description of the scope in engineering or product development projects.

Attribute: The attribute is the quality that the product should have. This includes aspects such as comfort, portability, durability, and so on. Attributes are closely related to nonfunctional requirements in IT and software development.

Functional Requirement: This is an action that the product (system) must perform under specific conditions. Functional requirements are typically used in IT and software development to describe the product scope.

Nonfunctional Requirement: This is a property or quality describing such properties as look and feel, usability, security, and legal restrictions that the product (system) must have. Nonfunctional requirements are typically used in IT and software development to describe the product scope.

Chapter Summary

In this chapter, I discussed the main reasons why I felt that a book dedicated to project scope management was long overdue on the market, including underdeveloped scope management domain, confusion among the project managers as to who should be responsible for requirements elicitation analysis and documentation, as well as the advent of the new multidisciplinary enterprisewide projects.

I also looked at a couple of real-life examples of multidisciplinary projects that upon close analysis turned out to include almost every department of the organizations that initiated them. Then the chapter proceeded to analyze the overall project performance over the past couple of decades and attempted to focus on the scope management root causes of our project challenges. I also shared certain scientific evidence that the investment in proper requirements elicitation and analysis can be very beneficial to every organization involved in projects.

Finally, I developed a shared vocabulary for the important terminology used throughout this book.

2

HISTORY OF SCOPE MANAGEMENT

Introduction

The history of design is an integral part of the history of scope management, and scope management is by definition inseparable from project management. Therefore, as soon as one of our distant ancestors decided that attaching a sharp-edged rock to a stick would make the job of killing his next meal so much easier, project scope management was born. For thousands of years afterward, engineering and construction went hand in hand competing to get ahead of each other, sometimes with engineering getting the upper hand and sometimes with architecture leaping forward with a new building design.

Sometime around the middle of the eighteenth century, the explosion of inventions and ideas more commonly known as the Industrial Revolution took place in Europe and introduced a multitude of new products to the market. With the introduction of new products, many new types of disciplines were developed; these included the electrical, chemical, transport, and manufacturing engineering fields, to name just a few. The 1950s are considered to be the birth of software development that followed soon after the invention of the first computers in the early 1940s.

The official birth of project management is a highly contested area, with some people thinking that the existence of the domain should be acknowledged once the entire science has been properly institutionalized, so they prefer to measure it from the establishment of the Project Management Institute (PMI) in 1969 or even from the time the first *Guide to the Project Management Body of Knowledge* (*PMBOK® Guide*) was released as a white paper in 1983. However, another group of practitioners (including myself) thinks that the science and art of project management, institutionalized or not, started as soon as one

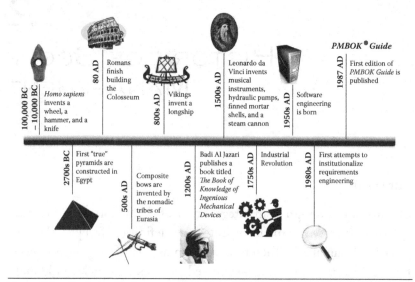

Figure 2.1   The design timeline.

of the representatives of *Homo sapiens* decided to create a new product in an endeavor that had a definite start and a definite end.

Let us then examine the history and the gradual progress of project scope management from the early days of humanity until the end of the twentieth century. A quick disclaimer: The events and the "products" examined on the next several pages (see Figure 2.1) have been selected for their "cool" factor and sometimes for their obscurity for the mass reader.

Brief History of Project Scope Management

Twenty-Seventh Century BC: Sneferu's Expensive Prototyping

The Egyptian pharaoh Sneferu, who lived approximately 4,600 years ago, reigned anywhere between 24 and 48 years, depending on which of the historians one chooses to believe. Aside from his long reign, he is mainly remembered as the father of classical Egyptian pyramid design. Egyptians had a variation of pyramids before his time. These were the famous step pyramids, or ziggurats as they were also known (see Figure 2.2). This design wasn't originally Egyptian but was rather borrowed from the more ancient Mesopotamian cultures such as Sumerian, Babylonian, and Assyrian.

After summoning his chief architect, whose name is lost in history, Sneferu ordered him to improve the design of the existing Meidum

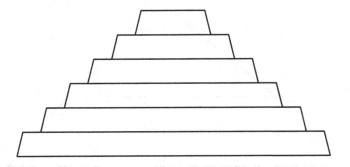

Figure 2.2   Step pyramid of Djoser.

step pyramid built by the famous Egyptian builder Imhotep for the pharaoh Huni. The idea was to fill up the steps in order to create a smooth "true" pyramid; unfortunately, due to engineering miscalculations, the entire structure collapsed (see Figure 2.3) and it was back to the drawing board for Sneferu and his team of designers. In the meantime, the 65-meter (213-foot) product of their project was labeled *el haram el kaddab* or "the fake pyramid" by the local population.

Sneferu, who was not one to be discouraged for very long, initiated the next project. This time, the goal was to build the true pyramid from scratch. Sneferu's architect elected to proceed with a 55° angle design, but at the height of approximately 40 meters it was discovered

Figure 2.3   Meidum pyramid.

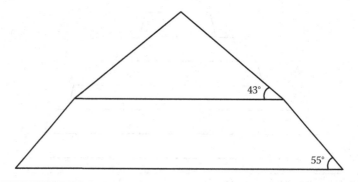

Figure 2.4   Bent pyramid.

that the structure was becoming unstable. In order to prevent the impending collapse, it was decided to change the slope of the pyramid from 55° to about 43° in the upper levels (see Figure 2.4). The resulting structure received a disparaging title, "The Bent Pyramid."

Finally, the third attempt paid off when Sneferu's architect, utilizing the lessons learned from the previous two failed attempts, decided on the 43° angle for the incline and a successful 104-meter (341-foot) structure was built. It is now known as the Red Pyramid and is considered to be the grandfather of all subsequent Egyptian true pyramids.

First Century AD: Building the Colosseum

The construction of the Colosseum started in 72 AD by the order of Emperor Vespasian and was completed only eight years later in 80 AD. At the end of the construction, the Colosseum, or Colloseo as it is called in Italian, was a stadium capable of seating 50,000 spectators, was 189 meters (615 feet) long, and was 156 meters (510 feet) wide. The building was 48 meters tall with a base area of 24,000 m² (6 acres). The Colosseum was used for gladiatorial contests and public spectacles such as mock sea battles, animal hunts, executions, re-enactments of famous battles, and dramas.

Because the Colosseum was conceived as the largest stadium of its time both in terms of size and capacity, there was one key problem that the Roman architects had to solve. Theoretically increasing the capacity of the stadium is not very complicated: one just has to make it wider, longer, and taller, that is, basically expand it in all three dimensions. Having said that, the practical implementation was met with certain limitations. One can't continue expanding the length and the width of a building indefinitely, inasmuch as this would result in some spectators being too far from the action. Hence, the architects had to consider expanding the stadium upwards to accommodate more rows. But here lies a serious problem: Increasing the height of the building to the required 48 meters implied that the structure would be too heavy to support itself. And that is when the Roman construction team came up with the ingenious decision to use arches instead of solid walls.

Up to that time, the arch design had been known for quite a while; it had been used by the Etruscans and several other ancient civilizations. But the Romans managed to take the arch design to the next level. What they created as a result of this design exercise was the three rows of 80 arches, each one of them stacked one atop another (see Figure 2.5).

Figure 2.5 Colosseum.

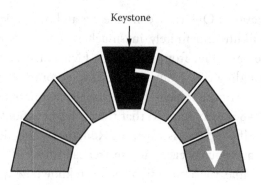

Figure 2.6 Arch construction.

The arch design allowed eliminating the tensile stresses in spanning a great amount of open space. Introduction of the keystone enabled the builders to ensure that all the forces were resolved into compressive stresses much better handled by both stone and concrete (see Figure 2.6). There are multiple benefits to the arch design; arches can bear relatively high weight while staying light. Also, a purely project management aspect of using arches in construction is that once the workers build the first arch, they need little supervision or guidance when building the next ones. Hence, arch building can be assigned to a relatively unskilled group of workers, and the skilled artisans can be diverted to more interesting tasks, such as creating statues or carvings.

Fifth Century: Composite Bow Design

Sometime around 500 AD, humanity faced another seemingly unsolvable problem. The existing self bows (i.e., the bows made from one piece of wood) were no longer adequate for the needs of soldiers. This was especially true in the regions where cavalry tended to outnumber the infantry or foot soldiers, which was typical for Asian people and tribes inhabiting what is now southern Russia and the former Asian republics of the Soviet Union (see Figure 2.7).

The body armor worn by adversaries became so robust that they required larger, more powerful bows to be able to penetrate the armor. Yet, on the other hand, large bows were not very well suited to being used by mounted riders. Hence the problem: How can one create a bow that is at least as powerful as larger self bows or longbows but are much smaller?

Figure 2.7 Ottoman horse archer.

Eventually, our ancestors came up with an ingenious solution: a composite bow! The wooden core, albeit much smaller, was retained to provide the bow its shape and stability, but the Huns, Magyars, Mongols, and Turks added a couple of things to the design of the bow. First, thin planks of animal horn were glued on the inner side, called the belly, of the bow (see Figure 2.8). Because horn is less bendable than wood, it is capable of storing more compression energy. Also, the composite bow designers laid the sinew, soaked in animal glue, in layers on the back of the bow because sinew can extend farther than wood, once more allowing for more energy storage.

What was the end result of this project? There was an inscription found on a stone stele in Siberia that claimed, "While Genghis Khan was holding an assembly of Mongolian dignitaries ... Yesungge (Genghis Khan's nephew) shot a target at 536 m!"

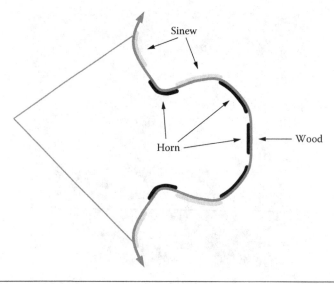

Figure 2.8   Composite bow.

Tenth Century: Story of a Viking Longship

Vikings, the ancestors of modern Swedes, Danes, and Norwegians, experienced a renaissance of their own sometime around the beginning of the eighth century. A fairly small (compared with other European nations) group of warriors and explorers managed to reach and plunder cities and villages in England, Scotland, Ireland, Russia, France, Spain, Portugal, Italy, Africa, and Asia (see Figure 2.9).

Historians and linguists recently discovered that every modern English settlement whose name ends in *by*—Corby, Crosby, Grimsby, Haxby, Maltby, Rugby, Selby, Spilsby, Wetehrby, and so on—was probably founded by the Vikings. It is widely believed that a Norseman named Rurik founded the first royal dynasty in Russia in 862 AD that ruled it until 1598 AD. And yes, Ivan the Terrible was one of Rurik's descendants.

William the Conqueror, or William the Bastard as he was known before the Battle of Hastings, was a direct descendant of the Vikings who settled in Normandy two centuries prior to the invasion of England. By the way, the same Normans managed to invade and rule Sicily for a couple of centuries before yielding to the German dynasty sometime in the thirteenth century.

Figure 2.9   *Guests from Overseas* by Nicholas Roerich.

In addition, Vikings settled in the Faroe Islands, Ireland, Iceland, Scotland, Greenland, and Canada. They even reached the powerful Byzantine Empire, where again for several centuries they formed the backbone of the ferocious Varangian Guard, the personal bodyguards of the Byzantine emperors.

So, here is a legitimate question: How could a fairly small group of people with, let's be honest, the somewhat backward technology of the eighth century get to such far reaches of the world? It turns out that Viking nautical engineers pioneered several revolutionary boat designs. These included the introduction of the keel made from a naturally curved wood; usage of overlapping (clinker) planks (see Figure 2.10); and the combination of the sail and oars, which made these longships light, fast, shallow, and yet sturdy enough to travel across the oceans (more about the Viking ships in Chapter 8).

Twelfth Century: First "Do-It-Yourself" Book

Badi Al Jazari was born in 1136 in the city of Jazirat ibn Umar. Fairly early in his life, he assumed the role of chief engineer at the Artuklu Palace, the residence of the Turkish dynasty that ruled Eastern

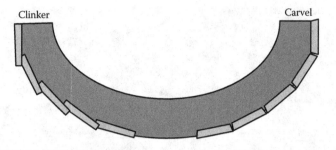

Figure 2.10 Viking boat, clinker versus carvel.

Anatolia at the time. Sometime at the end of the twelfth century, Al Jazari published a book titled *The Book of Knowledge of Ingenious Mechanical Devices*, where he describes 50 mechanical devices alongside the instructions on how to build them.

The book includes the "recipes" for various camshafts, several types of pumps, a drink-serving waitress, a hand-washing machine, a peacock fountain, a musical robot band, and an assortment of designs for clocks—including the most famous Al Jazari creation, the Elephant Clock (see Figure 2.11).

Fifteenth Century: Leonardo da Vinci

Leonardo da Vinci was born in 1452 in the town of Vinci. Because he was an illegitimate child, he had to adopt his town's name as his surname; *da Vinci* means "from Vinci" in Italian. Leonardo started his professional life as a painter and went on to work for the Duke of Milan, a cardinal at the Vatican, and the king of France, not to mention the famous (or infamous) Borgia and Medici families.

In addition to his painting job, Leonardo mastered anatomy, optics, botany, geology, cartography, and mathematics. However, one of the main bodies of work left by Leonardo was in the field of engineering and design. Here is a partial list of Leonardo's inventions:

- Measuring devices:
  - An adjustable drawing compass
  - A clock that measured minutes as well as hours
  - An improved scale
  - An odometer that measured distance traveled by a wagon
  - A pedometer that measured the distance traveled by a walking person

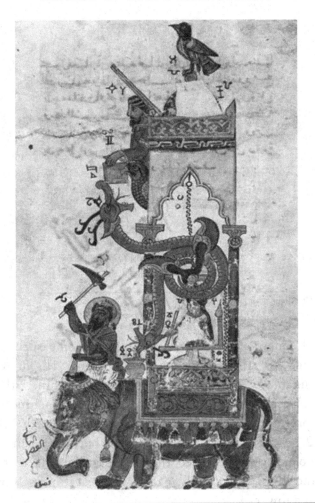

Figure 2.11   Elephant Clock design.

- An inclinometer that would measure tilt
- A hydrometer that measured humidity
- A anemometer to measure the speed of wind
- Tools
  - An adjustable monkey wrench
  - A mechanical saw that looks very similar to a modern jigsaw
  - Automatic shears
  - Devices that allowed rolling copper and tin into thin sheets
- A ratchet jack to lift heavy weights in construction (up to half a ton in weight)

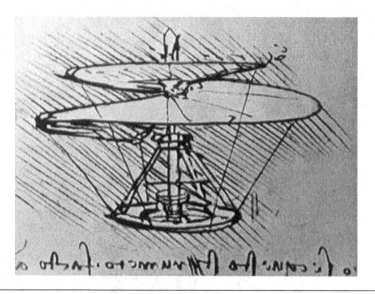

Figure 2.12 Helicopter design.

Once Leonardo had an inventory of tools and measuring devices, he directed his attention to the idea of human flight. Although he was unable to build the actual "flying machine," the scientist was able to design several models of flying machines, including the prototype of the modern helicopter he named "helix" (see Figure 2.12). Although the helix was not built, it is rumored that Leonardo not only designed the first parachute (a tent 24 feet across and high) but actually managed to test it himself by jumping from a tower.

Later in his life, while working for the Duke of Milan, Leonardo diversified into hydraulics and weaponry. His inventions included locks for canals, a pump that raised water from the river and distributed it through the castle pipes, a heating system for the duchess's bathroom, and a cooling system (this time for the duchess's boudoir). The Duke of Milan was involved in constant wars and battles with local Italian fiefdoms; therefore, Leonardo had to create the following weapons for his sponsor:

- Stink bombs that were mounted on arrows
- An assault chariot equipped with scythe blades to mow down enemy infantry

Figure 2.13   Tank design.

- A device for lighting cannon powder, some say a prototype of the modern cigarette lighter
- A fully functional tank that could move in any direction, and the guns mounted on it could point anywhere (see Figure 2.13)

Eighteenth Century: Industrial Revolution

It is considered by many historians that the beginning of the Industrial Revolution can be attributed to the English engineer and inventor Thomas Savery, who constructed and patented a low-lift combined vacuum and pressure water pump that generated about one horsepower.

From that point on, the Western world exploded with new engineering ideas, inventions, and discoveries. First, the mechanized cotton spinning machine* managed to increase the output of one human worker by a factor of 1,000. The next string of inventions improved the efficiency of steam engines so that they used between one-fifth and one-tenth as much coal. Chemical engineers of the time vastly improved the processes and the efficiencies of sulphuric acid production and sodium carbonate production. Another British engineer, John Smeaton, rediscovered concrete, a recipe that had been lost for 1,300 years. For a more complete list of the new designs, improvements, and discoveries made during the Industrial Revolution, see Table 2.1.

---

* http://en.wikipedia.org/wiki/Cotton-spinning_machinery

Table 2.1 Major Inventions of the Industrial Revolution

DOMAIN/INDUSTRY	INVENTIONS/SIGNIFICANT IMPROVEMENTS
Textiles	Flying shuttles
	Roller spinning machines
	Flyer-and-bobbin systems
	Carding machines
	Spinning mule
	Water frames
Metallurgy	Replacement of wood and other biofuels with coal
	Coal reverberatory furnaces
	Potting and stamping processes
	Puddling process
	Crucible steel techniques
Mining	Shaft mining (due to introduction of the steam engine)
	Water pumps
	Safety lamps
Steam power	Newcomen steam engine (see Figure 2.14)
	Savery steam engine
	Watt–Bolton steam engine
Chemicals	Production of sulphuric acid by the lead chamber process
	Production of sodium carbonate
	Development of bleaching powder
	Development of portland cement
Machine tools	Workshop lathes
	Cylinder boring machine
	Planing machines
	Slotting machines
	Shaping machines
Other	Gas lighting
	Glass making
	Paper machine
	Seed drill
	Canals
	Roads
	Railways

Geographically, although it started in England, the new wave of inventions quickly spread into the rest of Europe, including Germany, France, Belgium, and Russia (to name a few), and across the oceans to the United States, Canada, and Japan. It can be argued that the birth of modern engineering in general and the conceptual design in particular can be directly attributed to the original English inventions.

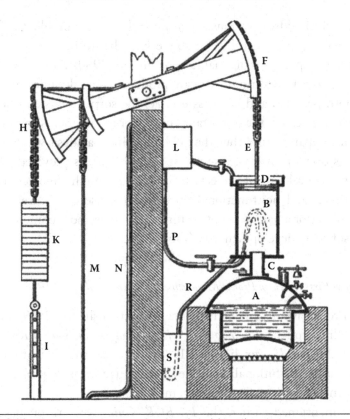

Figure 2.14 Newcomen steam-powered engine, circa eighteenth century.

Another very interesting fact: Recently, based on historical data kept by historians and modern economic analysis methods, scientists came up with a very interesting conclusion. It turns out that the GDP per capita figures remained pretty stagnant around the world from 1 AD until 1700 AD. But in the course of less than a century, the population income increased severalfold.

Twentieth Century: Software Engineering

The 1940s gave the world the first computer; initially the instructions guiding their operations were wired into the machines. However, practitioners quickly realized that this design was not flexible at all and came up with the "stored program architecture."

Thus, sometime in the following decade, software development was born with languages such as FORTRAN, ALGOL, and COBOL designed to address various scientific and business problems. Things progressed fairly smoothly (or so we were led to believe) until software development went mainstream in late 1980s and early 1990s, with hundreds of various software products being designed and built for both personal and business use. As the software systems became more complicated, the importance of proper requirements engineering became apparent, and thus the field of business analysis was born.

This domain over the course of several decades provided IT and software development project managers with methodologies such as functional and nonfunctional requirements, use cases, user stories, and so on (for a partial list of requirements tools and techniques in IT and software development, see Table 2.2).

Twenty-First Century: Project Management Institute and the PMBOK® Guide

The Project Management Institute was established in 1969, and the first edition of the *Guide to the Project Management Body of Knowledge* (*PMBOK®Guide*) saw light in 1987. This was the first attempt to define and institutionalize all key knowledge areas of project management, including scope management.

As mentioned earlier, the *PMBOK®Guide* went through several editions—one to three, to be more precise—without putting enough stress on the requirements elicitation and analysis aspects of the project scope definition, but the fourth release of the book, which was published in 2008, finally included the "Collect Requirements" process in the project scope management knowledge area.

Chapter Summary

In this chapter, we traced the history of project scope management, especially the requirements and the design aspects of it through human history. We started with the "pyramid prototyping" exercises by the ancient Egyptians, examined the design of the Roman Colosseum and the impact of the arch structure, and looked at the design of the composite bow invented by the Asiatic and Turkish tribes. Next, we analyzed the ingenious design of the Viking longships and the first engineering and design "do-it-yourself" book published by Badi Al Jazari in the twelfth century.

Table 2.2 Software Development Tools and Techniques

TYPE OF TECHNIQUE	DEFINITION	EXAMPLE
Functional Requirements Analysis	Elicitation and capture of the functions of a software system or its component including all relevant sets of inputs, the behaviors, and outputs	*The user shall be able to add a desired product to the shopping basket.*
Nonfunctional Requirements Analysis	Elicitation and capture of the qualities of the system, including usability, maintainability, security, performance, portability, etc.	*The process of adding the product to the basket shall take no more than one second.*
Use Cases	A list of steps, typically defining interactions between a user (actor) and a system, to achieve a goal	*Search for an item in the product catalog.*
User Stories (Agile Development)	One or several sentences that capture what a user does or needs to do as part of his or her job function, usually follows "As a <role>, I want <goal/desire> so that <benefit>"	*As a financial analyst, I want to generate a sales report by region so that I can provide updated information to my management.*
Business Rules Analysis	Elicitation and capture of the business rules (including both operative and structural) governing the business and other operations of the organization	*A local state (province) tax amount is calculated as total sum of all taxable items in the order multiplied by the local state (province) sales tax.*
Data Dictionary and Glossary	A centralized repository of information about data such as meaning, relationships to other data, origin, usage, and format	***Field Name:*** *UserID* ***Data Type:*** *Text* ***Data Format:*** *NNNNNNN* ***Field Size:*** *7* ***Description:*** *Unique seven-digit number represented as text* ***Example:*** *9712343*
Data Flow Diagrams	A graphical representation of the "flow" of data through an information system, modeling its process aspects	N/A
Interface Analysis	Identifies the interfaces between solutions or solution components	N/A

We then examined the life and the astonishing list of inventions and revolutionary designs introduced to this world by Leonardo da Vinci, who worked in fifteenth century Italy and France. The eighteenth century brought about the Industrial Revolution, where the majority of the modern engineering domains, save for electronics and computer engineering, were born.

The twentieth century was marked by the birth of software engineering, which in turn introduced a plethora of new techniques and methodologies including functional requirements analysis, nonfunctional requirements analysis, use cases, user stories, business rules analysis, data dictionaries, data flow diagrams, and interface analysis, to name a few.

Finally, we examined the role of the Project Management Institute and the *Guide to the Project Management Body of Knowledge (PMBOK®Guide)* and their impact on the domain of project scope management.

3

WRITING PROJECT
CHARTERS

Historical Perspective: The Sheep and the Oil

Close to the end of 1940, the head of the Soviet chief intelligence directorate (GRU) General Golikov summoned his deputies and issued two orders that were puzzling at first glance. First, the analytics department of the military intelligence was charged with a task of compiling weekly data on the situation in the European sheep industry, including amounts of mutton sold by the producers and the volatility of prices. The second order required Soviet undercover operatives to collect oily rags discarded by the German troops after cleaning their weapons, especially in the Eastern part of Europe. Both of these orders were immediately implemented by the GRU, an organization so secretive that the mere existence of it was not acknowledged by the Soviet government until 1991.

Why was the general so interested in these mundane and highly unusual, at least for military intelligence, matters? It turns out that in the late 1940s the Soviet Union was starting to get really concerned regarding the accumulation of the German infantry and motorized divisions along a newly created border that came into existence after the joint occupation of Poland by the Soviet and German troops a year earlier in 1939.

Joseph Stalin, the Soviet dictator, was worried about Adolf Hitler's next step: Would he use these troops to attack the Soviet Union, as British Prime Minister Churchill had been insisting in his telegrams? Or was he just resting his armies as far away as possible from the Western Front while preparing for Operation "Sea Lion" (the invasion of England)? Not being the most trusting individual, Stalin summoned Golikov one day to the Kremlin and ordered him to come up with a reliable way of confirming or refuting the possibility of the potential German invasion.

After conferring with a group of his top analysts, the head of the GRU came up with the following logical construct:

1. Any army that is planning to attack the Soviet Union must prepare for the war accordingly and consider the country's landscape, transportation system, geography, and climate.
2. Western parts of the Soviet Union tend to get very cold in winter, with temperatures plummeting to −30°C and even −40°C.
3. Hence, before making the final push, an army—especially one based in central Europe, with its relatively mild climate—must arm and equip their soldiers accordingly.
4. German gun and machine oil tends to freeze at temperatures below −12°C.
5. German soldiers are currently equipped with winter coats that are not designed to withstand severe frost.
6. Hence, if Germany is to attack us, they absolutely must take these two actions:
   a. Develop a new type of oil and supply all its troops located near the German–Soviet border with it.
   b. Equip all the Eastern Front troops with warm overcoats capable of withstanding low temperatures.

The general also knew that at the time the only type of overcoat capable of keeping a human being warm in −40°C weather was one made out of sheepskin. If one has to supply six million soldiers (the size of the German invasion army), reasoned the general and his analysts, then how many sheep would have to be slaughtered in Europe?

And the answer is "A lot!" From an economic standpoint, what would happen to the sheep industry markets if millions of sheep would simultaneously start getting slaughtered around the continent for the sake of their skins? The price of the sheepskins would skyrocket, and the price of mutton would plummet.

Let us now revisit the original orders issued by General Golikov. He wanted the oily rags discarded by the German soldiers to be collected and delivered for analysis in Moscow and a weekly report on the situation in the sheep industry.

What his subordinates told him week in and week out was that the prices of both mutton and sheepskin remained stable and that the German army was still using the "old" type of oil. On the basis of these two facts, Golikov came to the only possible conclusion: Germany indeed was not ready to invade and hence would not invade the Soviet Union.

The irony of this situation is that Hitler decided to attack the Soviet Union without any preliminary preparations for the cold weather. Initially, the Soviets suffered several disastrous defeats and were able to stop the Germans only near Moscow. However, by the time German troops reached the Soviet capital in the winter of 1941, the German soldiers were suffering from bitter cold, and their weapons (including tanks, artillery, and airplanes) were refusing to function properly because the gun oil would freeze and jam all the equipment.

There are many project management lessons one can deduce from this case study; however, because this is a book dedicated to project scope management, let us concentrate on this aspect alone.

One of the key areas of the project charter is the section dedicated to the project's goals and objectives, where the project manager (or the project champion, depending on the situation) should outline the key features of the project scope.

Therefore, the objectives section of the German project charter (aka, the plan for Operation Barbarossa) should have described several key features of this undertaking. This feature list should have probably included direction of strategic army thrusts; stockpiling the materiel; and accumulation of the troops, tanks, and artillery (and it did). However, the answer to a very simple and seemingly obvious question, "How are we going to address the problem with severe winter conditions in the country we are planning to invade?" was completely missed.

Dual Role of the Project Charter

What Is a Project Charter?

The project charter is usually defined as a statement of the scope, objectives, and participants in a project. A good project charter is expected to provide a high-level overview of project roles and responsibilities, project objectives, main stakeholders, and the authority of the project manager. It serves as a reference of authority for the future of the project.

It is also viewed as a formal document recognizing the existence of the project at both the portfolio management and project management levels.

Portfolio Management Perspective

From the point of view of portfolio management, the project charter should contain a brief discussion of the project feasibility or validity, probably inherited from the business case. The points justifying the project in the business case should be revisited and adjusted accordingly because more information becomes available to the project stakeholders as the project evolves from the business case to the project charter stage.

In the most simplified of forms, the project charter may contain a financial analysis of the proposed project. For example, if the cost of building a villa for sale is estimated to be $100,000 and the projected sales price is expected to be $150,000, then the return on investment (ROI) calculation may look something like this:

$$ROI = (\$150,000 - \$100,000)/\$100,000 = 50\%$$

However, this approach is deficient for a number of reasons. First, it relies exclusively on financial estimates that are notoriously inaccurate. Studies conducted in the project management domain indicate that project cost and resource estimates can oscillate between +300% and −75% on some projects, and one can argue that the projected revenues on any endeavor can sometimes be subject to even greater variations.

Second, the usage of financial models *a priori* assumes that the company has only financial goals in mind. For example, it is practically impossible to justify a significant investment in the telecom network infrastructure using financial modeling exclusively. The costs of such undertaking are readily available and typically very high, whereas the monetary benefits are very vague and spread over time.

Third, purely financial models fail to consider such important factors as risk, strategic alignment, customer attractiveness, technical feasibility, and fit to the company's supply chain, just to name a few.

Therefore, the more mature approach is to justify the project using a scoring model that incorporates several variables that are important to the organization. An example of such a matrix and the resulting score of each project candidate taken from a large European telecom company are presented in Tables 3.1 and 3.2.

Table 3.1   Telecommunications Company's Project Portfolio Scoring Model

SELECTION CRITERIA	1 POINT	5 POINTS	10 POINTS	KILL?
		POINTS AWARDED		
Strategic Fit	Fits at least 1 of the strategic criteria	Fits 2 to 3 strategic criteria	Fits 4 to 5 strategic criteria	Yes
Financial	Low	Medium	High	No
Technical Feasibility	Difficult A lot of external expertise is required	Medium difficulty Some external expertise is required Only internal expertise is required	Easy	No
Market Attractiveness	Low Very few requests from customers	Medium Average number of requests from customers	Strong Multiple requests from customers	No
Resources	70+ person-months	10–69 person-months	Less than 10 person-months	No

Table 3.2   Scoring of Project Candidates

	4G	NETWORK UPGRADE	UNDERGROUND
Strategic Fit	10	10	5
Financial	10	1	5
Technical Feasibility	1	1	5
Market Attractiveness	5	1	5
Resources	1	1	5
TOTAL	**27/50**	**14/50**	**25/50**

Project Management Perspective

From the project management perspective, the project charter is the first document that attempts to outline at least at a high level the key parameters of the project and answer the following questions:

- What are the key features of the final product or service? What features are outside our scope?
- How much time do we have to deliver the project?
- How much money will our management allocate to the project and how much do we actually need?

- What human resources will be required?
- Who are the key stakeholders of this project?
- What are the risks and the constraints associated with this undertaking?
- What assumptions can we make?

Furthermore, the project charter will act as a foundation for two other key project documents: the requirements document and the project plan. The requirements document will build the detailed project scope (i.e., detailed requirements) based on the high-level features outlined in the project charter. The project plan will, using both the project charter and the requirements document, build the scope, time, cost, and other management sections of the document that will govern the delivery of the product.

What Is Included in the Project Charters?

Problem and Opportunity Statements

This section of the document should further itemize the topics mentioned in the "Portfolio Management Perspective" section of the chapter. Basically, the creator of the project charter should try to answer a very simple question: What problem are we trying to solve, or what opportunity are we trying to capture?

Here are several examples from the sample projects analyzed in this book. The first one deals with a proposed "Port Upgrade" initiative.

> Port Upgrade—Problem Opportunity Statement:
>> P: Lack of current container capacity considering the increased trade with Asian partners
>> P: Increase in operating cost due to limited capacity
>> P: Decrease in customer satisfaction levels
>> O: Increase revenues and cut operating costs
>> O: Improve customer satisfaction

The second example comes from the project charter created by the software company that was hired to develop the check-in software for a local airline.

Airport Check-In Kiosk Software:

   O: Divert customer traffic away from check-in attendants,
      thus reducing the costs
   O: Better quality of service; higher availability
   O: Faster passenger processing

In certain instances, especially when dealing with government-mandated, regulatory projects, the problem/opportunity statement may take another form, just as in the Mobile Number Portability project charter presented below.

Mobile Number Portability—Problem Opportunity Statement   The Mobile Number Portability project that would enable the wireless company customers to switch mobile providers freely and keep their phone numbers with company-unique prefixes has been mandated by the ministry of communications.

Goals and Objectives

When writing the Goals and Objectives section of the document, the project manager must attempt to provide the answers to the following questions:

   What do you want to accomplish and by when?
   What scope items (features) do you need to deliver?

Also, it is very helpful to utilize the S.M.A.R.T. methodology to improve the quality of the goals and objectives. The S.M.A.R.T. methodology implies that all the statements should be as follows:

- *Specific:* Be as specific and precise as possible on the desired final product or service to be delivered. For example, if the high-level features of the products are already known at the project charter stage, list them underneath the goals paragraph.
- *Measurable:* Quantify the results where possible and ensure you have a reliable system for measuring them. For example, rather than stating "large house," state "house with an area of 5,000 to 6,000 square feet."
- *Assignable:* The statement clearly reflects who will be responsible for the delivery of the project.

- *Realistic:* The goals and objectives should be attainable under current constraints.
- *Time related:* The time frames and possibly the key milestones are mentioned in the statement (including applicable ± qualifiers).

Let us examine one example from the real-life documents. The first one comes from the "Airport Check-In Kiosk Software" project mentioned earlier:

ABC Software Systems Goals and Objectives ABC Software Systems shall study, configure, and implement the Airport Check-In Kiosk software system for XYZ Airlines by September of 2010. The project scope shall consist of the following features (see Table 3.3):

Note: ABC Software Systems is responsible for the delivery of the check-in software; actual kiosk hardware shall be procured, designed, and delivered independently by XYZ Airlines and its vendors.

Is this entire paragraph specific enough? One can argue that it is indeed fairly specific, especially considering the early stages of the project. It mentions the system to be developed, provides the key features, and even discusses the scope exclusions.

With respect to measurability, the text does not contain any measurable characteristics; however, one has to admit that it is fairly difficult to impose any kind of measurability this early in the software development project. On the other hand, mentioning in how many of the kiosks the said system should be installed could have increased the overall quality of the statement.

The statement is clearly assignable, as it names ABC Software Systems as an entity responsible for the delivery of the project. Is this

Table 3.3   Airport Check-In Kiosk Feature List

FEATURE ID	FEATURE DESCRIPTION
F 1.0	Kiosk Menu
F 2.0	Traveler Identification
F 3.0	Traveler Reservation Search
F 4.0	Confirm or Change Seat
F 5.0	Pay for Luggage
F 6.0	Print Boarding Pass
F 7.0	Navigation

statement realistic? Well, if it was written, say, sometime in January of 2008, then most likely it is a realistic statement. It is completely possible to develop such a system in the course of 19 months. However, if the project charter in question was written in August of 2010 (compare this date with the desired delivery in September of 2010), then probably not.

Furthermore, as we already mentioned, the paragraph contains a very specific time frame, thus making it time related.

Rough Order-of-Magnitude Budget and Schedule

The Rough Order-of-Magnitude Budget and Schedule is one of the most difficult sections of the project charter to complete. The stakeholders, including the management of the company, expect the project manager to produce some concrete estimates with respect to the project budget, schedule, and human resources required. The expectations are also such that the numbers are anticipated to be as precise and as accurate as possible, although very little is known about the scope of the project.

Let us try to determine what "precise" and "accurate" mean with respect to project estimates. In normal language, these two terms are used interchangeably as synonyms. However, in the world of project management, they stand for two completely different things.

Precise means the exactness of the number presented and nothing more. For example, number 1,345.78 is more precise than number 1,345. Although *ceteris paribus*, the more precise number, is almost always preferable to the less precise number, this is not the case in project management with all the unknowns, assumptions, and risks inherent in every project, especially at such an early stage as project initiation.

The *accurate* number (or a range, to be more precise) is the array that includes the actual cost or the duration of the project. For example, the range presented as "The project cost shall be between $5,000 and $10,000" when the actual cost turns out to be $8,000 is a very accurate estimate. It is by no means precise but accurate.

The project management literature recommends the following ranges for project estimates developed at the initiation stage of the project:

- +300%; –75% for new high-risk ventures
- +75%; –25% for familiar and relatively uncomplicated projects

When these ranges are shared with people not too familiar with project management, especially customers and executives, the first reaction is usually that of disbelief, astonishment, and sometimes anger. "What do you mean by saying that you can't predict with better accuracy at this point of time? We need more precise (and obviously accurate) estimates right now!" is the statement, I am sure, heard by every project manager at least once in his or her life.

But to explain the situation, let us consider one very simple scenario. Imagine a construction company that builds only one type of a family home. It has a fixed style, floor layout, size, number of bedrooms, number of bathrooms, and even the location of the door frames. The only flexibility provided to the clients is the types of finishes and decorations. In other words, the types of paint; flooring; and bathroom and kitchen installations, including faucets, showers, countertops, and appliances, are dependent on the choice of the client.

Another factor to incorporate into our model: Let us assume that the construction company has already built hundreds of such homes, and they know that the average cost was $100,000 per project. So, the project manager (PM) from the construction company and the prospective client (C) meet, and the following dialogue takes place:

C: I saw your house plan and I really like it. Unfortunately I haven't spoken to my wife yet; hence, I can't tell you what kind of features she will pick with respect to flooring, bathroom, kitchen, and so on.

PM: Oh, no problem about that. I am sure we can arrange another meeting that includes your spouse to discuss all the finer details.

C: But just so that we are prepared, what is your estimate of the cost of the house?

We already know that the historical average price of this type of home is $100,000. So, would I be really outrageous if the project manager answers as follows?

PM: You know, without gathering and analyzing at least your high-level requirements, it would be somewhat difficult for me to provide you with a very precise estimate. At this point of time, I can tell you that the cost could be anywhere between $75,000 and $175,000 (i.e., –25%; +75%).

At first glance, this statement may appear to be a bit surprising. After all, all the parameters of the house are already known, except for several "insignificant" features. To answer this question, let us take a mental trip to the nearest hardware store and examine the prices of some of the items there.

The cheapest flooring type represented by the standard gray carpet can be found for the price of about $1 to $1.50 per square foot. However, if the customer decides to go with something like *Macassar Ebony*, the price of flooring increases to approximately $150 per square foot. What is the difference costwise between these two options? If we assume that the total area of the house is 3,000 square feet, here is what we get:

Cheap option: $1/sq ft × 3,000 sq ft = $3,000

Expensive option: $150/sq ft × 3,000 sq ft = $450,000

So, we see that just the flooring choice can almost quintuple the cost of the project. Just for the sake of argument, let us examine the options for the kitchen appliances. On the "economy" end of the spectrum, one can probably find the appliances for the following prices:

Refrigerator = $500

Stove = $750

Dishwasher = $300

TOTAL = $1,550

If one Googles "luxury kitchen appliances," the results would be quite different:

Refrigerator = $41,000

Stove = $47,000

Dishwasher = $3,000

TOTAL = $91,000

Once more, we have been able to illustrate that one single feature on this project can potentially add almost 100% to the original budget. So, how does the estimate of between $75,000 and $175,000 provided by the project manager look now?

It actually appears that he has been very reckless, to say the least. The cost of the project, depending on the future choices of the family, might have increased by the order-of-magnitude rather than 75 percentage points.

Hence, the ROM Budget and Schedule section should contain the preliminary estimates for the project budget, schedule, and resource requirements presented using appropriate ranges. It is also worthwhile to ask the stakeholders to assign importance factors to all three corners of the "project management triangle" to establish relative priorities among scope and quality, time, and budget. Priorities or importance factors are basically percentage weights that should add up to 100%:

- Scope and Quality Importance Factor: 50%
- Time Importance Factor: 30%
- Budget Importance Factor: 20%

Let us examine several examples from the real-life project charters:

CRM System Implementation
  ROM Budget and Schedule:
    Budget: $1,500,000 ± $750,000
    Timeline: 2 ± 0.5 years
  Importance Factors:
    Scope and Quality: 30%
    Budget: 50%
    Time: 20%

Airport Check-In Kiosk Software
  ROM Budget and Schedule:
    Budget: $100,000 ± $50,000
    Timeline: 6 ± 2 months
  Importance Factors:
    Scope and Quality: 50%
    Budget: 30%
    Time: 20%

Stakeholder Register

The project stakeholder is usually defined as an entity (person or organization) that could be affected—either positively or negatively—by the outcome of the project. Stakeholders can be actively involved on a given project or play a passive role by getting occasional project-related communications. One of the key responsibilities of a project manager is to identify all the project stakeholders as soon as possible on the project and include them in the "Stakeholder Register."

Why is this step so important? First, project stakeholders usually act as requirements suppliers on a project. Omitting just one stakeholder can lead to an omission of an important requirement or even a group of requirements. One example is a project that took place at one of the largest telecommunication companies in Europe. The sales and marketing team identified a need for a new type of product. The project received an approval from the executive committee, and the team was designated by the department heads.

The project team included representatives from the sales, marketing, IT, engineering, and fraud departments. During the requirements stage of the project, the fraud department representative requested to add a specific feature involving collecting additional customer information that would have potentially prevented future scams. The entire team understood the issue, added the feature to the scope of work, and successfully implemented it at the end of the project.

Right before the project was supposed to go "live," the legal team representative, who had been accidentally omitted from the stakeholder list, appeared on the project manager's doorstep and announced, "You can't go ahead with that feature! We looked at the fraud department's requirements, and, according to the laws of this country, we can't collect this information about our clients."

That statement alone put an end to the entire project with dozens of people involved and thousands of person-hours invested. It basically boiled down to the fraud department saying that they simply can't approve the project without this specific feature, whereas the legal team justifiably insisted on the simple fact that the feature was illegal. And although both sides were right in this argument, the entire initiative had to be scrapped with a lot of person-hours and money wasted.

When compiling a stakeholder list, the project manager should consider at least the following groups of people and other entities:

- Project manager
- Project team
- Direct customers and clients
- All internal departments of the company

Table 3.4 Stakeholder Register

TITLE	NAME
President and CEO	Clayton Bring
VP Marketing	Hugh Mery
Project Manager	Serena Didomenico
VP IT	Roslyn Mussman
Director, Finance	Alejandra Vendetti
Director, Sales	Sofia Tacker
Director, Human Resources	Max Litz

- Government regulatory agencies
- Investors
- Shareholders
- Labor unions
- Suppliers
- Competitors

The stakeholder registrar is usually presented in a form of a table with at least the stakeholder title and his or her first and last name, in most cases adding the person's contact information such as e-mail address and phone number. For a sample stakeholder register, please see Table 3.4.

Project Feasibility/Justification

As mentioned earlier, there are several ways to approach providing the information for this section of the document. The worst possible way would be just to get away with some general statements about "improving profitability," "increasing customer satisfaction," or "growing our company's market share." Here is an example of such a feasibility discussion presented in the CRM Implementation Project mentioned earlier in this book.

CRM Implementation Project
The CRM Implementation Project is expected to generate the following benefits for the ABC Financial Services:

1. Company is expecting to increase its revenues via cross-sell and upsell capabilities resulting from this venture
2. Company is expecting an improvement in the levels of customer service
3. Company is expecting an increase in the number of products offered to the customers

Why is this version of the project feasibility the worst? Well, it would be very difficult for the company executives to examine the results of this endeavor, say, a couple of years after the project implementation. Some of the questions that may be asked are

- What was the impact of the new CRM systems on the revenue?
- How will we measure that impact?
- Did our cross-sell and upsell capabilities increase and by how much?
- What exactly is the "improvement of customer service" and what kind of impact has it had on our bottom line?
- How many new products and services have been implemented as a direct result of the CRM system implementation?

The better approach would imply using some kind of financial model such as internal rate of return, net present value, or return on investment, as was discussed earlier in this chapter. However, due to the low reliability of financial forecasts on both the cost and revenue sides as well as one-sidedness of the financial-only approach, this not the best way of presenting the project feasibility either.

This brings us to a proper "portfolio management based" approach that at least includes a calculation of the project score based on some kind of scoring model developed by the executive team. See the section "Portfolio Management Perspective" of this chapter for an example of such a scoring model.

The way it can be presented might look something like this excerpt from the project charter created in one of the leading pharmaceutical companies:

Considering the fact that our project portfolio scoring model awards points in the following manner (see Table 3.5).

Our "Development of drug X" project proposal points have been allocated in the following manner (see Table 3.6).

Risk Management

A lot of confusion exists in project management circles regarding constraints, risks, and assumptions. This section defines each one of these important risk management categories and provides several examples of each.

Table 3.5   Pharmaceutical Company's Project Portfolio Scoring Model

SELECTION CRITERIA	POINTS AWARDED (MAXIMUM POSSIBLE 30)			KILL?
	1 POINT	5 POINTS	10 POINTS	
Innovativeness (financial benefits vs. risks)	Low benefits High risks	High benefits OR Low risks	High benefits AND Low risks	Yes
Candidate for China/ Brazil/Russia?	Only 1 of the countries	Any 2 of the countries	All 3 of the countries	No
Resources	More than 70 person-years	50–70 person-years	Less than 50 person-years	No

Constraints   Constraints are the things that limit your options with respect to the successful delivery of project products or services. They typically, but not exclusively, include deadlines, budgets, availability of resources, and so on:

> "The product must receive an approval rating of 97% from the user focus group."
> "The final product must be delivered by September 30, 2015, in time for the Christmas shopping season."
> "The budget of the project was capped at $250,000."

Table 3.6   Project Candidate Score Calculation

	POINTS RECEIVED	COMMENTS
Innovativeness (financial benefits vs. risks)	10/10	Financial Benefits—High • The project is estimated to target at least two million potential patients around the world. Risks—Low: • According to our technical experts, it is possible to develop this drug using only in-house resources. • From a technical standpoint, the scope of the project involves adjusting the existing drug in order to fine-tune it to the new markets.
Candidate for China/Brazil/ Russia?	5/10	The drug is a candidate for two of the three target markets—China and Russia.
Resources	10/10	According to our technical project team experts, due to the relative simplicity of the project, the estimated resource investment is between 20 and 35 person-years.
TOTAL POINTS	**25/30**	

Table 3.7 Constraints

CONSTRAINT ID	CONSTRAINT DESCRIPTION
C1	The project must be completed by March 2012.
C2	The home must obtain an ENERGY STAR certification from the independent ENERGY STAR partner.

An example of the constraints from the "Energy Efficient House" project can be found in Table 3.7.

Risks Risks are the uncertain things that can jeopardize the project success; that is, "bad" things may happen on your project, but you are not entirely sure they will:

> "There is a distinct possibility that the ministry of communications may change the list of the requirements necessary for the successful delivery of the project."
>
> "There is a possibility of the major contractor's employees going on strike."

Note that when the probability of risk reaches 100% it becomes either a constraint or a scope item. An example of the risks from the "Energy Efficient House" project is shown in Table 3.8.

Assumptions Assumptions are typically "good" things that are supposed to happen on your project, but you are not entirely sure they will happen. For example:

> "We assume that all the resources required for the successful delivery of this project will be available."

Table 3.8 Risks

RISK ID	RISK DESCRIPTION
R1	The project will involve new techniques and technologies poorly known to ABC Construction; this could lead to costly mistakes and time overruns.
R2	There is a possibility that the energy-management experts, whose knowledge is essential to this project, will not be readily available on the market.
R3	There is a possibility that, due to its complexity and newness, the project will not be finished by the March 2013 deadline.

Table 3.9 Assumptions

ASSUMPTION ID	ASSUMPTION DESCRIPTION
A1	It is assumed that the project "Rainforest" team shall have access to the most experienced architects, designers, and construction specialists available to ABC Construction.
A2	It is assumed that the original budget of $400,00 ± $150,000 will not be changed or downgraded in any way.
A3	It is assumed that the project "Rainforest" team shall be able to outsource energy-efficiency nodules freely to external energy management specialists.

"We assume a timely delivery of the product blueprints out-sourced to the external design company."

Typically, it is beneficial to start with constraints first because they are definite, well-known aspects of the project and then move on to risks. Items that do not fall into the "Constraints" or "Risks" categories can fall into the "Assumptions" bucket. Needless to say, if an item is mentioned in one of the groups, it should not be duplicated in other ones.

Table 3.9 shows an example of the assumptions from the "Energy Efficient House" project.

Chapter Summary

We started this chapter with a discussion of the role the project charter plays in the project life cycle by examining its purpose and its role in both the portfolio and project management domains.

Then we looked at the contents of the project charter by examining its subsections. In "Problem and Opportunity Statements," we discussed the importance of presenting the problems to be addressed or the opportunities to be seized.

In the "Goals and Objectives" section we discussed how to present the goals of the project properly and the key high-level features that will act as a foundation for the future scope.

Presentation of the preliminary estimates was analyzed in the "ROM Budget and Schedule" section of the chapter. We reinforced the importance of presenting wide ranges of figures when providing the estimates for project costs and duration so early in the life cycle.

The chapter also focused on the importance of identifying all relevant stakeholders right at the very beginning of the project. We also discussed the dangers of omitting key stakeholders or groups of stakeholders and the kinds of potential risks it may present.

Finally, we looked at preliminary steps in the Risk Management section of the project charter, where we discussed constraints, risks, and assumptions.

REQUIREMENTS, CUSTOMERS, USERS

Historical Perspective: "New Account Opening" Project

This story started with a CIO of a large international bank being transferred from the European headquarters to the US division. As a part of his settling in a new country, he had to visit a bank—the one he worked at, of course—and, according to his expression, "transfer his British accounts to the local branch of the institution."

He assumed that it would be a matter of simply swiping his debit card followed by the bank teller transferring his accounts from the branch in the United Kingdom to the local one. To his great surprise, he found out that the American branch had no idea whatsoever as to who he was. In addition, it turned out that the branch in the United States had to send a request to the UK branch and ask for a hard copy of his files to be sent via mail to the United States.

So, needless to say, the CIO stormed into the office the next day proclaiming that, "We all live in the twenty-first century and something needs to be done about this situation." This is how the "New Account Opening" project (or NAO) was born.

Because this was an executive "pet project," it was expected that the project would be "fast tracked" or, in other words, rushed as much as possible. Thus, one of the strategic decisions made at the very beginning was to cut the "time wasting" by not talking to the actual tellers. It was decided that the requirements analyst should have a couple of meetings with several branch managers of the bank to investigate how the current systems worked and what could be done to improve them.

The requirements were collected, analyzed, documented, and validated with the designated group of branch managers. The project moved into the execution stage and was delivered on time and on budget, more or less. The problems started during the actual deployment of the NAO system when the tellers working at the branches started claiming, "But this is not how it should work!"

In a rush to deliver the project as soon as possible, a fatal mistake had been made: Branch managers, although very experienced and knowledgeable, had not worked as tellers probably for more than 7 to 10 years, and a lot of things can change in the course of 10 years when it comes to banking systems! So, what they actually did during the requirements elicitation sessions was share the features that were needed a decade ago rather than the modern requirements. In other words, the project team committed one of the most common and fatal mistakes one can do on the project: focusing on talking to the customers only, rather than both customers and actual users of the final product.

Therefore, in this chapter we spend some time talking about requirements owners, including stakeholders, customers, and users as well as the types of requirements and their taxonomies.

Requirements

Taxonomy

This section of the chapter should probably be started with a special explanation or even a disclaimer that should have come earlier in this book. The word *requirements* is unfortunately firmly associated with the IT and software development fields only. What this book will do, it is hoped, is attempt to change this tendency and reintroduce this term and concept to all other industries where project management plays an important role.

There is unfortunately a lot of inconsistency in the naming and the hierarchy of the scope components from industry to industry and sometimes even from one book to another. So, it would be worthwhile to try to tabulate and compare if not all then at least the major naming conventions for product scope definition (see Table 4.1).

The requirements management domain is by far the most advanced in the technology field into which the requirements (see Figure 4.1) are traditionally broken:

- Business Requirements (or problems, or objectives)
- Features (epics in the Agile world) and

Table 4.1   Requirements Taxonomy in Various Industries

| | INDUSTRIES | | |
REQUIREMENT GRANULARITY	INFORMATION TECHNOLOGY OR SOFTWARE DEVELOPMENT	ENGINEERING, ARCHITECTURE, OR PRODUCT DEVELOPMENT	MULTIDISCIPLINARY PROJECTS
Very High Level	• Business Requirements • Problems • Objectives	• Objectives • Problems • Business Requirements	• Business Requirements • Problems • Objectives
High Level	• Features • High-Level Requirements	• Features • Technical Requirements	• Features • Components

Detailed Level	• Functional Requirements
	• Nonfunctional Requirements
		• Functions
		  o Performance
		  o Value
		  o Size
		  o Safety
		  o Special
		• Attributes
		• Behaviors
			• Requirements

Other	• Use Cases • User Stories • Constraints • Business Rules • Data Dictionaries	• Constraints • Business Rules	• Constraints • Business Rules

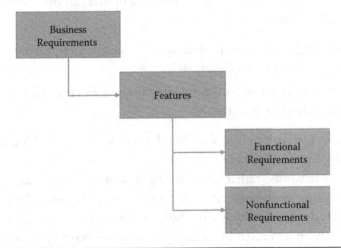

Figure 4.1   Software requirements taxonomy.

- Functional and Nonfunctional Requirements (user stories in Agile)

Requirements analysts in the IT and software development fields also have tools such as use cases, constraints, business rules, and data definitions to define the detailed level requirements better.

Here is an example of such a hierarchy; Let us assume that a small business producer of, say, scented candles decides at one point that she wants to sell them online. What is the resulting Business Requirement?

- BR 1.0 "We need to sell our products online."

Features that naturally flow from it include but are not limited to:

- F 1.1 "Customer Login"
- F 1.2 "Product Catalog"
- F 1.3 "Search Function"
- F 1.4 "Shopping Basket"
- F 1.5 and so on

The features are later broken into functional and nonfunctional requirements. For example, Feature 1.4 (Shopping Basket) can be broken into the following functional and nonfunctional requirements:

- FR 1.4.x "The user shall be able to add products to the shopping basket."
- NFR 1.4.x "The process of adding a product to the shopping basket shall not exceed 1 s."

Purely engineering projects tend to divide their requirements into the categories shown in Figure 4.2.

An engineering company producing home appliances may come up with the following objective:

- OB 1.0 "To produce a device that is capable of washing and drying the clothes in one cycle"

In other words, rather than having a separate washer and dryer, we are trying to design a new machine that can first wash the clothes and then dry them without any human intervention. For the sake of simplicity, let us pretend that there is only one wash cycle available; that is, we treat all clothes the same way regardless of whether they

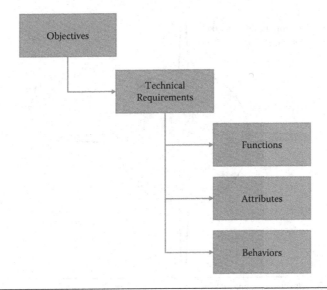

Figure 4.2 Engineering requirements taxonomy.

are whites, colors, or delicates. The resulting technical requirements for this device may look something like this:

- TR 1.1 "Adding water and detergent"
- TR 1.2 "Soaking the clothes"
- TR 1.3 "Agitating the clothes"
- TR 1.4 "Discharging the dirty water"
- TR 1.5 "Rinsing the clothes"
- TR 1.6 "Spinning"
- TR 1.7 "Agitating wrung clothes"
- TR 1.8 "Drying"

The technical requirements for TR 1.3 may look like this (see also Figure 4.3):

- FCT 1.3.1 "The agitator shall spin back and forth."
  - ATR 1.3.1.1 "The spin amplitude shall be ±180°."
- ATR 1.3.1.2 "The agitator speed shall be 45 oscillations per minute."

There is no universal agreed-upon structure for the requirements taxonomy and management on the multidisciplinary or enterprise projects, but on the basis of our previous experience, we recommend recording and organizing them as shown in Figure 4.4.

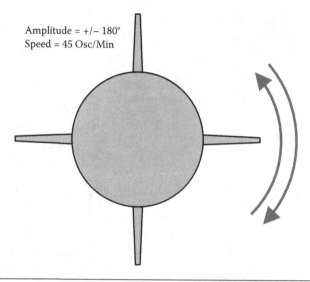

Amplitude = +/− 180°
Speed = 45 Osc/Min

Figure 4.3 Washing machine agitator.

For example, a very large retail supermarket chain that decided to open a new store in San Francisco, California, might formulate its objective or business requirement in the following fashion:

- OB 1.0 "Our company needs to open a new store in San Francisco, California."

What are the potential resulting components of this project? Well, the project team will probably need to find a piece of land at an appropriate location and rent or buy it. Then, the new building will have to

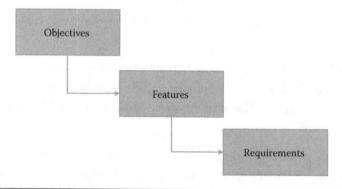

Figure 4.4 Multidisciplinary projects requirements taxonomy.

be designed and built. Once the building is ready, the IT people will have to go in and install all the necessary equipment, servers, and networks that have (it is hoped) been procured beforehand. By the time the store is ready to open, several other things will have to happen. First, the team will need to hire and train new employees to work at the store. Second, they will have to order the merchandise and conduct a PR and marketing campaign targeting local markets. Finally, the store-opening ceremony would probably have to be organized. If we write down all these deliverables in the requirements language, here is what we would get at the end of our exercise:

- F 1.1 "Location procurement"
- F 1.2 "Building construction"
- F 1.3 "IT installations"
- F 1.4 "Store staffing"
- F 1.5 "Merchandise acquisition"
- F 1.6 "Marketing"
- F 1.7 "Opening ceremony"

Now, let us pick one of the features listed above, say, Feature 1.6, and try to drill deeper into it to unearth more granular deliverables.

- Req 1.6.1 "Marketing in newspapers"
- Req 1.6.2 "Flyers"
- Req 1.6.3 "PR campaign on TV"
- Req 1.6.4 "Contest on a local radio station"

The feature titled "Marketing" was broken into four more manageable requirements, including newspaper marketing, flyers, PR campaign on TV, and a contest on a local radio station.

As can be seen from the above examples, all these approaches are fairly similar: One starts with a few business objectives, requirements, or problems and tries to drill down into them to figure out the next level: the components or features. In Chapter 13, we discuss how these granular scope components become inputs into the work breakdown structures that are used to define the project scope.

An interesting observation to mention here: One of the companies I worked for in the past had a very interesting rule regarding the highest level of the requirements hierarchy—the objectives or business requirements. They were governed by the following rule that has been strictly enforced:

> If you have more than two business requirements (objectives) in your project, then you probably have more than one project at hand.

This rule was implemented to avoid piggybacking—that is, when a project sponsor tries to squeeze in an extra, typically unrelated, project in the form of an additional objective or even a feature onto the main project.

As far as the naming conventions are concerned, they are the most rigid in the IT and software development world, where they have been somewhat deeply entrenched since the 1980s. Engineering and construction industries, although much older fields, tend to have a more flexible approach to naming conventions. And finally, multidisciplinary projects have very few or no rules at all regarding requirements taxonomy. Therefore, one of the most important things for any company is to agree on one of the naming conventions—it doesn't really matter which one—and stick to it for all its projects.

One additional disclaimer to make: It is possible that a company that chose the

$$\text{Objective} \rightarrow \text{Feature} \rightarrow \text{Requirement}$$

model may discover that in certain cases it will have to integrate one or more other approaches into the one originally selected. For example, if the project consists of the three components

- F 1.1 "Marketing"
- F 1.2 "IT"
- F 1.3 "Engineering"

The project manager may discover that it is more appropriate for her to continue calling Marketing subcomponents "requirements" but to expand the IT feature using functional and nonfunctional requirements and the Engineering feature using functions and attributes. In other words, the requirements hierarchy may end up looking something like this:

- F 1.1 "Marketing"
  - Req 1.1.1...
  - Req 1.1.2...
  - Req 1.1.3...

- F 1.2 "IT"
  - FR 1.2.1...
  - FR 1.2.2...
  - NFR 1.2.2...

- F 1.3 "Engineering"
  - FCT 1.3.1...
  - ATR 1.3.2...
- ATR 1.3.3...

Types of Requirements

Hierarchical Approach One of the most common ways of sorting requirements is by their detail level. This approach is demonstrated in Table 4.1 and Figures 4.1, 4.2, and 4.4.

The scoping process is started with determining business requirements also called objectives or problems. Then, each objective is drilled down into to figure out the components or features of which it consists.

Engineering Approach Another approach, more typical for the engineering and product development sectors, is to divide requirements into the following categories:

Prescriptive requirements specify values for the attributes of the designed object. For example, they may state that:
The step of a ladder shall be made of Grade A fir and have a thickness of ≥ 0.75 in.

Note: Prescriptive requirements are somewhat similar to the nonfunctional requirements used in IT and software development.

The next type is the *procedural requirements* that describe procedures for calculating attributes or behaviors of the product. For example: "The maximum bending stress σ_{max} shall be calculated according to the following formula":

$$\sigma_{max} = \frac{Mc}{I}$$

Note: Procedural requirements are comparable to the business rules used in IT and software development.

Finally, the performance requirements specify performance levels that must demonstrate successful functional behavior. For
example, a *performance requirement* may look something like this:
"The step of a ladder shall support up to 300 lbs."

Note: Performance requirements are not unlike the functional
requirements used in IT and software development.

Conscious, Unconscious, and Undreamed-of Requirements Approach   One
of the popular ways of grouping requirements is by dividing them
into conscious, unconscious, and undreamed-of requirements.
Trawling for *conscious requirements* is typically the easiest. These
scope items are normally uppermost in customers' minds; they are
almost always indicative of something your customer is trying to create or improve. For example, a small business owner who is trying to
increase his revenue stream by selling products on the Internet will
undoubtedly mention a website with a product catalogue, shopping
baskets, and the ability to make payments using most popular credit
cards. Therefore, it is very likely that these requirements would be
the first ones mentioned by the stakeholders during one-on-one
interviews with the project manager, thus making such requirements fairly easy to catch.

Unconscious requirements are a bit more difficult to extract because
they are so common and familiar to the stakeholder that he frequently
fails to mention them, assuming that everyone is aware of them.
Again, using the small business owner example, including the value-
added tax into the final price of the product sold via the Internet could
be considered common knowledge by the business owner. Yet a web
developer may not possess sufficient understanding of accounting to
add this requirement to the scope of the project.

Unconscious requirements are one of the most difficult to elicit
inasmuch as they frequently go unmentioned by the stakeholders.
Only inquisitive and thoughtful questioning and follow-up walk-
throughs can unearth all the unconscious scope items.

Undreamed-of scope items are the things that could be very useful
to the customer, but for whatever reason (typically a lack of technical
expertise) he is not aware of their existence. Once more, returning to

the website example, the small business owner may not be aware that all credit card–related information must be encrypted and protected according to industry standards. The burden of informing him about this regulation and thus adding an extra requirement lies on the project manager's shoulders.

Departments Involved or Domains Approach   Many larger organizations have achieved good results by breaking down their project requirements by the departments or business sections involved in the project. For example, the store-opening project mentioned earlier may have its scope broken down in the following manner:

- F 1.1 "Real Estate"
- F 1.2 "Construction"
- F 1.3 "IT"
- F 1.4 "Human Resources"
- F 1.5 "Marketing"
- F 1.6 "Public Relations"

Systems Approach   Certain organizations, especially the larger ones with a significant IT infrastructure, sometimes prefer to break down the projects by the systems involved. For example, one major banking core system upgrade that involved close to 300 separate systems connected to the central one was divided by systems requirements:

- F 1.0 Core System
  - Req 1.1
  - Req 1.2
  - Req 1.3

- F 2.0 System A
  - Req 2.1
  - Req 2.2
  - Req 2.3

- F 3.0 System B
  - Req 3.1
  - Req 3.2
  - Req 3.3

Target Audiences Approach   Sometimes it is useful to categorize the requirements according to the target audiences, including user requirements, customer requirements, other stakeholder requirements, and regulatory requirements. For example, the Mobile Number Portability project mentioned earlier in this book can be broken into the following categories of features:

- User Requirements
  - The requirements of the actual customers of the wireless company

- Customer Requirements
  - The requirements of the members of various wireless company departments

- Other Stakeholder Requirements
  - The requirements of other wireless companies in the market

- Regulatory Requirements
  - The requirements imposed by the ministry of communications

Information Technology or Software Development Approach   The field of IT and software development contains probably the largest collection of requirements categorization methodologies. The classical approach is to divide requirements into

- Functional Requirements
- Nonfunctional Requirements (more on this in Chapter 7)

These requirements are frequently supplemented by

- Business Rules
- Data Definitions
- Constraints

Use cases are also a popular approach of documenting the requirements, especially the ones describing the interactions between humans and the systems. The use case is typically a list of steps defining interactions between an actor (human) and a system to achieve a certain goal (e.g., to print a label or to obtain a boarding pass). Use cases are also frequently supplemented by business rules, data definitions, and constraints.

Agile methodologies, so popular recently, use a technique called "user stories" that are used to capture both functional and nonfunctional requirements. User stories are typically expressed in the following format:

As a <role>, I want to <goal/desire> so that <benefit>

where

- Role: A human or a system
- Goal: Some kind of action to be taken
- Benefit: Benefit for the role expected to be derived from the action

For example:

"As a store clerk, I want to swipe a customer credit card and initiate the payment so that the customer can pay for his purchases."

Table 4.2 contains the summary of the requirements categorization approaches along with their suitability for various situations and industries, with three stars denoting a great fit; two stars, a satisfactory fit; and one star, a poor fit.

Which one of the above categorization approaches should be used? Unfortunately, there is no straightforward answer to this question, and it falls into the art of project management rather than the science. However, it seems that using the hierarchical approach coupled with whatever is appropriate considering the scope being analyzed works the best for most projects.

What Is the Requirements Engineering Process?

Let us spend some time analyzing the requirements engineering process as it is defined in the software development field. Although it is understood that this approach has its roots in IT, there is no reason why it can't be at least referred to for better understanding in other fields.

Figure 4.5 describes the requirements engineering process as it is viewed in the IT and software development fields. Requirements engineering consists of requirements development and requirements management. In its turn, the requirements development area consists of requirements

Table 4.2   Requirements Categorization Approaches

REQUIREMENTS CATEGORIZATION APPROACHES	INFORMATION TECHNOLOGY OR SOFTWARE DEVELOPMENT	ENGINEERING, ARCHITECTURE, OR PRODUCT DEVELOPMENT	MULTIDISCIPLINARY PROJECTS
Hierarchical			
• For example:			
o Business Requirements	★ ★ ★	★ ★ ★	★ ★ ★
o Features			
o Requirements			
Engineering			
• For example:			
o Prescriptive Requirements	★ ★	★ ★ ★	★
o Procedural Requirements			
o Performance Requirements			
Psychological			
• For example:			
o Conscious Requirements	★ ★ ★	★ ★ ★	★ ★ ★
o Unconscious Requirements			
o Undreamed-of Requirements			
Departments/Business Domains			
• For example:			
o Marketing Requirements	★ ★	★	★ ★ ★
o Training Requirements			
o IT Requirements			
o Operational Requirements			
o Legal Requirements			
o Construction Requirements, etc.			
Systems			
• For example:			
o System A Requirements	★ ★	★	★
o System B Requirements			
o System C Requirements, etc.			
Target Audiences			
• For example:			
o User Requirements			
o Customer Requirements	★ ★	★ ★	★
o Other Stakeholder Requirements			
o Regulatory Requirements			

Table 4.2 Requirements Categorization Approaches (Continued)

REQUIREMENTS CATEGORIZATION APPROACHES	INFORMATION TECHNOLOGY OR SOFTWARE DEVELOPMENT	ENGINEERING, ARCHITECTURE, OR PRODUCT DEVELOPMENT	MULTIDISCIPLINARY PROJECTS
Technical			
• For example:			
o Functional Requirements	★ ★ ★	★	★
o Nonfunctional Requirements			
o Use Cases			
o User Stories, etc.			
Design			
• For example:			
o Technical Solutions	**AVOID**	**AVOID**	**AVOID**

elicitation, requirements analysis, requirements specification (or documentation), and requirements validation. Requirements management contains requirements tracking and requirements maintenance.

The typical scope definition process from the requirements management perspective is as follows: First, the requirements are elicited

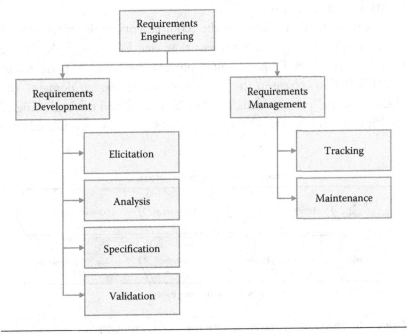

Figure 4.5 Requirements engineering process.

(some people prefer the term "extraction" instead) from the users and customers. Then, the entire requirements pile has to be sorted through, and the scope components have to be classified and arranged according to the preferred hierarchy. Frequently, a need arises to clarify some of the less obvious points by engaging in extra elicitation sessions with the customers.

Afterwards, the requirements have to be documented properly in some kind of a specifications document. Before the document is baselined and passed on to the project manager and the rest of the technical team to create the work breakdown structure followed by the scheduling and budgeting, the specifications have to be validated with three different groups of people: the customers, the project team, and preferably the requirements owners (more on this in Chapter 14).

Once the actual "hands-on" work starts on the project, the requirements analyst is responsible for tracking the requirements and their maintenance, as a significant percentage of the scope components will probably change and new features will be added to the original scope on any given project. Her job is to process all the changes to the product scope and maintain the requirements document as the requirements grow and change.

It is worthwhile to compare the requirements engineering process with the project scope management flow (see Figure 4.6). As can be seen, the "Collect Requirements" process corresponds perfectly to the "Elicitation" phase in the requirements engineering domain. The "Define Scope" process includes all of "Analysis" and the beginning of the "Specification" stage. Work breakdown structures are finalized once

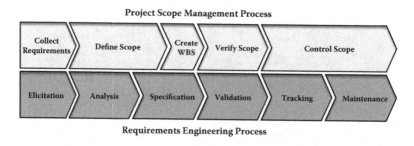

Figure 4.6   Project scope management versus requirements engineering.

the "Specification" phase is complete. "Verify Scope" and "Validation" correspond to one another perfectly, and "Control Scope" includes both "Tracking" and "Maintenance."

Who Is a Requirements Analyst?

Let us try to define one of the most enigmatic roles on modern projects: the role of the requirements analyst. Who is this person who is responsible for one of the major areas of any project? As mentioned before, in the software development industry this role is performed by a business or systems analyst.

In product development, this mission very frequently falls on the shoulders of engineers or designers—by the way, they are frequently people with purely technical backgrounds, both education and experiencewise. Hold that thought for a while; we will come back to it shortly.

In construction, this role is performed by the architects and interior designers. Once more, they are people with very technical backgrounds, architects probably more so than designers, who as a rule have not been trained to elicit requirements from the customers or users.

In multidisciplinary projects, the role of the requirements analyst is even more obscure; sometimes it is performed by the project manager, and sometimes the product scope is defined by the technical representatives of each of the departments participating in the project. Once more, in both cases it is very unlikely that project stakeholders received any kind of requirements training.

For the purposes of this chapter in particular and the book in general, we do not concentrate too much on what the requirements analyst's title should be or whether it is a separate role on every project or if it should be performed by a project manager or a technical expert. The only thing this book advocates is that there must be at least one person on the project team who is trained in proper requirements elicitation, analysis, and documentation. So, who is the requirements analyst? He has to perform several roles at once. He has to be a translator, because he is responsible for capturing the requirements expressed in the language of the user or customer (typically a nontechnical language) and translating it to the language understood by the technical project resources.

For example:

>"*The car must be really fast.*"

converts to

>"*The car shall be able to travel at a speed of up to 100 mph.*"

She has to be a keen observer, because she has to observe the work performed by the user from the user's perspective rather than from the technical resource's perspective. The requirements analyst has to be an interpreter of the work to be performed—in other words, someone able to reveal the essence of work, not its incarnation.

For example:

>"*The bottle opener must be rectangular in shape.*"

converts to

>"*The bottle opener shall be able to open bottles with both round and rectangular necks.*"

Very frequently, the requirements analyst is someone who invents better ways of performing the work described by the user.

For example:

>"*The dryer should have different drying cycles to accommodate different types of loads.*"

converts to

>"*The dryer shall have three different drying cycles (small, medium and large loads).*"

and

>"*The dryer shall have a dryness sensor that will shut the device down once the laundry is completely dry.*"

The requirements analyst is also a scribe who should be able to record the results of the analysis in the form of stakeholder-under-standable requirements specifications and analysis models that are necessary, verifiable, attainable, unambiguous, complete, consistent, traceable, concise, and prioritized.

For example:

"We want our house to be energy efficient."

will convert to that shown in Table 4.3.

Table 4.3   Energy Efficiency Requirements

FEATURE ID	REQ ID	REQUIREMENT DESCRIPTION	PRIORITY
F 6.0	R 6.1	The building shall be built from sustainably harvested wood.	Nice to Have
	R 6.2	The insulation materials used shall range from R-20 to R-30 in the walls and from R-50 to R-70 in the ceilings.	Must Have
	R 6.3	The basement and the foundation shall also be insulated.	Should Have
	R 6.4	The builder shall locate as many electrical appliances in the basement as possible.	Nice to Have
	R 6.5	The builder shall use vapor-retardant materials in construction of the walls.	Must Have
	R 6.6	The smaller windows (less than 9% of the floor area of the room) shall be located on the north, east, and west sides of the building.	Must Have
	R 6.7	The windows on the north, east, and west sides of the building shall be made of the glass with low solar heat gain coefficient (SHGC).	Must Have
	R 6.8	The larger windows (approximately 12% of the floor area of the room) shall be located on the south side of the building.	Must Have
	R 6.9	The windows on the south side of the building shall be made of the glass with high SHGC.	Must Have
	R 6.10	All the potential air leaks everywhere in a home's thermal envelope shall be sealed.	Must Have
	R 6.11	Heat recovery ventilators (HRV) or energy recovery ventilators (ERV) shall be installed in the house.	Should Have
	R 6.12	ENERGY STAR–certified furnace shall be installed in the house.	Should Have
	R 6.13	ENERGY STAR–certified appliances shall be used in the house.	Should Have

What Does the Analyst Do?

One of the most important responsibilities of the requirements analyst is to challenge the business context of each requirement requested by the stakeholders. This necessitates considerable courage on the part of the analyst, because in many instances the customers and users are not really keen on answering questions such as "Why exactly do you want this feature in the final product?" or "What is the benefit of this component to the organization?"

Requirements experts are responsible for identifying the project stakeholders, customers, and users from whom the requirements will be elicited. They should master a multitude of requirements elicitation techniques, including interviewing, marketing surveys, problem reports analysis, Joint Application Development (JAD) sessions, and apprenticing, to name a few, and know what combination of the techniques is to be used in a given situation (more about this topic in Chapters 5 and 6).

Requirements experts should also be capable of the detailed requirements analysis by asking a massive amount of questions to unearth all the finer details of the requirements provided by the stakeholders, to discover the requirements that have been omitted by the users, and to understand dependencies between the features requested by various groups of customers (see Figure 4.7).

After the requirements have been "found" and analyzed, they should be documented in such a format that is specific and unambiguous

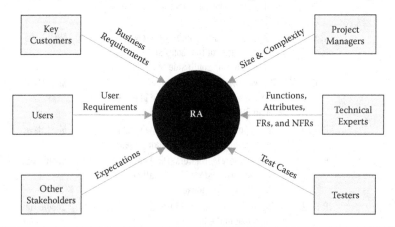

Figure 4.7   What does the analyst do? (FR: functional requirement, NFR: nonfunctional requirement, RA: requirements analyst.)

enough for the technical resources on the project but yet simple enough that they are clear to the nontechnical users and customers.

The scope analyst must be adept at running validation workshops, including customer walk-throughs, technical team inspections, and peer reviews, to catch all the deficiencies and mistakes earlier rather than later in the process when the cost of each mistake simply skyrockets (more on this topic in Chapter 15).

He is also responsible for requirements prioritization sessions with all the key project stakeholders to assign importance factors to all the scope components. Again, this is a process requiring significant integrity and bravery, because it is not unusual for the stakeholders to demand that all the requirements be assigned the highest possible priority (more on this topic in Chapter 6). Finally, the requirements analyst, frequently in tandem with the project manager, tracks and maintains all requirements once the project moves into the execution and control phases.

What Skills Would You Need?

Requirements experts should possess several key skills that should enable them to perform the job properly. Listening skills are at the top of the list inasmuch as a big portion of the requirements are gathered by having one-on-one and one-on-many conversations with key project stakeholders, including customers and users. Closely related to listening skills are the interviewing and questioning abilities that allow the scope analyst to extract conscious, unconscious, and undreamed-of requirements from the stakeholders.

As mentioned earlier, analytical skills are also very important for the requirements expert because she is supposed to sift through a big pile of generic requirements and sort them (see Figure 4.8) according to their hierarchy and type (i.e., functions, attributes, functional requirements, business rules, etc.). Furthermore, the analyst is supposed to watch out for requirements necessity, verifiability, attainability, ambiguity, completeness, consistency, traceability, conciseness, and prioritization, just to name a few (more about these topics in Chapter 6).

The scope expert must be a skilled facilitator because he will be responsible for conducting numerous meetings and sessions with the stakeholders and frequently acting as an arbitrator when the discussions get a bit heated, and believe me, they will. Having great

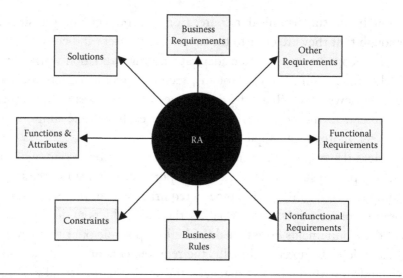

Figure 4.8 Sources of requirements. (RA: requirements analyst) (Adapted from Wiegers, K.E. *Software Requirements* [2nd ed.]. Redmond, WA: Microsoft Press, 2003.)

interpersonal skills also helps navigate out of the hairy situations that will surely arise on projects!

The requirements expert must possess keen observation skills especially when the work includes observing other users at work and attempting to come up with additional or even improved product functionality. As stated above, excellent communications skills including both written and verbal, are also very important.

Finally, the most important and unfortunately the most overlooked aspect of requirements analysis: There exists a misconception, especially at the senior levels of management, that a talented and experienced technical expert—be it a programmer, engineer, architect, designer, or any other type of professional—can become a good requirements analyst without training, resource materials, mentoring, and coaching.

Requirements Owners: Customers, Users, and Stakeholders

Introducing the Requirements Owner

We should probably start this section of the chapter with one of the most important definitions of this entire book. This is the point of time when the mysterious person who, for the lack of my imagination, was called the "requirements owner" is introduced to the audience. Why do we highlight this point so much?

The problem is that so far the fields of both engineering and software development have stressed the importance of listening almost exclusively to the actual users of the final product. However, with the emergence of larger, more sophisticated multidisciplinary projects in the past decade or so, listening just to the voice of the user will probably not suffice any more.

Consider the following example: A local port authority decided to implement a "Coast Power" project that would allow the cruise ships moored at the docks to shut down their diesel engines and connect to a land-based electrical grid. Who are the users of this service? They are the cruise ship crews and port employees responsible for the maintenance of the entire system. But would it be sufficient to collect just their requirements in order to define the "Coast Power" project scope? The obvious answer to this question is an unequivocal "No," and here is why.

Who are the high-level stakeholders of this venture? The are definitely the port authority; the cruise ship companies; federal, state, and municipal governments; and the local power company. Is it possible that all of them would have business and technical requirements in mind as well as constraints, business rules, and attributes that are likely to affect the scope of this project?

What would happen if the requirements analyst fails to talk to all three levels of government that do not act as users on the project but most definitely will have multiple rules and regulations governing the building of large electricity grids? Would the energy company providing the actual electricity have certain components it would want implemented before this project is complete?

Who Should We Talk To?

A question that gets asked frequently, especially on large and complicated projects, is "Who should I include in scope discussions?" This is a very complicated matter. Setbacks in the form of cost overruns and missed deadlines are pretty common because the right group of people (or even a single person) was not consulted properly at the scope definition stage.

An example of this scope definition problem is as follows: The project in question was fairly small by this organization's standards—less than $1 million. It involved installing a new high-tech gate on one of the terminals. The project was initiated by the security and engineering departments, who managed to get through all the phases of the project and were in the final stages of execution. About a week before the deadline, one of the engineers suddenly "remembered" that the new gate had to be operated remotely and should be properly "hooked up" to their computerized terminal operations system. The IT department was contacted and told in no uncertain terms to "connect" the gate to the existing software system by the planned deadline. The "computer guys," while collectively scratching their heads, dropped many of the tasks on their current projects and came to a very disheartening (at least for the security team) answer: Software that operated the gate was not the same as the system they were running; hence, they would need about a month or two to study it and integrate both packages properly. This story serves as a perfect example of what can happen when the project manager neglects to include all the relevant stakeholders during the detailed scope definition phase.

The first collective group of primary stakeholders are the clients (aka, "sponsors"), customers, and the future users of the product or service you are trying to build. Clients have the final say in the product scope discussions with respect to what the product does, how it does it, and how sophisticated or simple it should be because they are the ones financing the project.

Customers are also important because they (one hopes) will pay for your product and walk out of the stores with it under their arms. Or, they may ignore it and decide to buy the competitor's product. Therefore, it is very important that you understand their real needs.

End users could be a different group from customers; that is, purchasing can be done by one group of people and actual usage by another (think of millions of parents buying video games for their kids during the Christmas season). On a more serious note, it is typically the users of the product or service who possess the deep knowledge and expertise in the area to provide the project manager with real detailed requirements.

Other groups of stakeholders can include company management, subject matter experts and consultants, project team members, inspectors, legal experts, public opinion, government, and last—but definitely not least—adjacent departments within the organization.

Why Do We Neglect the Customer?

I have seen it happen on numerous occasions: It is a common behavior within the profession when project managers and their team of technical experts decide either independently or after being pressured by their management to ignore one or more stakeholder groups in their detailed scope definition efforts.

Some of the common excuses for this behavior by teams are

- "We are afraid the stakeholder will find out too much about the problems we are having and the mistakes we made, rather than seek their help in overcoming the difficulties."
- "We are too busy to take time out to communicate and coordinate with our stakeholders."
- "We think/pretend it is harder when we involve the stakeholder."
- "We think we can do it without the stakeholder."
- "We believe stakeholder involvement costs too much money and time."
- "There are personality conflicts with key stakeholders."
- "Our own management won't let us."
- "We are already late with some of our deliverables! Talking to the stakeholder will waste more of a valuable project's time."

Note: In this particular discussion, stakeholders include clients, customers, end users, company management, and subject matter experts, among others.

Project managers should be aware of these "excuses" to ignore the voice of the stakeholder and must be ready to defend their decisions to invest the necessary time and effort into building proper project scope. The value of investment in requirements can be clearly demonstrated by the study conducted by Barry Boehm to determine the relative costs of fixing an error at various stages of the project (for a detailed discussion of the "cost of mistake" concept, please refer back to Chapter 1).

The question that project managers should be asking their overly hasty team members, managers, and other project stakeholders is

"Would you like to spend one hour discussing the scope with me now, or would you rather spend between 40 and 1,000 person-hours fixing our scope omissions and defects closer to the end of the project?" (See Figure 1.6, "Cost of mistakes" in Chapter 1.)

How Do We Find the Requirements Owners?

There are multiple ways for the requirements to "find their way" to the scope analysts (see Figure 4.9). They can be communicated via the sales department to the product manager, who bundles all the high-level features and passes them on to the requirements analyst for further investigation. At many product companies, this is the preferred channel of communication between the requirement owners and the scope experts.

Sometimes the requirements owner can have a chat with his manager, who is authorized to approach the requirements analyst directly and either pass on the information to her directly or arrange for a meeting with the original requirements owner.

The requirements can be communicated to the procuring manager, who in turn can initiate a conversation with the marketing or sales department of the vendor company to describe the key features of the

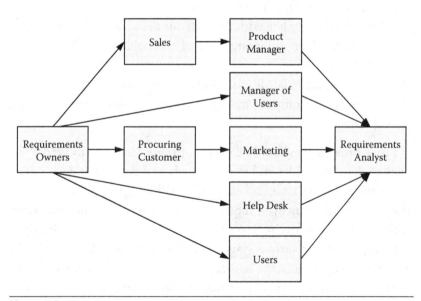

Figure 4.9 User–to–requirements analyst communication lines.

product or service required. A lot of professional services companies operate in such a manner.

Requirements owners in some cases have a direct channel of communication with the company help desk that, among other tasks, has a responsibility to accumulate all problem reports and submit them to the requirements experts for further analysis.

Finally, in certain cases the requirements owners get to chat with the scope analysts directly without any intermediaries between them. This can happen on a variety of projects, especially internal and multidisciplinary ventures.

There are several groups of stakeholders that need to be considered when assessing who specifically could be a requirements owner (see Figure 4.10). In general, stakeholders represent the highest level of requirements owners. They can be divided into real project customers and other stakeholders who do not necessarily possess any requirements but are still interested in a successful completion of the project.

The customers are in turn divided into actual product users and their managers—that is, people who do not necessarily use the product of the project but supervise those who use it, so their opinions may also be of value. The users can be divided into three distinct groups: favored users, secondary users, and other users. Obviously, the favored

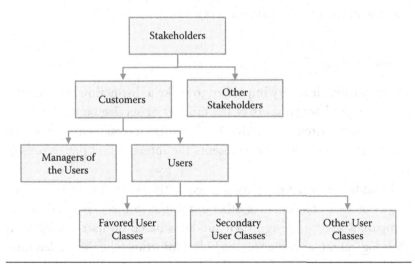

Figure 4.10   How do we find the users? (Adapted from Wiegers, K.E. *Software Requirements* [2nd ed.]. Redmond, WA: Microsoft Press, 2003.)

users class receives the most preferential treatment when requirements are collected.

How does one find the requirements owners? In general, whoever performs the role of the requirements analyst on the project should not be afraid to ask questions such as

- "Who is the subject matter expert in this area?"
- "Who, do you think, should be able to answer my questions with respect to this topic?"
- "If you don't have this information, who would have it?"

Once the pool of requirements owners is complete, the analyst can divide them into different classes based on the following characteristics:

- Their profession or the job they perform
- Frequency with which they use the product (service) of the project
- Domain experience
- Their expertise with the product or service to be delivered
- Features they use
- Tasks they perform in support of their business processes
- Access privilege or security levels

Once the classes have been established, the requirements analyst may select representatives for each user class and agree and understand who the real decision makers are.

Customers versus Users Discussion

In many cases, it is very important to make a distinction between the customers and actual users of the product or service being designed, even if the requirements analyst is "forced" to interact with the paying customer who supposedly represents the interests and preferences of the actual users.

In addition to the story mentioned at the beginning of this chapter, let us look at a couple of other examples. In the 1950s, several toy companies used to design their products based on user testing with their logical target audience: the kids. Unfortunately, they failed miserably because the products had to be attractive to the actual buyers:

the parents. So, for quite a while the toy manufacturers had to design the toys to be attractive to the parents.

Unfortunately for the toy companies, things changed sometime in late 1990s with the advent of e-commerce when children could buy products directly online without any intervention from their parents. However, some companies failed to adjust their requirements-gathering methodologies for the new toys and had some serious issues. They neglected to realize that over the course of 50 years, the kids had turned from just users into customers and users.

Another example was related to me by a student of mine who used to work in the real estate business. She mentioned that there is a rule known to all the realtors and custom-home builders: It doesn't matter who the paying customer is; do not try to finalize the sale or the detailed home design until the key user (wife) has examined them and provided all parties involved with her approval.

Partnership Agreement

Experience shows that it is always a good idea to educate the requirements owners about the requirements elicitation process and attempt to establish some ground rules for future engagements. Here is a list of topics a scope expert might want to discuss with the stakeholders:

- We will communicate our problems openly and as early as possible.
- We will resolve problems and make decisions at the lowest possible level.
- We will maintain a professional atmosphere and respect.
- We will always remember that there is no such thing as a stupid question.

Although the first three rules are fairly self-explanatory, it is important to point out the significance of the last tenet. Unfortunately, it is a somewhat common perception that an analyst or a project manager who asks "too many" questions somehow projects an image of unprofessionalism or even incompetence.

"You are asking too many questions; the customer might think you have no idea what you are talking about!" I have heard this phrase uttered many times in corporate environments. Sadly in many instances, unprepared clients may indeed conclude that the project experts are ignorant. On the other hand, abstaining from asking these questions may, and most likely will, lead to omitted, misunderstood, or misplaced scope components that will come back with a vengeance sometime during the execution, or, God forbid, during the closeout stages of the project.

Chapter Summary

We started this chapter with an in-depth examination of the types of requirements, including the hierarchical, engineering, departmental systems' target audiences, and the software development approaches. Then, we spent some time learning about the requirements engineering process and how it is aligned with the project scope management phases. We also discussed the role of the requirements analyst, his or her responsibilities, and the skills required to perform these functions.

Furthermore, we talked about the different types of requirements owners, including the customers, users, and stakeholders. We also described the dangers of neglecting the customers and various ways of identifying the requirements owners.

Finally, we recommended that on every project the project team led by the project manager and the requirements owners establish ground rules for all future engagements on the project, including professionalism, problem resolution, and open communications.

5

HIGH-LEVEL SCOPE ELICITATION

Historical Perspective: University in the Desert

A government of one of the countries in the Gulf region decided to embark on a project of building a multicampus university in several, at times remote, locations. It was decreed that the said project should take five years to implement and the cost should be around US $200 million. It was not completely clear, even after talking with several people actually involved in the endeavor right from the very beginning, whether these constraints were just "dropped" from the very top of the government levels or were at least very high-level estimates generated by a qualified party.

The scope of the project, at least at a very high level, was also thought to be well understood. It included the following requirements:

- Engineering design of all five campuses (both conceptual and final)
- Construction of classrooms and lab training facilities
- Construction of dormitories
- Procurement and installation of all necessary equipment
- Setup of a new IT infrastructure including several data centers
- Design, development, and delivery for over 100 new courses
- Setup and customization for a web e-learning portal

The primary contractor decided to proceed with five different vendors to be responsible for different parts of the scope of the project. As a result, each vendor was requested to provide his version of the solution with respect to his vertical area of expertise. The primary contractor decided simply to aggregate individual scopes provided by the vendors into one united program scope. Consequently, no thought was given to proper integration between different scopes.

Finally, it turned out that the original request for proposal (RFP) issued by the customer neglected to mention that the university would be constructed in an open desert with no water, electricity, sewage, or roads. And because the primary contractor neglected to verify the existence (or absence, to be more precise) of all these ingredients, the budget and duration for the project mentioned in the original contract were, to say the least, inadequate.

Ultimately, by the time the contract was signed and all five subcontractors led by the primary contractor arrived on the construction site, there were a lot of complaints, accusations, and threats of court action thrown around. Finally, it took the involvement of an external consulting company who had to intervene and to establish, among other things, proper requirements elicitation and analysis techniques in order to create one united program scope and revised budget and timeline resulting directly from it.

Why is this story being mentioned at the beginning of the "High-Level Scope Elicitation" chapter? The lessons that one is expected to learn from this case study are

- Scope components and features missed at the very beginning of the scope elicitation process can, and usually do, turn into nasty surprises sometime during the execution stage of the project.
- Scheduling and budgeting for the project without a good understanding of the scope of work is a futile effort.
- And finally, a project manager should not under any circumstances ignore the interdependencies of the various scope components.

Sources for Requirements

Requirements Elicitation Is Not Easy

I frequently employ an exercise when teaching my courses: I ask the audience members to think for one moment of their idea of a "dream home." I ask them whether they thought about this before; the majority of them agree that yes, indeed, over the course of their lives they have given this topic a lot of thought and can envision this building pretty well.

Then, I tell them that they now have to sit down with me, and I am willing to invest as much time as needed, and describe the house to me in detail, down to the type of flooring in the kitchen and living room, color of the walls in the master bedroom including the exact shade, specific type and model of faucets in the bathrooms, molding in the dining room area, and so on. The goal of this exercise is that at the end of it I should have a detailed blueprint of the building and the bill of materials, including product SKUs (stock-keeping units), with which I can go to, say, Home Depot and purchase all the necessary supplies. After a couple of minutes, someone in the room exclaims, "But that is impossible! How can you expect us to know all the little details about the house?"

Why am I telling this story? The reason is that thinking that one can easily come up with a complete list of detailed requirements at the beginning of the project is self-deception. Requirements elicitation is a long and at times painful process of probing, asking questions, analyzing the preliminary results, coming up with more questions, and investigating again.

Furthermore, once the technical experts sit down to have any kind of requirements elicitation interaction with customers or users, they (the users) do not necessarily provide the analysts with a structured model of requirements that follows a predefined taxonomy. In other words, the customers rarely start these conversations by saying, "I will cover all the high-level business requirements first, followed by product features. And at the very end, I will provide you with all the functions and attributes of the product."

Those who have at least once been involved in a project know that this scenario is practically unheard of. What really happens is the user tells us a narrative that includes different types of information belonging to all levels of the requirements hierarchy (see Figure 4.8). Here are some of the examples of such information exchanges that I have witnessed:

From a conversation with a real estate agent wanting to improve her website:

> You can't get to the "All Properties" page from any secondary page unless you keep clicking [the] "Back" button several times (depending on where you are in the application). Also, we don't like the "Search" function. ... You can only search houses based on their location. What about price ranges, type of house, and number of bedrooms. Also, the current search is too slow ... Is there anything you can do to speed it up?

What information is contained in this short paragraph? The real estate agent wanted to provide the website visitors with a convenient way of getting back to the home page. Furthermore, she needed the search criteria to be expanded to include location, prices, type of house, and number of bedrooms. She was also a bit concerned about the website performance.

The analysis of this fairly simple monologue unearths at least two functional and one nonfunctional requirement. The improved version of the actual captured requirements may look something like this:

- FR 1.1 The "All Properties" page shall be accessible from each secondary page.
- FR 1.2 The user shall be able to search for property by the
  - House location and/or
  - Price range and/or
  - Type of house and/or
  - Number of bedrooms

- NFR 1.2 The property search shall take no more than two seconds.

And here is an example from the world of engineering—a conversation between a representative of the marketing team and the design engineer:

The current corkscrew bottle opener is inadequate for several reasons. Firstly, the customers want a bottle opener that will fit the bottles with square bottle necks. Also, it has been reported that the screw itself is a bit wobbly, which frequently leads to the destruction of the cork. Another complaint that we had is that the device is too heavy and too big. Can you see if you can decrease the weight and the size of the bottle opener? And by the way, the new device should still conform to our corporate branding standards.

What kind of requirements can we find here? According to the marketing manager, the improved version of the corkscrew bottle opener should fit square bottles, be more stable, and still conform to the corporate branding standards, presumably color and shape. There is also a request to decrease the size and the weight of the opener. Let us see if we can record all these features in a proper—functions (FCT) and attributes (ATT)—project scope management format:

- FCT 1.1 The bottle opener shall fit square as well as round bottle necks.
- FCT 1.2 The screw shall deviate by no more than 1/16 of an inch.
- ATT 1.3 The bottle opener shall weigh no more than 100 grams.
- ATT 1.4 The bottle opener shall fit into a 5 × 3 inch box.
- ATT 1.5 The bottle opener shall conform to ABC Ltd. corporate branding standards.

As shown in Figure 4.8, there can be several different types of requirements that can be "thrown" at the requirements analyst:

Business Requirements: Where the customer or user typically states what benefits (financial or other) she expects from realization of the project:
"Increase market share by 25%."
"Save $1,000,000 by eliminating manual report generation."

Functional Requirements: When the user defines what the final software product should do in specific circumstances:
"If the credit card is not authorized, the issue shall be communicated to the customer."
"The user shall be able to sort the list alphabetically."

Nonfunctional Requirements: When the user describes the quality of the system, for example, how fast or how secure the financial transaction should be.

Functions: When the user defines what the final product should do in specific circumstances:
"The ladder shall support up to 300 lbs."
"When the fire alarm lever is pulled, the fire alarm sound shall be activated throughout the building."

Business Rules: Where the user describes a business policy or procedure:
"Must comply with PCI security standards."
"Must add VAT to the purchase price."

How to Elicit Requirements

Elicitation Methodologies

Interviews Interviews are probably one of the most popular elicitation techniques. Having one-on-one or one-on-many discussions with clients or users is a popular start for the requirements elicitation stage on many projects. In Chapter 4, we already discussed the best ways for identifying the users. Later, in the "Unearthing High-Level Requirements" section of this chapter, we talk about various requirements extraction techniques that can be used during interviews.

There are two types of interviews a project manager or a requirements analyst could conduct:

- Informal interviews
- Structured interviews

Informal interviews have a relatively unstructured setup where the project manager might start the conversation with sentences such as "Please tell me about what the system should be able to do" or "What is your vision for the new container terminal we are about to build?"

In the case of structured interviews, the requirements analyst has a list of prepared questions that allow him to combine the structure/consistency of a survey with the flexibility of an informal interview. Interviews are one of the most efficient ways of collecting requirements on almost all types of projects.

Documentation Documents that describe current or competing products, especially if they had certain success in the market, can be quite useful. For example, a layout and a list of features of a successful convention center halfway around the world can provide designers and architects with a few interesting and useful ideas.

Document analysis can be useful on larger IT, product, and interdisciplinary projects.

Requirements Specs Analysis of the requirements specifications written for the previous versions of the product can be very helpful in identifying important requirements, especially the review of the "Nice-To-Have" features and of the "Parking Lot" section of the documents, which possibly may reveal some interesting features that have been deemed not important in the previous release of the product.

Review of the requirements specifications comes in handy on product and software development projects.

Problem Reports/Enhancement Requests   Analysis of the help desk problem logs is one of the best ways of unearthing valuable and needed requirements. Having a conversation with the field people (e.g., maintenance) who deal with customers on a daily basis can also be very helpful in discovering features that are needed in the market. Finally, frequent interactions with the sales department can be very useful to the project team in deciding what components are of importance in future product releases.

Problem reports/enhancement requests can come in handy on internal IT, software development, and product development projects.

Marketing Surveys/Focus Groups   This category includes marketing surveys, focus groups, questionnaires, and interviews. The firsthand data are gathered directly from the people to determine what they expect from a product or service. Statistically a properly placed survey of about 100 people should give an approximate picture of an entire US market (about 300 million people). Enlarging the survey size to 1,000 participants would, according to statistics, give you a fairly accurate picture of the entire population.

Having said that, it is important to understand that certain weaknesses in the design of the surveys may lead to false responses. Potential root causes include "group think," where some people in the sample are psychologically "forced" or peer pressured to provide the same answers as the rest of the people in the group. Also, leading questions in the surveys can skew the results of the experiments.

To avoid these situations, try to ask open-ended questions to catch all the possibilities or iterate between "how" and "why" questions. Focus groups involve allowing a design team to observe the response of appropriately selected users to the specific product design. Marketing surveys focus group approach can be useful on all types of projects.

Market Trends   Many organizations, especially those in product development, like to start their development quest by looking around themselves and trying to understand how their competition is interpreting the market requirements and trying to address those needs.

Some of the questions such organizations might ask are

- Who are the products aimed at?
- What trends exist?
- What are the differences in cost, range, shape, and so on?
- Which ones are more successful and why?

In addition, the information can be found in marketing reports or trade directories, historic trends, and even political and macroeconomic factors.

Product and software development companies are the first ones that come to mind with respect to employing market trend analysis. Having said that, a large company could initiate a major interdisciplinary project just because they saw a specific trend in the market. For example, a port authority may decide to build a new cruise ship terminal because they saw a potential increase in the number of ships arriving and departing from their city.

Observing Users   Observing users at work, or apprenticing, is a technique that dates back to medieval times when a master craftsman (the user in our scenario) was being watched by the apprentice (the requirements analyst). The analyst sits by the user and learns the job by making observations, taking notes, drawing process diagrams, and asking questions. It is even possible that the "apprentice" gets to do some tasks under the supervision of the master to even better understand the processes involved.

The trick used here is that an average person is not typically very good at describing step-by-step processes when not actually being involved in the performance of the tasks. However, this job of describing the steps becomes much easier while he or she is in the middle of doing it. The job of the "apprentice" is to receive the running commentary and to ask the following questions whenever the explanations provided by the user are unclear:

- Why did you do that?
- What does this mean?

- How often does this happen?
- What happens if ... ?

The beauty of this methodology is that it can be used on almost all projects: IT, software development, engineering, product, and interdisciplinary ventures.

Scenario Analysis   Scenarios are the descriptions of business processes where the story is broken into a series of steps or scenes that take place between the user and the system or between two users. Here is an example of a "Check the Passenger onto the Flight" scenario that describes the interaction between the passenger and the airline employee:

1. Locate the passenger's reservation.
2. Ensure the passenger is correctly identified and connected to the right reservation.
3. Check that the passport is valid and belongs to the passenger.
4. Attach the frequent flyer number to the reservation.
5. Allocate a seat.
6. Get correct responses to security questions.
7. Check the baggage onto the flight.
8. Print and hand over the boarding pass and bag tags.
9. Wish the passenger a pleasant flight.

Events and Responses   Sometimes the requirements can be recorded in the event–response table format. An *event* is some action taken by the user or another system that must stimulate the system for a certain action or *response*.

Let us consider a seemingly simple example; a normal kitchen stove, or the buttons that operate the oven, to be more precise (see Figure 5.1). As can be seen, the panel consists of five buttons: "Up," "Down," "Bake," "Grill," and "Clear All." Our job is to foresee all possible combinations of events (in this case, users pushing various buttons) and responses (what the oven should "do" in response to these actions by humans). Table 5.1 lists all possible events that can take place with the panel and all possible responses to the aforementioned events.

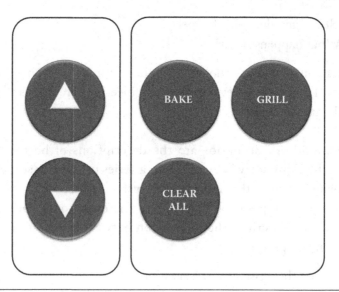

Figure 5.1   Stove buttons.

Table 5.1   Oven—Events and Responses

EVENT ID	EVENT DESCRIPTION	INITIAL SYSTEM STATE	SYSTEM RESPONSE
1.1	"Bake" button is pushed	Oven is not in use.	Produce a beeping sound and initiate the lower heating element at the temperature of 200 degrees.
1.2	"Bake" button is pushed	Oven is in the "Grill" mode.	Produce a beeping sound.
2.1	"Grill "button is pushed	Oven is not in use.	Produce a beeping sound and initiate the upper heating element at the lowest of two available temperatures.
2.2	"Grill "button is pushed	Oven is in the "Bake" mode.	Produce a beeping sound.
3.1	"Up" button is pushed	Oven is not in use.	Produce a beeping sound.
3.2	"Up" button is pushed	Oven is in the "Grill" mode and the heat is at "Low."	Produce a beeping sound and reset the temperature of the upper heating element to the highest of the two available temperatures.

Table 5.1 Oven—Events and Responses (Continued)

EVENT ID	EVENT DESCRIPTION	INITIAL SYSTEM STATE	SYSTEM RESPONSE
3.3	"Up" button is pushed	Oven is in the "Grill" mode and the heat is at "High."	Produce a beeping sound.
3.4	"Up" button is pushed	Oven is in the "Bake" mode and the heat is at less than 500 degrees.	Produce a beeping sound and increase the temperature by 10 degrees.
3.5	"Up" button is pushed	Oven is in the "Bake" mode and the heat is at 500 degrees.	Produce a beeping sound.
4.1	"Down" button is pushed	Oven is in the "Grill" mode and heat is at "Low."	Produce a beeping sound.
4.2	"Down" button is pushed	Oven is in the "Grill" mode and heat is at "High."	Produce a beeping sound and reset the temperature of the upper heating element to the lowest of the two available temperatures.
4.3	"Down" button is pushed	Oven is in the "Bake" mode and the heat is at more than 200 degrees.	Produce a beeping sound and decrease the temperature by 10 degrees.
4.4	"Down" button is pushed	Oven is in the "Bake" mode and the heat is at 200 degrees.	Produce a beeping sound.
4.5	"Down" button is pushed	Oven is not in use.	Produce a beeping sound.

Psychology Understanding human psychology has recently become a very important asset in defining the project scope. For example, understanding child psychology is essential in the design of toys. This is especially important lately, because in the past several decades the process of buying toys itself has undergone a key transformation. Again, it is not the parents who are making decisions to buy toys for their kids; it is the children who find these toys (frequently online) and purchase them with or without their parents' explicit knowledge.

Another field that is utilizing the latest developments in psychology is, surprising to many people, e-commerce. We all shop on the Internet for books, clothing, tools, and electronics, but very rarely do we realize how the site designers manage to manipulate and direct us using subtle but very powerful psychological tricks. Here are some of them:

- *"Buy" and "Add to Cart" buttons*: Do you ever notice how large and colorful they are? Do you really think it is just a design quirk of the user interface specialist? And yet it has been proven that color, size, and even irregular shape have a proven, measurable impact on products added to cart, checkout initiation, and checkout completion.
- *Free Shipping versus Savings*: Do you think that $10 in money saved is always better than $6.99? The conventional answer to that question is "Yes," but a professor from Wharton School of Business found that consumers preferred free shipping worth $6.99 in savings over a $10 discount on the product. And smart e-commerce retailers take full advantage of this irrational behavior.
- *Lump Sum versus Distributed Payments*: By the same token, when offered to buy a warranty for an additional $15, most customers declined that offer. But guess what they did when they were offered to pay $2 per month for the next 12 months for the same warranty?
- *Usage of "Will"*: The e-commerce psychologists argue that the statement "Shampoo X will calm itching and will reduce redness" is much inferior to "Shampoo X calms itching and reduces redness." Some peculiar process in our brains forces us to believe the second type of statement way more than the first one.

As mentioned earlier, this technique could probably be quite useful in software and product development, although it is possible to employ it on certain multidisciplinary projects as well.

Brainstorming Brainstorming can be a very effective technique if used properly. There are several rules and guidelines on how to conduct the brainstorming exercises:

- Get participants from a wide range of disciplines and experiences.
- Present them with a well-articulated problem.

- Explain that judgment; evaluation; criticism; and, most important, debate must be suspended.
- The goal is to produce as many ideas as possible; that is, at that point of time the team is aiming for quantity over quality of ideas.
- Participants must be encouraged to present unconventional, unique, crazy, and wild ideas.
- Keep in mind that the sessions must be fun. It is very unlikely that the people will get creative if the project manager says, "I want to hear marketable ideas only."

The idea of the brainstorming exercise is to capture as many ideas as possible (sometimes new ideas will flourish from the ones mentioned earlier) and then filter out and select the best solution(s) to the problem at hand.

Brainstorming is a universal tool and works well on practically every type of the project.

Competitive Products Benchmarked This process involves designers looking at similar products that are already available and trying to evaluate how well those products perform certain functions or possess certain attributes. The technique is fairly useful in software and product development as well as in some construction projects.

Reverse Engineering This is a somewhat controversial technique that involves disassembling the existing (frequently competing) product and trying to understand how it was designed in the first place. Engineering and new product development projects seem to be the prime candidates for the reverse engineering technique.

Cool Hunting This technique is widely used in the product development industries, especially the ones targeting youth markets. The key premise of this approach is that the trends currently considered to be "cool" by the younger generation have a significant probability of becoming mainstream in the next several years, or even months, in the world of high technology.

Thus, *cool hunting* is a combined term that describes a variety of techniques, such as living in the subgroups and observing their behavior in the context of the rules of sociology and psychology. The requirements analysts are supposed to notice what the youngsters are wearing, how they are receiving information, and what communication methods they use, just to name a few. Obviously, the role of social media websites such as Facebook, for example, cannot be ignored.

Then, the analysts are supposed to make predictions as to where the future trends will be directed based on the data collected. Cool hunting is probably more suitable for software development and new product design projects.

Crowd Sourcing   The idea behind the crowd sourcing method is to get as many opinions about the product from as many people in one's target markets as possible. Several years ago, this approach would imply fairly large expenses for those willing to invest in this type of requirements elicitation. Nowadays, with the amazing growth of social networking sites—including Facebook, LinkedIn, and Twitter, to name a few—collecting the opinions of several hundred if not thousands of people has become a matter of one post and a waiting time of several days or even hours.

All that is left to the analyst is to sift through all the posts left by potential customers and collect the key features of the future product. As in the case with cool hunting, crowd sourcing is probably most common in software and product development industries.

Targeting   Realizing who exactly your customer is (i.e., the target market) and starting by creating his profile would probably be a very intriguing step for many companies. Sometimes these profiles are straightforward and unsurprising; for example, one would not expect to see many retirees in the video games market or to sell golf clubs to people with an income of less than $30,000 per year.

On the other hand, I remember one instance when a North American–based charity thought for the longest time that their donors were typically older people with low incomes residing in blue-collar neighborhoods. Almost 20 years later, they hired a marketing company to conduct an analysis of their donor base and, to their great surprise, discovered that their typical donor was between 35 and 50 years

Table 5.2 Comparison of Methodologies across Industries

	INFORMATION TECHNOLOGY, SOFTWARE DEVELOPMENT PROJECTS	ENGINEERING, CONSTRUCTION, PRODUCT DEVELOPMENT PROJECTS	INTERDEPARTMENTAL MULTIDISCIPLINARY PROJECTS
Interviews	★★★	★★★	★★★
Documentation	★★	★★★	★★
Requirements Specs	★★	★★	★
Problem Reports	★★	★★★	★
Marketing Surveys	★★	★★	★★
Market Trends	★★★	★★★	★★★
Observing Users	★★	★★★	★
Scenario Analysis	★★★	★★★	★★★
Psychology	★	★★	★
Events and Responses	★★★	★★★	★★★
Brainstorming	★★★	★★★	★★★
Product Benchmarking	★	★★★	★
Reverse Engineering	★★	★★★	★
Cool Hunting	★	★★	★
Crowd Sourcing	★★	★★	★★
Targeting	★★★	★★★	★★★

Note: Three stars denote great fit, two stars are average fit, and one star is poor fit.

old, earned higher income than the national average, and resided in mixed white collar and immigrant parts of town. Needless to say, their marketing efforts and campaigns needed quite an adjustment after that discovery!

Table 5.2 compares the effectiveness of various requirements elicitation methodologies in information technology, engineering, and multidisciplinary projects.

Unearthing High-Level Requirements

Importance of Questions The ability to ask the right questions is the science and the art on which scope elicitation depends. One of my favorite exercises to conduct is to ask the class attendees a very simple but very tricky question:

I am sure most of you have used a check-in kiosk at the airport. Do you think, having used this device, it is an easy or a difficult thing to create, especially the software side of it?

The answer always invariably is that it should be a fairly straightforward and simple process. As one of my corporate clients put it, "You identify yourself with a passport and get the boarding pass. How difficult could it be?"

Let us review some of the questions an experienced requirements analyst will ask in the process of eliciting requirements for this particular process. Let us assume that the key steps in this process are

1. Initiate the program.
2. Identify yourself.
3. Find the reservation.
4. Check visa.
5. Check in luggage.
6. Select a seat.
7. Select a meal.

Table 5.3 shows some of the questions that may be asked just for the first three steps in the process.

This simple example is designed to demonstrate how something seemingly very simple can, with the help of several well-targeted questions, suddenly grow in size exponentially. In my own extensive project management experience, the failure to ask these (at times extremely

Table 5.3   List of Potential Questions for the Airline Kiosk

1. Initiate the program
What options will the user have to identify himself/herself?
2. Identify yourself
With a Passport:
- Do all passports follow the same encoding standard?
  - o If not, then how many standards exist?
- What happens if the machine is unable to read the passport?
- If the machine is able to read the passport, what happens if:
  - o Passport is real and not expired?
  - o Passport is real but expired?
    - Will the user be issued a boarding pass if this is an international flight?
    - Will the user be issued a boarding pass if this is an internal flight?

Table 5.3 List of Potential Questions for the Airline Kiosk (Continued)

o Passport is fake?
- ▪ Should the kiosk notify the police?
  - • Does this mean that every device needs an interface with an airport police department?
  - • Does this imply that we need to deploy some kind of software in the airport police headquarters?
- ▪ What should the kiosk "do" while the police are being notified?

With a Credit Card:
- • What types of credit cards will the machine accept?
- • Will the device rely on the information recorded on the magnetic strips? or
- • Communicate and confirm the information with the credit card company?
  - o Does this mean that we need a secure interface with all the credit card companies?
  - o Do we need to encrypt the data exchanged between the kiosk and the credit card companies?
- • What happens if the machine is unable to read the credit card?
- • What happens if the card is expired?
- • What happens if the card is fake?

With the Airline Frequent Flyer Card (AFFC):
- • Will the device rely on the information recorded on the magnetic strips? or
- • Communicate and confirm the information with the airline?
  - o Does this mean that we need a secure interface with the airline?
  - o Do we need to encrypt the data exchanged between the kiosk and the airline?
- • What happens if the machine is unable to read the AFFC?
- • What happens if the card is expired?
- • What happens if the card is fake?

3. Find the reservation
- • How will the user find his or her reservation?
  - o Will it be done via a combination of the Name and the Reservation Number?
  - o Will the Name be extracted and saved from the previous "Identify yourself" step?
- • What should the system do if the Name is found but not the Reservation Number?
- • What should the system do if the Reservation Number is found but not the Name?
- • What should the system do if there are two different reservations for the same person?
- • What should the system do if the person is not traveling alone?
- • What should the system do if the reservation is found?

annoying) questions at the very beginning of the project led to a severe underestimation of the scope of work to be done. A small scope led to low project budget forecasts and aggressive timeline estimates. And at some point of time in the execution stage, someone uttered the proverbial, "Oops, I guess we didn't think about that!"

Structure for Defining Preliminary Scope   One of the first most important steps in building the project scope is to understand the key components or features of the project. It is a fairly simple exercise if the project manager has the right people in the room (see the "How Do We Find the Requirements Owners?" section in Chapter 4) and knows what questions to ask. Based on my own experience, this is the moment of truth where in the course of one or two hours a project can go from "Hey, this is just a small thing that should take no more than a couple of months" to "Oh my God, we never realized we had to do so many things to succeed on this project!"

Let us consider several examples of different types of projects and how the high-level scope definition was initiated on them. By the way, these examples stay with us for the rest of the book; by the time we reach the last chapter, we will have developed a project charter, requirements documentation, requirements management plan, requirements traceability matrix, project scope statement, and work breakdown structure for almost every case study mentioned below.

First, we have the "Airport Check-in Kiosk" project, a purely product-oriented software development endeavor. In this case, ABC Software Systems was hired to develop the software for the first-ever airport check-in kiosks for XYZ Airlines. After several initial meetings between the project team members and the customers and users, the high-level scope for the project was defined as shown in Table 5.4.

The software was supposed to have a menu screen (Feature 1.0) as well as a way for the traveler to identify herself to the system (Feature 2.0); find her reservation (Feature 3.0); confirm or change the seat preassigned to her (Feature 4.0); pay for her luggage, if necessary (Feature 5.0); and print her boarding pass (Feature 6.0). An extra

Table 5.4   High-Level Features—Airline Kiosk

FEATURE ID	FEATURE DESCRIPTION
F 1.0	Kiosk menu
F 2.0	Traveler identification
F 3.0	Traveler reservation search
F 4.0	Confirm or change seat
F 5.0	Pay for luggage
F 6.0	Print boarding pass
F 7.0	Navigation

Table 5.5 High-Level Features—Energy Efficient Home

FEATURE ID	FEATURE DESCRIPTION
F 1.0	West Coast style
F 2.0	Five bedrooms
F 3.0	Four bathrooms
F 4.0	Square footage: 3,500–4,500 square feet
F 5.0	Two floors
F 6.0	Energy efficient

feature (Feature 7.0) called "Navigation" was created to unite all the relevant nonfunctional requirements and certain navigational logic applicable to all the screens of the application.

The second example is a "West Coast Style Energy Efficient Home" project that falls into the category of product development, engineering, and construction undertakings. In this case, the construction company was expected to design and build a five-bedroom, four-bathroom West Coast style energy efficient (ENERGY STAR certified) home (see Table 5.5).

In the next endeavor, for the "Port Upgrade" project that falls into the category of multidisciplinary (or enterprise) projects, the high-level scope looked something like that shown in Table 5.6.

In this particular case that port authority's internal stakeholders chose to dissect the upcoming project by department-specific scope components. Here the project scope involved an acquisition of a suitable piece of land (Feature 1.0) followed by finalization of all legal aspects of the purchase (Feature 2.0). While the building was being

Table 5.6 High-Level Features—Port Upgrade

FEATURE ID	FEATURE DESCRIPTION
F 1.0	Land acquisition and environmental cleanup
F 2.0	Legal aspects
F 3.0	Public relations (including federal, state, and municipal governments)
F 4.0	Marketing (including Chinese, Japanese, Indian, and Korean markets)
F 5.0	Planning—facility design
F 6.0	Construction
F 7.0	Engineering
F 8.0	IT components
F 9.0	Logistics (including building a road and bus connection)
F 10.0	Security

designed (Feature 5.0), the PR department had to initiate communications with the federal, state, and municipal governments (Feature 3.0). Also, business development specialists at the port had to start a marketing campaign targeting Asian markets, especially Japanese, Korean, and Chinese shipping companies (Feature 4.0).

The actual construction component (Feature 6.0) also implied cooperation of the internal engineering and IT teams (Features 7.0 and 8.0) with the construction contractors to deliver the building computer networks, hardware, and software deployments. Furthermore, the logistics department was responsible for building a road and a bus connection to allow for delivery and removal of cargo from the port (Feature 9.0). Finally, due to strict regulations at the federal government level, the project included a significant security component involving fencing, cameras, electronic gates, and the like (Feature 10.0).

The "CRM Implementation" project undertaken at a European financial institution can be labeled as a multidisciplinary (enterprise) project with a strong IT component. In this particular scenario, the IT department of the organization was charged with the deployment of a new CRM (customer relationship management) system. Once again, initially it was perceived as a pure technology project where only minimal involvement of the rest of the departments would be required.

However, even the first joint stakeholder meeting discovered that the project was much more complicated than it appeared before (see Table 5.7). First, four front-end modules of the CRM system were supposed to be configured and deployed at four different departments: call center (Feature 1.0), business intelligence department (Feature

Table 5.7   High-Level Features—CRM System

FEATURE ID	FEATURE DESCRIPTION
F 1.0	Call center module
F 2.0	Business intelligence module
F 3.0	Campaign management module
F 4.0	Direct marketing module
F 5.0	Data warehouse integration
F 6.0	Data cleanup
F 7.0	Updates to the standard operating procedures
F 8.0	Training

2.0), campaign management team (Feature 3.0), and direct marketing department (Feature 4.0).

In addition, the new system had to be integrated with the existing data warehouse (Feature 5.0), and a considerable data cleanup factor had to be considered (Feature 6.0). Also, standard operating procedures of at least the call center, business intelligence, campaign management, and direct marketing departments had to be updated by their respective team members (Feature 7.0). Finally, certain employees from the above-mentioned four departments as well as the IT team had to be trained in usage and maintenance of the new software (Feature 8.0).

And finally, a "Mobile Number Portability" project example. A government of one of the European countries mandated that starting on a specific date all mobile customers would be free to switch from one mobile provider to another while keeping their phone numbers, including prefixes.

Initially, the project was perceived as a purely technical venture where, according to one of the executives, "Network engineers and IT people had to make several minor adjustments to the existing setup." However, the first-ever requirements exercise with all the key stakeholders in the room led to the following discovery (see Table 5.8).

First of all, it turned out that the organization needed to obtain, install, and configure additional hardware for its information technology, networks, and value-added services departments. Also, significant changes were required to the way the mobile contracts with customers were set up.

Table 5.8 High-Level Features—Mobile Number Portability

FEATURE ID	FEATURE DESCRIPTION
F 1.0	Infrastructure upgrades—IT
F 2.0	Infrastructure upgrades—networks
F 3.0	Infrastructure upgrades—value-added services
F 4.0	Changes to contract management
F 5.0	Tariff changes and risk analysis
F 6.0	Changes to standard operating procedures
F 7.0	Training of personnel
F 8.0	Call center capacity extension
F 9.0	Market research and campaigns
F 10.0	Software changes—IT

Sales had to reassess their tariffs and conduct risk analysis as well as design and implement the necessary changes to the sales and logistics processes. A lot of changes to the standard operating procedures were expected, and they all had to be documented properly either in new or existing manuals. As a result, many different groups of employees within the organization had to be trained in new procedures.

Furthermore, the existing call center had to be increased in size inasmuch as the company was expecting a major increase in the number of calls because customers were now free to switch from one mobile provider to another.

Marketing, most importantly, had to prepare the entire organization for the fact that the competition in the market was going to increase drastically and to conduct market research and design new campaigns.

And finally, there was a certain amount of application development work to be done by the developers on the information services team.

One interesting aspect of this project: At the beginning, when management perceived it to be "just a technical thing to be implemented by the IT and networks teams," it was estimated to be a 10 to 20 person-month effort. However, at the end of the planning stage the forecast "cost" had been revised to 200 to 300 person-months!

Types of Questions to Ask   So, now that we know what the preliminary scope should look like, let us look at the multitude of questions the project manager or the requirements analyst should be asking to unearth all the requirements—conscious, unconscious, and undreamed-of—that would comprise the project scope.

Questions can be divided by type (see Table 5.9) into direct, open-ended, clarifying, and leading questions. Direct questions are aimed at getting specific information out of the user or customer. Here are some of the examples of direct questions:

- What should the capacity of the new container terminal be?
- What weight should the ladder support?
- How many products should the new e-commerce platform support?
- What should the airport check-in system do if it cannot recognize the passport?

Table 5.9 Types of Questions

TYPES OF QUESTIONS	WHAT DO THEY DO?	EXAMPLES
Direct Questions	Questions seeking specific information	"Why should the tax rate be set at 7%?"
Open-Ended Questions	Questions designed to stimulate the discussion and force the customer to disclose more relevant information	"What about the IT component of the project?"
Clarifying Questions	Questions that rephrase the speaker's words in order to clarify them	"In other words, what you are saying is …"
Leading Questions	Questions that propose a new action, an alternative, or an exception	"Can the customer identify herself to the system in any other way?"

Open-ended questions allow us to unearth the deviations from the normal or expected course of events (called alternatives or exceptions) that can have a dramatic impact on the scope of the project. Below are several examples of open-ended questions:

- Are there any other ways for the passenger to identify himself? (check-in kiosk project)
- What other features could become important on this project? (product project)
- What are some other uses for this ladder? (improved ladder project)
- Are there any other ways for the customer to find the product on the website? (e-commerce project)

Clarifying questions are important because the users are typically not very disciplined with respect to requirements elicitation; they are allowed to use vague and ambiguous language, whereas project managers and requirements specialists are not:

- What did you mean by "the ladder should be sturdy"? (improved ladder project)
- When you said, "Passengers will never use their frequent flyer card to identify themselves," did you actually mean "never" or can it happen on occasion? (check-in kiosk project)
- Did I hear you saying that there must be at least two roads and one bus connecting the new container terminal to the mainland? (port upgrade project)

Table 5.10   Questions to Ask—Part 1

QUESTION	REASONS	WHAT HAPPENS IF THE QUESTION IS NOT ASKED?
Why are we creating this product or service?	To make sure there is a clear understanding of the needs and benefits for the project, as well as the problems the stakeholder is trying to solve.	The wrong solution may be delivered.
What happens if we don't create this product or service?	An alternative way of asking the question above.	The wrong solution may be delivered.
Who is the original owner of this feature or requirement?	You have to know who the original initiator of the feature or requirement in question is.	You may end up eliciting requirements that have been distorted by going through the chain of command.
What problem are we trying to solve?	As a representative of the technical team, you may have a much better (cheaper, faster) solution that the customer is not aware of.	You may end up delivering the wrong solution by blindly following what the customer demands instead of understanding his or her needs.

Finally, leading questions help us in discovering both missing high-level features as well as more detailed requirements that might have been missed because they are "obvious" to the customer but not readily noticeable to the project manager.

Tables 5.10 and 5.11 contain several other questions that should probably be asked every time a project manager or requirements analyst sits together with his or her customers.

Critical Thinking   There is another absolutely crucial aspect of requirements elicitation that, in my opinion, requires a complete overhaul of one's brain. The problem here lies in the fact that sentences and expressions that would appear to be absolutely normal and acceptable by regular people must be met with a due portion of skepticism and questioning by the project managers or analysts.

I always joke with my project management training attendees that by the end of the first day they will all be turned from *Homo sapiens* into the *"Homo projectus"* because they will undergo a psychological breakthrough and develop certain "allergies" to certain words and expressions in the course of the class that will be considered abnormal by the rest of their coworkers and family members. Let us look at some examples.

Table 5.11   Questions to Ask—Part 2

QUESTION	REASONS	WHAT HAPPENS IF THE QUESTION IS NOT ASKED?
What other features (requirements) can be affected by this?	Hidden interdependencies between various features of the project may exist.	You can miss important interdependencies or even contradictions between various scope components.
What is our budget?	You need to gain a high-level understanding of the amount of money at your team's disposal.	There could be a significant discrepancy between the desired scope of the project and the budget.
When do you need this product or service to be delivered?	You need to gain a high-level understanding of the key project milestones.	There could be a significant discrepancy between the desired scope of the project and the time at the team's disposal.
If you don't know the answer to this question, then who does?	You need to make sure you are getting the correct information from the right person or group of persons.	You may end up talking to the messengers instead of real requirements owners. As a result, you may end up with the wrong information.

Unspecified Information: Does the phrase "We get sales reports" seem like a normal and acceptable thing to say? After all, we do hear it all the time when we chat with executives, sales, marketing, and business development people.

Imagine now that you are in charge of developing a system that will, among other things, provide the business development department with sales reports. A "normal" person upon hearing the phrase "We get sales reports" will probably just nod her head, write down something along the lines of "Provide sales reports to the business development team" in her notebook and move on to the next questions.

Homo projectus, on the other hand, will (and should) produce the following questions upon hearing that statement:

- Is it just you who gets the reports or your entire department?
  - Do just specific employees within your team get these?
  - Are other departments privy to these reports?
  - If yes, then who in other departments gets them?

- What do you mean by "get"?
  - Are the reports printed out and mailed to you or are they faxed?
  - Do you receive them by e-mail?

- In what format?
- Do you have a software package that produces them automatically?

- What is a sales report?
  - What kind of information is contained there?
- Do you just have one type of report or several?

We ask these questions because we need to know

- Who specifically will be getting these reports.
- How and in what format will these reports be transferred to the readers.
- What constitutes a sales report and how many types of report exist.

The readers of this book are encouraged to examine Table 5.12 for some further examples (by the way, all are taken out of real project management documents) of unspecified comparisons and generalizations.

Table 5.12 Critical Thinking

TYPE OF STATEMENT	SAMPLE STATEMENT	SAMPLE QUESTIONS

Unspecified information	"We get sales reports."	• Who is "we"?
		  • Is it you or your entire team?
		  • Is it just the specific employees from your team who get these reports?
		  • Will other departments have access to these reports?
		  • If yes, then who in other departments should get them?
		• What do you mean by "get"?
		  • Are the reports printed out and mailed to you?
		  • Are they faxed?
		  • Do you receive them by e-mail?
		  • In what format do you receive them?
		  • Do you have a software package that produces them automatically?
		  • Is it a "push" or a "pull" type of information?
		• What is a "sales report"?
		  • What kind of data fields are contained there?
		  • Do you just have one type of the sales report or several?

Table 5.12 Critical Thinking (Continued)

TYPE OF STATEMENT	SAMPLE STATEMENT	SAMPLE QUESTIONS

Unspecified comparison	"The container terminal should be improved."	• Improved how?
		  • Are we comparing it to the existing terminals at your port or your competitors?
		  • Should it become the best in the world?
		  • Improved in what way?
		    • In terms of size, overall container capacity, logistics, usage of computer technologies, security?
		  • Who decided that it should be improved?
		  • What is the reasoning behind this decision to increase square footage or overall container capacity or to improve logistics, usage of computer technologies, and security?

Generalization	"The new retail outlet should be located at the major intersection in the northern district of the city."	• Why should the outlet be located at the major intersection?
		  • If you are looking for high-traffic areas, have you considered other locations, such as malls or shopping plazas?
		• What happens if you can't find a space for rent or sale at the major intersection?
		  • Will the project be abandoned?
		  • Will the opening of the new store be postponed until you can find a suitable location?
		    • What kind of drop-in revenue are you anticipating if we open the outlet at another location?
		  • Would it still be profitable?

Some Cautions about Elicitation

"Losing" the Stakeholders

Finally, some general tips about high-level scope elicitation. First, the project manager has to make sure that all the stakeholders, customers, and user classes have been identified. Collecting the input from too few representatives could and most likely would lead to missed and overlooked features and components.

For example, in the "Mobile Number Portability" project, the executives of the organization in question formed their opinion about the scope of the project by initially perceiving it as a purely technical endeavor and thus spoke only to several directors of the IT department. As a result, the marketing, sales, call center, and training components of this project were completely ignored at the initial stage.

Listening to Only a Few Representatives

Hearing the voices of only the loudest, most opinionated customers is also a perennial problem that has negatively affected many projects. As mentioned earlier, I once witnessed a large account-opening software project at a major bank start with basically a couple of vocal branch managers stating that there was no need to "waste time" and talk to all the bank's tellers. "We have been working at the branches for 15–20 years; we can tell you everything there is to know about the account-opening systems."

The project manager agreed with the branch managers and elicited the requirements only from them, overlooking one little problem: The last time the managers had to interact with the system was at least 10 years ago! And a lot of things changed in that decade, both in banking operations and especially with respect to software capabilities.

Requirements versus Design

When eliciting the requirements, project managers frequently come across stakeholders' ideas for a possible solution rather than the description of the underlying problem they are attempting to solve. An experienced requirements expert should always make every effort to interpret what is requested by the customer, thereby uncovering the essence of the problems. Let us examine an example to demonstrate how this principle might work in real life.

A company producing high-end cameras decided, based on the feedback of their customers, that they needed to include battery chargers in the camera kits they sell because all their products use batteries. Because the company had no in-house expertise on battery charger manufacturing, their management decided to outsource the production of these devices to another firm. The following conversation took place at the meeting of the manager from the camera company and the representative of the supplier:

Manager: We would like you to design and manufacture several types of battery chargers for us.

Representative: What types of chargers do you have in mind?

Manager: Well, we produce cameras that utilize several different sizes of batteries; they include AAA, AA, C, and D types. So, we need at least one type of charger manufactured for each battery size.

There are two possible scenarios for this conversation to progress further. Let us examine both of them.

Scenario 1

Representative: No problem, we will start working on the designs for all these types of chargers right away.

Manager: Great, I hope to hear from you soon!

Scenario 2

Representative: So, what you are saying is that your company will need four different types of chargers because your devices use four different battery sizes, right?

Manager: Yes, that is the case.

Representative: Would you be open to the idea of having one battery charger that would accommodate all four types of batteries?

Manager: What do you mean?

Representative: Well, there are several ways we can approach addressing this issue. We can design a charger with several different slots for batteries of different sizes. Alternatively, we can build a charger with a sliding clamp that the customers would be able to adjust based on the batteries they are using. Another option available to us is to use springs instead of clamps; they will "automatically" adjust to the battery size.

Manager: I never thought about those possibilities! Would that mean that the cost of design and production is going to decrease?

Representative: Oh, absolutely. Instead of four different chargers, we will have to design just one. And because order quantity is going to increase drastically, we would probably be able to extend a volume discount to your organization.

What happened in the first scenario? The representative of the battery charger manufacturing company simply accepted the design solution imposed by the client instead of focusing on his underlying needs. The essence of the problem at hand was not the different types of chargers, but rather different sizes of the batteries their cameras were using.

On the other hand, in the second case, the representative asked a clarifying question, thus confirming that the client really cared about being able to recharge the various battery types they used. Therefore, having a much greater experience in the domain, he was able to come up with three possible universal solutions to the customer problem:

- Chargers with different slot sizes
- Chargers with sliding clamps
- Chargers with springs instead of clamps

And the final and very important question to ask here: In which case do you think the customer was happier at the end of the conversation? In addition, in which of the scenarios did both the customer and the supplier save and make a lot of money, respectively?

"Don't Ask Too Many Questions" Advice

I have personally witnessed on many occasions the following situation: An experienced project manager or requirements analyst is sitting down in the first meeting with the customers and users and proceeds to ask a lot of questions. At some point, typically during the break, he is approached by a representative of senior management, who tells the project manager to "tone it down with questions a bit," because the more questions one asks, the less professional and knowledgeable he looks.

This is unfortunately a very common occurrence that can lead to serious issues with whole high-level features on the project being overlooked at the very beginning and thus leading to wrong forecasts with respect to budgets, schedules, and efforts required.

Chapter Summary

In this chapter dedicated to high-level scope elicitation we have described various requirements elicitation methodologies including interviews, documentation, requirements specs, problem reports, market surveys, and the like.

Then we learned about the importance of asking the right questions and "initiated" from the requirements perspective five different projects including the "Airport Check-In Kiosk Software," "CRM System Implementation," "Energy Efficient House," "Mobile Number Portability," and the "Port Upgrade" projects.

Finally we covered the topics dedicated to certain deficiencies one may encounter during the requirements elicitation process including losing the stakeholders, listening to too few representatives, and getting into the design stage too early in the project.

6

DETAILED REQUIREMENTS ELICITATION

Historical Perspective: Burj Al Arab

The Burj Al Arab (The Arab Tower) hotel was built in 1999 in Dubai, United Arab Emirates. This project was conceived at the very top of the UAE government as a venture that would assist in transforming the country and the state from an exclusively oil-based economy to the trade- and tourism-based market.

The ruling family of Dubai gambled (and by all accounts won) that the conversion into an international hub of trade and tourism should start with a "wow-type" project that would demonstrate to the rest of the world that the Gulf country

- Can undertake ambitious projects and see them to completion
- Has a rich cultural and historic heritage
- Has the supply of and the demand for luxury hotel accommodations

The project that lasted for five years, from 1994 to 1999, delivered a 321-meter (1,053-foot) structure (see Figure 6.1) that is now the fourth tallest hotel in the world. The Burj Al Arab stands on an artificial island 280 meters (920 feet) from Jumeirah Beach and is connected to the mainland by a private curving bridge. The shape of the structure is designed to mimic the dhow's (type of local boat) sail. It is very frequently referred to as the world's only seven-star hotel although the company managing it refuses to even acknowledge the fact that they were the ones who started using this epithet. The Burj Al Arab is one of the most photographed buildings in the world and definitely played a vital role in putting both Dubai and the United Arab Emirates on the world map.

Figure 6.1   Burj Al Arab.

The purpose of this case study is to attempt to take this enigmatic and grandiose product and try to reverse engineer the requirements elicitation process from the few high-level business requirements to general features to detailed technical requirements. Let us start with what the business requirements for this project may have looked like (see Table 6.1 and Figure 6.2).

As can be seen, the project of enormous size and complexity can be "diminished" to only three business requirements: the new building

Table 6.1   Burj Al Arab Business Requirements

BUSINESS REQUIREMENT ID	BUSINESS REQUIREMENT DESCRIPTION
BR 1.0	Has to become a national icon for the UAE
BR 2.0	Has to be located offshore
BR 3.0	Has to be a luxury hotel

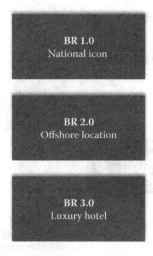

Figure 6.2 Burj Al Arab business requirements.

has to be a national icon, it has to be located in the water, and it has to be a luxury hotel. Surprisingly enough, there are only three features resulting from the above-mentioned high-level requirements (see Table 6.2 and Figure 6.3):

- The building shall resemble a dhow's sail.
- The building shall be built on the man-made island.
- The building shall meet or exceed the current requirements for a six-star hotel as defined by the European Hotelstars Union.

Once we reach the features level and drill deeper into the detailed requirements, things start getting more interesting and complicated at an exponential speed (see Table 6.3). Feature 1.1 results in a multitude of technical requirements (we listed only the first 10) describing all the relevant attributes of the hotel. They include but are not limited to its height, shape, and so on.

Table 6.2 Burj Al Arab Features

PARENT BR	FEATURE ID	FEATURE DESCRIPTION
BR 1.0	F 1.1	The building shall resemble a dhow's sail.
BR 2.0	F 2.1	The building shall be built on the man-made island.
BR 3.0	F 3.1	The building shall meet or exceed the current requirements for a six-star hotel as defined by the European Hotelstars Union.

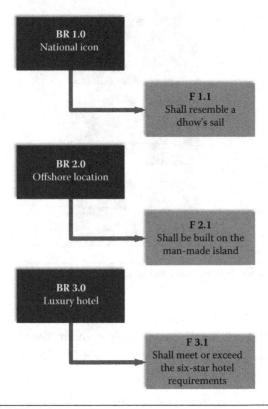

Figure 6.3   Burj Al Arab features.

The second group of requirements is dedicated to the description of the artificial island on which the hotel would be built; they include the island shape, location, height, protection mechanism, and the attributes of the road connecting the island to the mainland. Once again, only the first six of many more requirements have been listed in Table 6.3.

The last group of requirements, although probably the largest compared to other two, was the easiest to collect: The requirements for the six-star hotel can be downloaded from the European Hotelstars Union website at any point of time; some of them are listed in Table 6.3.

What was the point of this reverse requirements engineering exercise? Although I obviously can't guarantee that this was exactly the way the requirements for this project were documented,

Table 6.3 Burj Al Arab Detailed Requirements

PARENT FEATURE	REQUIREMENT ID	REQUIREMENT DESCRIPTION
F 1.1	REQ 1.1.1	The concrete structure shall have exposed diagonal steel wind bracing.
	REQ 1.1.2	The concrete structure shall be triangular in plan.
	REQ 1.1.3	The concrete structure shall be founded on piles that penetrate the sea floor.
	REQ 1.1.4	The accommodation wings shall enclose the two sides of a triangular atrium that runs up the full height of the accommodation floors.
	REQ 1.1.5	The third side, facing the shore, shall be enclosed by a glass screen.
	REQ 1.1.6	Lights illuminate the exterior of the hotel in varying colors throughout the night.
	REQ 1.1.7	The atrium shall be no less than 180 meters high.
	REQ 1.1.8	The hotel shall have 28 double floors.
	REQ 1.1.9	The hotel shall have approximately 200 bedroom suites.
	REQ 1.1.10	The hotel shall be approximately 300 meters in height.
	REQ 1.1.x	...
F 2.1	REQ 2.1.1	The man-made island shall be located 290 meters off the Dubai coast.
	REQ 2.1.2	The island shall be triangular with sides of 150 meters in length.
	REQ 2.1.3	The island shall be built off the sea bed in 7.5 meters of open sea.
	REQ 2.1.4	The island shall be protected by armor that absorbs the waves without throwing water onto the island.
	REQ 2.1.5	A road shall connect the island to the mainland.
	REQ 2.1.6	The road shall be curved.
	REQ 2.1.x	...
F 3.1	REQ 3.1.1	Only high-grade materials shall be used in construction and decorations.
	REQ 3.1.2	The hotel shall have at least one gourmet restaurant.
	REQ 3.1.3	Every room shall have a safe.
	REQ 3.1.4	The hotel shall have a gym.
	REQ 3.1.5	Every room shall have a PC with Internet access.
	REQ 3.1.x	...

it demonstrates that even large and complicated projects that deliver awesome landmark products can be broken down into fairly easy and mundane subcomponents that can be easily processed by the design team (architects and engineers, in this particular case).

Detailed Requirements Elicitation Methodologies

Before we get into the detailed discussion of tools and techniques of the detailed requirements elicitation, it must be noted that they are not very different from techniques described in Chapter 5, just slightly more appropriate for going deeper to a more granular level of the product scope.

Wallpapers

Using wallpapers is one of the easiest ways to gather detailed requirements. It is low tech and efficient and could potentially involve every person at a company. All that the project manager (or the requirements analyst) has to do is find a high-traffic area such as a lobby or a corridor next to, say, a cafeteria and attach large sheets of paper to the walls or even install special dry-erase coating and invite all the stakeholders to leave their comments.

It could be a good idea to "seed" the conversation by listing all the key features of the new product or service. For example, if the project were expected to deliver a West Coast–style energy efficient home, the "seed" list of features could look like that shown in Table 5.5.

What will most likely happen is that some of the stakeholders will leave their feedback, others will comment on the feedback provided by others, and the discussions may get very lively. Another trick the project manager or requirements analyst could use is to announce a prize for the most useful comment.

At the end of several days, the project team will be left with a lot of highly relevant and somewhat organized feedback (especially if they bothered to list the high-level features) that can be analyzed and converted into detailed requirements. This methodology is especially useful for internal large multidisciplinary or product development projects where a lot of in-house feedback has to be generated fairly quickly.

Wikis

Wikis are a natural, albeit more hi-tech, extension of the wallpapers discussed earlier in this chapter. They operate on the same principle as Wikipedia, a very popular website where anyone can create or update an article of interest. The good news is that there are quite a lot of software products out in the market, some of them free, that can be deployed fairly easily and enable the project teams to start engaging on requirements-related discussions.

The only possible limitation of using wikis is that not all the people are technologically savvy enough to know how to leave and edit their comments. Having said that, this problem can be addressed by coupling the "wallpaper" approach with the wikis. This way, the techies can use the online forums, and the rest of the people can use the old and reliable markers.

Brainstorming Revisited

Let us spend a bit more time discussing brainstorming and how it can be employed by the project teams to identify detailed requirements. To be brief, brainstorming is a way to generate a lot of ideas—many of them completely crazy—most of which will be later discarded.

It is recommended that brainstorming sessions involve between four and ten people because fewer than four participants does not provide the project manager with sufficient "critical mass," whereas when the number of participants exceeds ten, the crowd might get a bit unruly. Another aspect to keep in mind is that the organizer of the brainstorming session should ensure that the group he is assembling is as diverse as possible with respect to age, position within the organization, sex, insiders versus outsiders, and so on. This approach ensures the maximum variety of inputs.

The process involves the following steps:

- Step 1: The facilitator formulates the problem in a form of a question (the problem should not be too narrow).
- Step 2: The participants spend some time thinking about the problem presented to them.

- Step 3: The participants express their ideas on the cards (succinct and one per card).
- Step 4: Each participant quickly presents his or her idea (no criticism is allowed).
- Step 5: The facilitator tries to combine and sort the ideas and generate new ones.
- Step 6: The process is repeated until an acceptable solution is reached.

The general rules applicable to brainstorming are

- Rule 1: No criticism is allowed.
- Rule 2: A larger quantity of ideas is wanted.
- Rule 3: Crazy ideas are welcome.
- Rule 4: All ideas should be kept short and snappy.
- Rule 5: Combining ideas to improve them is highly encouraged.

Let us consider a simple brainstorming example. A manager of the product company walks into the war room and describes the following problem:

Many of our customers have the following challenge: They have a limited number of keys to their house or apartment per family. Sometimes they can't cut additional keys because the building management does not allow it, and sometimes they feel that providing their kids with the extra copies of the keys may be dangerous because they tend to lose them.

So, our goal is to come up with a device or method that will enable the family to safely share the limited number of house keys among them.

What kinds of ideas can the participants come up with?

1. Hide the key under a doormat.
2. Hide the key in a fake flowerpot.
3. Leave the key with neighbors.
4. Design a doormat with a hidden pocket.
5. Install a small safe by the door.

Secure Key Storage

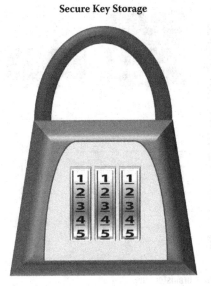

Figure 6.4   Secure key storage.

6. Install a small safe on the door disguised as a mailbox.
7. Rent a mailbox nearby and leave the key there.
8. Install a PIN code lock on the door.
9. Install a fingerprint lock on the door.
10. Create a small key storage that can be opened with a PIN code and locks onto the door handle (see Figure 6.4).

Let us try to determine what most likely happened during this brainstorming exercise. The participants started with three distinct groups of ideas that can be generally divided into the following broad categories (see Figure 6.5):

• Hide the key (ideas #1 and #2).
• Keep it at a safe location away from the door (ideas #3 and #7).
• Install a new kind of lock that does not require a key (ideas #8 and #9).

The "doormat" and "fake flowerpot" ideas led to the "doormat with a hidden pocket" and "small safe by the door" ideas. The "rent a mailbox nearby" proposal combined nicely with the "small safe by the door" suggestion and gave birth to the "small safe disguised as a

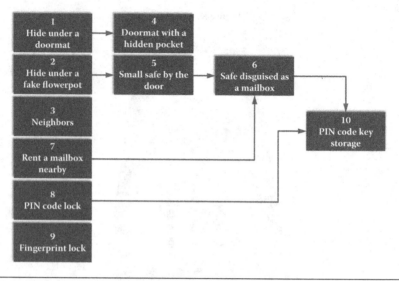

Figure 6.5   Key storage brainstorming.

mailbox" design. Finally, after realizing that hiding the key in any way is probably unsafe, leaving the key with the neighbor is too cumbersome, and changing the locks is too expensive (and probably won't be allowed by the building strata anyway), the brainstorming exercise participants combined the "safe" and the "PIN code" idea to come up with the small key storage that can be opened with a PIN code and locks onto the door handle design.

Flowchart Diagrams

Flowchart diagrams are used to describe an algorithm or a business process by providing a visual representation of a step-by-step solution to a given problem or a task. There are several different approaches and methodologies for creating the flowcharts, but they all include the following components:

- Start and End symbols: Usually represented by a small circle or an oval
- Arrows: Show the flow of the process
- Processes: Represented by rectangles and contain processing actions (e.g., "Add A to B" or "Ask customer for an ID")
- Condition or Decision: Represented by a diamond and always contains a question that must be answered by "Yes" or "No"

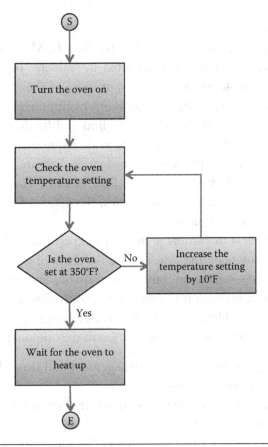

Figure 6.6   Flowchart sample: Set oven temperature.

Here is an example of a very simple process of setting the oven temperature to 350°F (see Figure 6.6). The process starts with the user turning the oven on. Then, he has to check the oven temperature setting. If the setting is lower than 350°F (for simplicity, we are assuming that 350°F is the maximum), then the user must increase the temperature setting by 10°F by pushing on the "Temperature Up" button on the panel. After each adjustment, the user must loop back to the question in the diamond "Is the oven set at 350°F?" and check the condition. The series of operations continues until the desired temperature setting is reached.

This is obviously one the most primitive examples of the flowchart use. For a more complicated example, see "Airport Check-In Kiosk" project requirements specifications under the Downloads tab on the Taylor & Francis Group/CRC Press website at http://www.crcpress.com/product/isbn/9781482259483.

5 Whys Method

The "5 Whys" method originated in the Toyota Motor Corporation and is rumored to have been invented by Sakichi Toyoda himself. It postulates that to get to the real root cause of the actual problem, one needs to ask on average five questions beginning with "why." The methodology was initially invented to find and fix defects in Toyota cars, but it recently became popular with requirements analysts as well. The architect of the Toyota Production System, Taiichi Ohno, described the "5 Whys" method as "the basis of Toyota's scientific approach ... by repeating why five times, the nature of the problem as well as its solution becomes clear."

The objective is to encourage the scope expert to avoid assumptions and imposed solutions and instead trace the chain of causality from the random request—which can come in the form of a feature, requirement, design element, business rule, assumption, constraint, and the like—to the underlying problem or need. Here is an example of how the afore-mentioned method helped the analyst get to the original problem:

- We need to install project management and time-sheet soft-ware on all our desktops.
- *Why* (do you think that you need to install project management and time-sheet software)?
- Because we need to have a better handle on managing our projects.
- *Why* (do you think that you are not handling your projects properly)?
- Because many of our projects are late and overbudget.
- *Why* (do you think your projects are late and overbudget)?
- Because our project managers are inexperienced.
- *Why* (do you think that your project managers are inexperienced)?
- Because they lack proper training, especially in the areas of estimation, negotiation, and planning.
- *Why* (do you think they lack proper training)?
- Because the senior management perceives an investment in project management training and certification as a "waste of time and money."

In this particular case that actually took place in real life, the analyst was able to deduce, by using the "5 Whys" method, the real problem at the company: lack of properly trained, experienced project managers.

User Scenario Method

The user scenario method originated in the software development sector but recently spread quickly to other areas of business. It involves taking a trip through the whole process of using a particular product or system and making yourself a critically observant user. The whole concept is very similar to the idea of apprenticeship discussed in Chapter 5.

It implies trying to see the product or service from different perspectives, including customers, operators, management, maintenance, and other stakeholder groups. On larger projects with multiple stakeholder groups, this process can take several trips. There are several other dimensions in addition to the stakeholder one that the requirements analyst may decide to consider. These include what happens with the product or service

- In day versus night
- In dark versus light environments
- In busy versus free times of the day or season
- In hot versus cold temperatures
- In dry versus humid weather
- Before versus after the use
- When used by experienced versus inexperienced users

The number of dimensions one may need to consider is pretty much infinite and varies greatly from situation to situation and from project to project.

What the requirements analyst is expected to do is to embed herself into the user team and record actions, thoughts, comments, and impressions. Carrying a recorder or a notebook could be quite beneficial. The analyst can start the process by observing the experienced user working with the product to understand the key procedure and operations. It would be a very interesting approach to attempt either to ask an inexperienced user to work with the product or even to try to use it yourself, because you may end up making the mistakes an experienced user wouldn't.

A fascinating story was shared with me by an elderly electronics engineer who started his career at a secret Soviet research facility back in the 1960s. He was one of the junior technical resources on the project developing a brand-new portable military radio system:

> We were finishing the project and conducted all the tests related to distance, clarity and strength of the signal, system capabilities in various weather conditions, the ease of use, and even its weight. All of the tests have been passed with flying colors.
>
> Finally, we were told that a three-star general who happened to be a World War II veteran will be conducting the final verification and "user acceptance testing." On one hand we were a bit nervous, and on the other, full with youthful cockiness, especially fueled by the series of successful internal tests.
>
> The general arrived at our facility and looked a bit bored and generally unimpressed while we were going through all the prescribed testing procedures. Finally, he exclaimed, "OK, all the parameters look fine, but I do have one last test remaining I need to conduct personally." And then, without any warning he approached the radio, picked it, and threw it against the wall with all the force he could muster.
>
> "Now, check if it still works," he said. We tried to activate the radio, but unfortunately it was completely dead.
>
> "You, guys, don't get out of your offices much, do you now?" the general inquired. "Have you ever observed how eighteen year conscripts load army trucks? I want this system to be robust enough to be dropped from the height of three or four feet and still work!"

What this example demonstrates is that interactions with the users in "field conditions" are often absolutely essential to the success of the project. The requirements analysts should go out and meet the users in the field, get them to describe each step as they are using the product or the service, and remember that nobody can talk better about what they do and why they do it than they can while in the middle of doing it.

Some questions that may be helpful in the process are

- Why did you do that?
- What does this mean?

- How often does this happen?
- What happens if this feature does not work?
- What other ways of accomplishing the tasks can you mention?
- In which way can the thing go wrong?
- What can prevent you from accomplishing your task?

JAD

Joint application development (JAD) sessions also originated in the high-tech sector but recently have spread into other industries as well. The idea behind this concept is that the user representatives and the technical project team members work together aided by the facilitator. Some studies suggest that using JAD sessions can decrease the dreaded scope creep by half. There are several key participants in the JAD sessions:

- *Executive Sponsor:* Typically, this is a fairly senior person on a project (possibly a product champion) who has the power to make important strategic decisions and provide overall direction to the team.
- *Subject Matter Experts:* They are the actual users of the final product or service as well as the people who possess the information about what the final product should do and how it should do it. They comprise one of the most important groups in the meeting who will do most of the talking.
- *Facilitator:* This person runs the meeting by directing the flow of discussions and prepares the agenda and the list of follow-up tasks. Typically, the role is performed by the requirements analyst or the project manager.
- *Scribe:* This person records all the proceedings of the session.

JAD sessions usually require the following preparation steps:

- *Review the project charter (and, if applicable the business case):* Identify the project objectives, critical success factors, assumptions, and constraints. Make sure the project charter (business case) is properly written, validated, and signed off.
- *Review the key high-level features*: Again, they should be captured in the project charter (business case).

- *Establish the schedule of JAD sessions:* They tend to be fairly long, anywhere between one and five days. It is recommended, however, that the first session is scheduled for at least three days, as it will take some time for the team to gel (one day), develop a common language (one day), and start working on the issues full time (one day).
- *Select the participants:* Identify the sponsor, subject matter experts (SMEs), facilitator, and the scribe.
- *Prepare a workshop agenda:* This is one of the most important steps. Using the feature list extracted from the project charter, prepare documentation, worksheets, diagrams, and even props that will help the participants understand the business function under investigation.
- *Present to the participants:* Familiarize all the participants with the project, including the information contained in the project charter (business case). A PowerPoint presentation could be very helpful to communicate all the relevant project information to all the participants in an organized manner.

Once the sessions start, the job of the project manager or the requirements analyst is to coordinate the workshop logistics, including projectors, whiteboards, PCs, tables, markers, masking tape, and flip charts, to name a few.

Best Trawling Techniques

Table 6.4 contains the comparative assessment of various detailed requirements elicitation methodologies and their effectiveness in different project situations.

Running Efficient Meetings

Importance of Communications

Efficient and effective communications are an important ingredient of every process involving managing people in general and project scope management in particular. Consider one of the earliest projects in human history, the Tower of Babel. The construction crew was doing fairly well in erecting the tower with "its top in the heavens." However, at some point the jealous deity Yahweh became

Table 6.4 Best Trawling Techniques

	INFORMATION TECHNOLOGY, SOFTWARE DEVELOPMENT PROJECTS	ENGINEERING, CONSTRUCTION, PRODUCT DEVELOPMENT PROJECTS	INTERDEPARTMENTAL MULTIDISCIPLINARY PROJECTS
Wallpapers	★ ★	★ ★ ★	★ ★
Wikis	★ ★	★ ★	★
Brainstorming	★ ★ ★	★ ★ ★	★ ★ ★
Interviews	★ ★ ★	★ ★ ★	★ ★ ★
User Scenarios	★ ★	★ ★	★ ★
Focus Groups	★	★ ★ ★	★
JAD	★ ★ ★	★ ★	★

Note: 1 star—poor fit, 2 stars—good fit, 3 stars—great fit

so displeased with human vanity that he decided to confuse their languages and to scatter the people throughout the earth. The lesson learned from that futile endeavor was, "If you can't communicate, you will most definitely not be able to succeed!"

Therefore, let us concentrate this section of the chapter on the art of running efficient project meetings in general and scope elicitation sessions in particular, the place where the destiny of the project is frequently decided by the stakeholders and where the collective soul of the project teams can be broken or inspired depending on the talent or lack thereof of the project leader.

How Formal Should One Get?

A question that is frequently being asked by both junior and seasoned project managers and requirements experts is, "How formal should we get when running the meetings?" In today's confusing world when different industries, companies, and even departments have diverse project management methodologies with respect to process agility and formality, many project managers are confused as to which approach would be more appropriate to their situation. Some of the questions asked by the project professionals include the following:

- Should I send out a meeting agenda before the meeting, or should I just let the stakeholders pick the topics they want to discuss?

- Do I have to record meeting minutes, or is it better to leave it to attendees to capture their preferences and tasks on their own?
- Should I let people discuss the important topic for as long as they need without imposing time limits?
- When it comes to project scope related meetings, am I a dictator, facilitator, or just a scribe?

The answer to all these inquiries is that each requirements analyst is expected to have a style of his own that no doubt has to be adjusted depending on the industry or company for which he finds himself working. For example, on smaller projects, meeting minutes are sometimes not recorded formally; rather, various "to do" and "issues" lists are written on a whiteboard or flip chart. Also, sometimes no formal invitations are sent via e-mail either because of the physical proximity of all the stakeholders or because it is customary to start every day with a "daily stand-up meeting."

On the other hand, on very large endeavors, meeting minutes are recorded formally in a project management office (PMO)-approved template, meeting agendas are distributed beforehand via e-mail, and the requirements expert is expected to keep a very accurate log of attendees and "regrets." Having said that, what is attempted in this section is to gather and systemize the best practices of conducting scope meetings and allow the analysts in the field to adjust the degree of formality according to their project realities.

Importance of Meeting Minutes

One of the most important documents that should be utilized by all project managers and requirements analysts irrelevant of the size and complexity of their projects is the meeting minutes. Unfortunately, this document is frequently ignored by many project leaders who cite various excuses in trying to justify their reluctance to document tasks, issues, and key discussion points examined during the stakeholder meetings.

Sometimes they argue that "Nobody reads them anyways" and therefore "Why waste time?" In other cases, project managers argue that their job is to facilitate the meetings and not act as scribes. Yet another justification frequently heard, especially from software development professionals, is that they don't want to appear too bureaucratic or as trying to dominate the "dynamic and agile environments."

What Are the Benefits of Meeting Minutes?

Anyone is free to agree or disagree with the earlier arguments; however, let us examine the benefits of using the meeting minutes templates. First, because all the topics, issues, and tasks are recorded in an organized fashion, nothing is ever omitted or forgotten. Also, meeting minutes can act as "to do" lists for all the customers and users.

Furthermore, there are awkward and sometimes very embarrassing pauses when a requirements analyst looks around the room and utters something along the lines of, "Hmmm, what else were we supposed to discuss today?" I do realize that the last example may sound silly to some, but I have been a participant in several such meetings in my professional life. Trust me, this is a painful thing to watch! Thus, having a properly captured agenda definitely helps in establishing your reputation as an organized professional.

In addition, a habit of keeping up-to-date meeting records frequently enables the project manager (sometimes involved on several projects concurrently) to prepare for the upcoming meeting quickly. All she needs to do is to review the minutes from the previous meeting and promptly refresh all the key points for the forthcoming get-together with the stakeholders.

Surprisingly enough, meeting minutes may help in dealing with difficult project stakeholders. I remember a situation when I joined a large bank where the concept of project management discipline was, let us say, "a fairly unknown entity." As a result, a small group of people continuously managed to sabotage the work of the project manager by claiming that they either had not been informed about their tasks or missed the e-mail messages. A simple "deployment" of the meeting minutes with requirements-related tasks, people responsible for them, and deadlines addressed both the attendance and overall discipline issues on the project. Interestingly enough, it was the peer pressure of the other customers and users that changed the situation on the project rather than any punitive actions of the project manager.

Some additional benefits of using meeting minutes are

- Nothing is ever omitted or forgotten.
- Meeting minutes can act as "to do" lists for all team members.
- There are no awkward pauses.

- They help in establishing your reputation as an organized professional.
- They enable the project manager to quickly prepare for the upcoming meeting.
- They improve attendance.
- They improve discipline.

How to Make Your Meetings Work

Table 6.5 contains some of the key tips on how to run effective project meetings for the project managers. Also, avoid booking "all-hands-on-deck" meetings whenever possible. For example, let us assume that a project manager needs to discuss two issues with his project stakeholders: topic A and topic B. In the first scenario, he invites all 16 stakeholders to a two-hour meeting. However, only seven people

Table 6.5   Tips on Running Meetings

WHAT YOU SHOULD DO	HOW TO DO THAT
Be a facilitator and establish a host position.	• Introduce people, clarify the agenda and start the discussion.
Listen and reflect.	• For example, "So, Mike, what I think you are saying is …"
Direct the conversation.	• Use the meeting agenda as a guide. • Publish the agenda/meeting minutes and stick to them.
Manage the meeting time.	• Suggest continuing offline. • Weed out issues for offline discussions.
Make a history.	• Use flip charts. • Use whiteboards. • Use meeting minutes to capture everything that happened in the meeting. • Keep a digital camera or even a cell phone handy to take photos of the whiteboards when leaving the meeting room or running out of space.
Establish a set of rules (and e-mail it to all participants).	• Interruption policy: With this policy in hand, the meeting facilitator can readily and politely silence the interrupters. • Setting time limits (e.g., two minutes per person per topic). • No personal attacks: Nobody objects in the calm beginning, but many will violate in the heat of events.
Reduce pressure; be calm and collected. Smile.	• No "Oh my God, we are all going to die!" screams.

are interested and can provide meaningful feedback on topic A, whereas six participants are worried about topic B. Let us pretend that three participants possess relevant knowledge on both issues. If the project manager decides to dedicate one hour per topic, then we have the following situation:

- Six people will be bored for the first hour.
- Seven people will be bored for the second hour.
- Three people will be kept "entertained" throughout the meeting.

Needless to say, the meeting atmosphere will be less than inspiring. In addition, 13 person-hours of valuable time will be wasted. Thus, an experienced project manager would rather book two separate one-hour meetings: one dedicated to the discussion of topic A and another to topic B.

Top Five Signs That You Are Done Collecting and Reviewing the Requirements

Interestingly enough, many requirements experts, even experienced ones, have trouble understanding when to stop gathering the requirements. "How do we know when it is OK to stop eliciting scope components? We are a bit concerned that if we stop talking, we may overlook some important features that may pop up in the project later and wreak havoc on our budgets and schedules."

Here are some of the telltale signs that the project team may consider in wrapping up their requirements gathering efforts:

- If the users can't think of any other requirements
- If the users repeat features and components that have already been covered
- If suggested requirements are all out of scope
- If all proposed requirements are low priority
- If the users are proposing features that should be included some time in one of the next releases

If the project manager or requirements analyst notices one or several of these symptoms during the requirements elicitation meetings, it could be a good idea to consider wrapping up the scope definition phase of the project.

Prioritizing Requirements

One of the most important actions for a project manager and the require-ments analyst to do closer to the end of the requirements stage is to pri-oritize all the scope components. It is very important that the project team members and other project stakeholders establish an understand-ing that all the scope components will be prioritized as soon as possible in the process. There are several very important benefits to this approach.

First, a simple discussion about how important one or the other feature is can shed some light on the overall vision of the product. For example, if when designing, say, a mobile phone the analyst was told that sturdiness, reliability, and ability to perform in extreme weather conditions were all high-priority factors, then probably he would be able to deduce that the intention of the company is to develop the device to be used by the military, explorers, and professionals working at remote locations.

If, on the other hand, a sleek design, a multitude of functions, and the ability to play video and music files were deemed to be of signifi-cant importance, then the requirements analyst can understand that the target market for the product is a younger urban well-to-do crowd.

Feature prioritization also allows for the early delivery of the prod-uct inasmuch as all the less important requirements are either omitted or postponed until the next release, thus allowing for the scope to be decreased and speeding up the project flow.

Prioritization can also reduce the riskiness of the project because lower priority but technically problematic requirements (and there are always quite a few of them on any given project) can be omitted from the future scope, thus decreasing the probability of technical chal-lenges at the later stages.

Games Your Stakeholders Can Play

Many customers and requirements owners still erroneously assume that the sole purpose of the project manager's existence is to cut the scope of the project at all costs. Thus, whenever the project manager or a requirements expert initiates a much-dreaded conversation regarding the priority of the project requirements, the stakeholders frequently exclaim something to the effect of, "Hey, all the requirements are high priority! Because as soon as we label some of them with 'medium' or 'low' priority labels they, are practically gone from the scope. They will almost certainly never be included into the final product scope."

Hence, some of the excuses used by the customers and users include the following:

- "We absolutely need all these features. You are a project management professional. Just make it happen somehow!"
- "It is not politically acceptable at our company to claim that a requirement has a low priority."
- "Our organization has always been known for its *we can do it all* attitude!"
- "I believe our technical people can tackle any challenges!"

One of the possible ways to deal with such a situation is to ask a simple question that sounds something like, "I understand that this requirement is of the highest priority to you. But, just for the sake of the argument, what would happen if we drop it? Would that automatically imply cancelling the entire project?"

Ways to Prioritize Requirements

Must Have, Should Have, and Nice to Have   One of the most effective ways to prioritize the project features and requirements is to break them into the following three categories:

- Must Have
- Should Have
- Nice to Have

The definition of the first grouping is very simple and straightforward: The requirement gets labeled with a "Must Have" only if the elimination of the requirement implies the cancellation of the entire project. For example, if our project were to design and build a car, dropping the "Engine" feature would deem the entire endeavor useless; the car can't travel without an engine. Hence, the "Engine" requirement would deservingly be stamped with the "Must Have" priority.

The "Should Have" grouping can be described as features and requirements that are really important, but their elimination from the scope would not automatically imply the cancellation of the entire project. For instance, having a power-windows function in the car is considered to be a very important capability for the modern auto industry. However, not including this requirement into the design of a new car would not automatically imply the cancellation of the entire project.

Finally, the third category includes all the "Nice to Have" features. The definition of this group is also fairly straightforward: These are value-adding requirements whose cancellation would not have a serious effect on the final outcome of the project. For example, sticking with the car theme we followed thus far, unless we are dealing with a very high-end model, built-in seat warmers are definitely a pleasant thing to have in your vehicle, but their absence is not going to have a serious impact on the sales.

Urgent/Not Urgent versus Important/Not Important   Another interesting approach for requirements prioritization is to look at them from two fairly different angles simultaneously. The dimensions considered in this model are the requirement importance and the requirement urgency. For the purposes of this model, "important" means that the project either will fail or would be seriously hindered if this feature were not included in the scope. Also, the feature or the requirement is considered to be urgent if the customer can justify that she needs it as soon as possible, that is, in the first version of the product or service. For example, if a company decides to develop a new smartphone, having Wi-Fi capability would be both important and urgent, because customers nowadays are very unlikely to buy a phone without this feature.

Next, after each component has been assessed on both the "urgent/not urgent" and "important/not important" elements, Table 6.6 can be used to categorize each requirement as "Must Have," "Should Have," or "Nice to Have." If the requirement is deemed to be both "Urgent"

Table 6.6   Requirements Prioritization

	IMPORTANT	NOT IMPORTANT
Urgent	Must Have	X
Not Urgent	Should Have	Nice to Have

and "Important," it gets a ranking of "Must Have"; if it is "Important" but "Not Urgent," it is deposited it into the "Should Have" pile. If the requirement is considered "Not Urgent" and "Not Important," we label the requirement as "Nice to Have" or even drop it completely. Finally, the "Urgent" but "Not Important" category implies that the requirement falling into that cell in the matrix must be ignored or cut from the scope of the project.

Market-Qualifying Criteria   Market-qualifying criteria are yet another alternative way of prioritizing the requirements. Sometimes certain features of the product or service are absolutely mandatory—frequently there is an explicit law requiring them—and it would be impossible to deliver the product or service to the market without them. Let us consider some examples. If a car company wants to sell its vehicles in California, it must ensure that its emission levels comply with the California Air Resources Board standards; otherwise, the car cannot be sold in that market.

For new home builders pretty much throughout North America, traditionally US and Canadian home buyers expect that the new homes or condos they buy should be equipped with the following six appliances: washer, dryer, refrigerator, dishwasher, microwave, and stove. And although it is still possible to sell the home without some of or all these devices, it is would significantly decrease the pool of potential customers.

Order-Losing Criteria   Sometimes the customers are quite vocal about what they specifically want in the future product or service and indicate to the vendor that unless those features make it into the scope, they would not be interested in acquiring the product.

For example, I remember a case where a company producing e-commerce platforms was told in no uncertain terms by several of its key customers that unless the new version of the software included cross-selling and upselling features (i.e., "The customers who bought this item also bought items X, Y, and Z"), they shouldn't even bother calling them. Naturally, the cross-selling and upselling components became the absolute "Must Have" ingredients on the next project.

Order-Winning Criteria   Order-winning criteria are yet another prism through which one can look at the relative importance of the requirements. It implies developing the features that give an advantage over competitors. For instance, some argue that the dominant market share owned by Android phones is partially because iPhones could not play YouTube videos. Others point out that BlackBerry phones could have been a bit more popular if they had the ability to have Skype communications software installed on them.

Expected versus Unexpected Features   It is possible also to divide the scope of the product into the following categories:

- Basic or expected features
- Unexpected features

Basic or expected features are the features that are expected to be inherent in the product by the users. For example, the users of the dryer expect the device to have at least a couple of drying cycles for different types of laundry and different load sizes.

On the other hand, the unexpected features, also referred to as "exciters," are the scope components that differentiate the product from other offerings by competitors. For instance, having a steam cleaning option on the dryer can be the "deal maker" that could entice the customer to buy the product.

Utilizing the Project Portfolio Management Technique   A project portfolio management technique called the "scoring model" can also be used to prioritize requirements. In this methodology, the stakeholders, both internal and external, have to agree on the scoring criteria that would be used to assess the requirements value. In our example (see Table 6.7) we have listed the following four criteria:

- Profit potential
- Marketability
- Ease to produce
- Intellectual property

Then, each of the factors was assigned a weight on a scale of 1 to 5. For example, the "Profit potential" factor as a very important ingredient

Table 6.7 Prioritization Using a Scoring Model

	PROFIT POTENTIAL	MARKETABILITY	EASE TO PRODUCE	INTELLECTUAL PROPERTY	TOTAL SCORE	PRIORITY
Weight	5	4	3	3		
Requirement A	5	5	5	5	75	2
Requirement B	5	5	4	3	85	1
Requirement C	4	3	4	2	57	3
Requirement D	3	3	3	5	43	5
Requirement E	4	2	1	3	40	6
Requirement F	5	3	4	4	46	4

in the overall algorithm got a weight of 5, whereas "Intellectual property" received a weight of 3.

Afterward, the score for each requirement was calculated as a weighted total of all individual scores; for example, the Requirement A score was computed in the following manner:

$$\text{Requirement A Score} = 5*5 + 4*5 + 3*5 + 3*5 = 25 + 20 + 15 + 15 = 75$$

According to the results from our table, Requirement B came in first place with 85 points, Requirement A was second with 75 points, Requirement C was third with 57 points, Requirement F was fourth with 46 points, Requirement D was fifth with 43 points, and finally Requirement E came in sixth with 40 points.

This implies that if the project team has resources and time for only two requirements, then Requirements B and A would be implemented. If they have resources and time for only four requirements, then it would be components B, A, C, and F that would go ahead.

Documenting Requirements

Criteria for Good Requirements

Once all the requirements have been gathered, it is time for the analyst to write the requirements specifications document. Although this book dedicates three of its chapters (7–9) to writing the requirements documentation in IT, engineering, and multidisciplinary environments, let us discuss the best practices that are applicable to all types of the documentation (see Table 6.8).

Each requirement listed in the document must be necessary. It may sound somewhat silly to question the necessity of scope components inasmuch as the stakeholders asked for them specifically in the first place, but industry studies show that as much as 50% of requirements can be cut from the scope of the project by asking a simple question such as "Do you really need this feature?" or "Would a project be a 'no go' without this component?"

The necessity of the requirement can also be checked in the following fashion: If one can trace the requirement back to the parent business problem via the parent feature and the relationship is still logical, then the requirement is most likely indispensable.

Each requirement must be verifiable, which implies that the requirement can be tested. This criterion is strongly related to the ambiguity discussed a bit later in this chapter. In general, if the requirement is not measurable, it is very unlikely that it would be verifiable. For example, requirements such as

- "The building shall be sustainable,"
- "The system shall be efficient," and
- "The light bulb shall save energy"

are not verifiable because different people can, and most likely will, have a different understanding of what "sustainable," "efficient," and "save energy" mean. On the other hand, statements such as

- "The building shall generate 50% of the energy it needs,"
- "The system shall decrease the account-opening process from 27 to 4 operations,"
- "The lightbulb shall have a luminous efficacy of at least 55 lumens per watt (lm/W),"

are completely verifiable because it is very easy to test whether they conform to the requirements imposed on them by the stakeholders.

The *attainability* simply means that the requirement can be implemented in the product or service considering all the limitations of either technology, budget, or time constraints of the project.

Ambiguity is defined as uncertainty or inexactness of meaning in language. Requirements ambiguity is one of the most dangerous time

Table 6.8 Dangerous Words to Avoid

DANGEROUS WORDS	WHAT TO DO ABOUT THEM	EXAMPLES
"Acceptable," "adequate," "satisfactory," "suitable"	Define acceptability and how the product and stakeholders can decide what is acceptable and what is not	Before: House of adequate size After: House area shall be between 2,500 and 3,000 square feet
"Efficient," "capable," "economical," "ecologically aware," "helpful"	Explain how efficiently the product performs operations or how easy it is to use	Before: Efficient engine After: Engine with a mileage of at least 235 miles per gallon
"Fast," "rapid," "swift," "speedy"	Specify minimum, maximum, and desired speed	Before: Fast car After: A car that is capable of speed of at least 217 miles per hour
"Flexible," "agile," "easily adaptable," "variable"	What specifically should the product do in response to specific changes in the environment or business objectives	Before: Flexible payments system After: A payments system that is capable of accommodating both prepaid and postpaid customers
"Improved," "better," "faster," "superior," "enhanced," "better quality"	Quantify how much faster constitutes adequate improvement	Before: Improved equipment After: Equipment capable of producing 1,000 gadgets per hour (instead of 200 gadgets per hour)
"Maximize," "minimize," "optimize," "capitalize on"	Provide maximum and minimum acceptable parameters for each value. You can also provide desired range	Before: The new spell-check software shall minimize the number of errors After: The new spell-check software shall detect at least 97% of spelling errors
"Seamless," "transparent," "graceful," "faultless," "flawless," "perfect"	Translate into observable product characteristics	Before: Seamless integration of System A with System B After: No more than 0.5% of transactions shall be misplaced after the integration of System A with System B
"Several," "few," "a number of"	How many? Provide a specific number or maximum and minimum acceptable parameters for each value	Before: The stadium shall have several entrances After: The stadium shall have 12 entrances
"State-of-the-art," "high-tech," "modern," "sustainable"	Define what this means	Before: The state-of-the-art library shall be built at the university After: The new university library shall have collection space, electronic workstation space, multimedia workstation space, viewing rooms and listening rooms, user seating space, staff work space, meeting space, auditorium or larger lecture space, and special use space

(continued)

Table 6.8 Dangerous Words to Avoid (Continued)

DANGEROUS WORDS	WHAT TO DO ABOUT THEM	EXAMPLES
"Sufficient," "ample," "satisfactory"	How much is sufficient?	Before: Sufficient number of user accounts shall be created After: The user accounts shall be created for all employees of the accounting and finance departments
"Support," "enable," "sustain," "facilitate"	Define exactly what functions would constitute support or enabling	Before: The new call center shall facilitate the customer care program After: The new call center shall be able to process X number of calls per day
"User friendly," "simple," "easy," "comprehensible," "idiot proof"	Translate into observable product characteristics	Before: The website shall be user friendly After: The website design shall conform to the current company GUI standards guide

Source: Adapted and amended from Wiegers, K.E. *Software Requirements*, (2nd ed.), Redmond, WA: Microsoft Press, 2003.

bombs in the specifications documentation and one of the most difficult ones to catch. Let me demonstrate it by sharing a couple of examples from my consulting practice.

The first story was conveyed to me by a senior manager of a construction company in Saudi Arabia. One of the services his organization provided was building luxury villas for the local business elite. At one point, the crew had finished erecting the walls of the house and building internal partitions. The building site was visited by the client, a vice president of large company whose wife happened to be pregnant at the time. The construction manager, whose command of both Arabic and English languages was, shall we say, poor, took him on a tour of the building. When they got to the master bedroom, the following conversation took place:

Construction Manager: And this room will serve as a master bedroom.
Client: (Pointing at one of the walls) And what is on the other side of this wall?
Construction Manager: There is another smaller room.
Client: Great! We will make it a baby room! And I want you to install a baby door over here (pointing to the wall again).

What do you think the client meant by "baby door"? Of course, he meant "the door through which my wife and I can get access to the baby's room." What do you think the construction manager, who was too intimidated to question the client about his intentions, installed? It was a door about a third of normal size!

"It was actually very embarrassing on two levels," said the manager who told this story. "First, the client was left with an impression that we have somewhat inadequate people working for us, and second, the door the construction manager installed ended up costing almost 10 times more because this was a custom order! And, of course, we had to fix this problem at our own expense."

Another example comes from a North American port authority whose CEO told the following ambiguity-related story:

> We were planning on building a cruise ship terminal. And somehow we allowed the expression "state-of-the-art" to sneak into the project charter. From the project charter, it was allowed to migrate to the requirements document and to the project plan.
>
> Now, we had the following stakeholders on the project: the federal government, state government, municipal government, several cruise ship companies, and the port authority itself. Do you think they all had one united vision of what "state-of-the-art" means or a dozen different ones? Some stakeholders insisted on expensive building materials, others wanted to automate pretty much every function of the building, and yet others wanted the facility to be 100% sustainable… It was a nightmare! We went $200 million over the budget because of just one phrase.

Completeness of the requirements is also one of the potential time bombs in any specification document and is quite difficult to catch. Complete requirement implies that all potential alternatives and exceptions in the requirements have been foreseen and addressed properly.

Consistent requirements are the specifications that do not conflict with other features and scope components.

Requirement *traceability* and *unique identifiers* are also closely linked because it would be fairly challenging to trace the requirements—especially on larger, more complicated projects—if they are not labeled properly (for example, BR 1.0, F 3.11, or Req 5.10.2).

Requirements should also be written in a *concise* manner with sentences being short and to the point and preferably in a simple, easy-to-understand language that can be "absorbed" by all types of audiences. It is also preferable that the requirements are written using *standard constructs* preferably with the verb "shall":

- "The building shall be 175 meters high."
- "The ladder shall be able to support loads of up to 300 pounds."
- "The system shall be available 99.9% of the time."

The requirements must be *design free*; in other words, they should not say how the requirement will be implemented (i.e., the technical solution), but only what is needed.

Finally, the requirements must be prioritized. For more on ways of prioritizing the requirements, see the section "Prioritizing Requirements."

Introducing the Concept of Measurability

Imagine that a representative of one of the Formula One teams walks into the office of the car engine design company and requests that they build an engine that will enable the car to go at a very fast rate of speed. Assuming there are no further discussions or clarifications, how easy or difficult would it be for the engine manufacturers to produce such an engine? For comparison purposes, let us consider another scenario. A representative of the Formula One team walks into the car engine designers' office and requests that they build him an engine capable of reaching the speed of 250 mph.

Which request would be easier to implement? Obviously, it would be the second one, because the engineers will have a very clear and tangible (measurable) goal that they can work to reach. Interestingly enough, most of the people reading this book would not have any challenges with identifying the proper way of forming the requirements for the Formula One car engine. It is very clear from the very beginning which version of the requirement is more appropriate for the real world.

But let us complicate things a little bit by employing a sample statement from the requirements document for a new city airport:

"The new airport terminal shall have a sufficient number of gates to accommodate all the flights during the peak travel periods."

Interestingly enough, when presented with the airport terminal statement, many professionals—including the executives, functional managers, and even project managers—find it way more acceptable than the one about the "fast car engine," which inevitably begs the question: "How fast should it be?"

Let us return to the airport example once more. Compare the earlier requirement with the following statement:

> "The new airport terminal shall have a sufficient number of gates to accommodate at least 300 daily flights, both arrivals and departures."

Or this statement:

> "The new airport terminal shall have 70 gates to accommodate at least 300 daily flights, both arrivals and departures."

If you were an architect or an engineer, which requirement do you think would be more helpful if you were about to start working on a terminal blueprint? In the second scenario, the project team would have to calculate the number of gates necessary to accommodate the number of arrivals and departures indicated in the document, whereas in the third example, the specific number of gates has already been clearly indicated.

Therefore, introducing measurability to the requirements documentation can be one of the key factors in improving the quality of requirements and avoiding future misinterpretations resulting in rework and budget overruns as the project progresses from the planning to the execution and closeout stages.

Imposing measurability on the requirements can be one of the most stressful exercises the project team can go through in the course of the project. On one hand, the project team has to identify all the "suspicious" words and expressions in the project documentation. These can include terms such as "adequate," "several," sufficient," and many others. Then, the project manager has to contact appropriate requirements owners and ask them the following question:

> "When you stated X, what exactly did you mean?"

Unfortunately, very frequently the stakeholders are reluctant to do that fairly early in the project because they either don't know the numbers required or are unwilling to accept the responsibility for providing them. As one of the executives told me, "What happens if I state that the airport needs to have 50 gates and then it turns out that 70 gates were required to accommodate all the airport traffic?"

Furthermore, providing answers to such questions typically implies a considerable investment of time, human resources, and finances. Think about how difficult it is to predict all the potential traffic at the yet-unbuilt airport, including the forecasts for the on- and off-seasons. Surprisingly enough, there are a lot of instances where senior management is reluctant to "waste money" or "delay the start of an important project" in order to obtain this important information.

How does one impose measurability on project documentation? One of the easiest ways of doing that is by asking the following question:

> "What would you consider to be a failure to meet this requirement?"

Let's examine this methodology using a real-life example. This conversation took place between me and a project manager working for a very large retail chain. He was responsible for one of the multiple "New Store Opening" projects, and I was assigned to peer review his project documentation.

Me: I see that your requirements document mentions that the team needs to maximize the number of working POS stations for the store's opening day. You need to impose some kind of measurability on this statement.

PM: This would be a very difficult thing to do. The management really strives to have all the POS stations working and fully operational for the store opening.

Me: OK, but as far as I know, these stations arrive from your suppliers. What happens if you unpack one of them and discover that it is deficient? Would the company postpone the opening of the new retail location because one of the 30 stations is not operational? They will probably just leave that terminal unmanned and direct all the extra traffic to the other 29 stations.

PM: Yes, that is exactly what is going to happen.

Me: So, the question you really need to ask them is, "What is the minimum acceptable number of working POS terminals for the store's opening day?" In other words, what is the threshold for them to postpone the opening of the store to another day? That number is your measurability parameter.

Chapter Summary

We started this chapter by examining various requirements elicitation methodologies, including wallpapers, wikis, brainstorming, flowcharts, the "5 Whys," and the user scenarios method as well as joint application development (JAD) sessions. We also talked about the importance of running structured meetings and the benefits of using meeting minutes to record and communicate project tasks, issues, announcements, and potential solutions to the problems at hand.

The next section of the chapter was dedicated to various ways of prioritizing requirements. Next, we discussed document requirements, including the criteria for good requirements and application of measurability.

7

DOCUMENTING REQUIREMENTS

Information Technology and Software Development Projects

Historical Perspective: The Story of A2LL

A2LL, the German social services and unemployment software system, was developed over the course of several years by T-Systems, a software department of the state telecommunications company, along with ProSoz, a smaller company of about 30 developers located in the town of Herten. The final product was delivered in the last quarter of 2004 and went live on January 1, 2005. The system consisted of the web browser front end, and the back end was based on 16 servers with four processors each.

Upon the deployment of the system in several large German cities, including Cologne, Hamburg, Frankfurt, and Berlin, the users at the welfare offices started reporting serious problems with the software. Some of the problems encountered are listed in Table 7.1. As a result of the deficiencies, the expert committee appointed by the German government concluded that the system was inadequate and started considering a new software system, just nine months after A2LL went live.

What are the lessons that can be learned from this project? It looks like the failure of this endeavor is rooted in the project team's inability to extract and document the proper system requirements (both functional and nonfunctional). After all, it is less likely (at least in my humble opinion) that the requirements were captured and included in the requirements specifications documentation properly but neglected by the developers.

Therefore, this chapter is dedicated to the best practices of documenting software requirements followed by an actual sample of the system requirements specifications document.

Table 7.1   A2LL Deficiencies

SYSTEM BUG DESCRIPTION	TYPE OF REQUIREMENT
If data entered into the form were incomplete (e.g., someone missed one of the many questions), the system automatically deleted the record after about three or four weeks.	Functional
Account numbers that were fewer than 10 digits in length were filled with zeros at the end of the string rather than at the beginning (e.g., 3225223 became 3225223000 instead of 0003225223).	Functional
The system was not capable of producing an "Analysis of Variance" report.	Functional
The system was not capable of producing a "Persons Who Received Too Much Money" report.	Functional
The system did not include the functionality to deal with the deductions for income from small jobs.	Functional
The system could not cope with one-time payments (e.g., schoolchildren purchasing books).	Functional
The system was not registering people properly with their insurance companies.	Functional
The system could not properly calculate insurance rates resulting in €25 million per month overpayment to the insurance companies.	Functional
There was extremely slow response time of the software.	Nonfunctional
There were extremely slow data-entry times.	Nonfunctional
Document printing was incompatible with many local stations.	Nonfunctional

Requirements Specifications Template

We have already discussed the best practices of capturing generic requirements in Chapter 6, but because requirements documentation follows slightly special rules in IT and software development, we review certain documentation rules and methodologies before proceeding to the analysis of an actual "Airport Check-In Kiosk" software example.

The traditional system requirements specifications document in IT and software development domains usually consists of the components listed in Table 7.2. It is important to point out that there are numerous software specification templates available in various textbooks, Internet sites, and other sources. They include various presentation formats of user classes, operating environments, constraints, assumptions, dependencies, and various interfaces, among others.

Readers have to keep in mind that the outline is only a recommended template, which they are free to change and adjust according

Table 7.2   Outline of the Requirements Document for the IT and Software Development Industries

- Introduction
  - o Purpose
  - o Intended Audience
  - o Project Scope
  - o References
- Product Description
  - o Product Features
  - o User Classes
  - o Operating Environment
- System Features
  - o System Feature X
    - Description and Priority
    - Stimulus/Response Sequences
    - Functional Requirements
- External Interface Requirements
  - o User Interfaces
  - o Hardware Interfaces
  - o Software Interfaces
  - o Communications Interfaces
- Nonfunctional Requirements
  - o Performance Requirements
  - o Security Requirements
  - o Other Software Quality Attributes

to the needs of their project. Another important disclaimer to make: Software requirements can be captured in a variety of ways. These include use cases, user scenarios, and user stories (on Agile projects). However, inasmuch as the functional and nonfunctional requirements approach is the oldest and the most traditional of all the methodologies, we concentrate on it in this book.

Functional Requirements

What Are the Requirements Writing Guidelines?

There are several simple rules that have to be followed when recording functional requirements. First, let's examine the concise writing rule. This rule consists of several subcategories. Statements should be short and to the point. They should focus on what the system must do rather than on how it should do it. One of the most difficult aspects to achieve is that the statements should not leave any room for interpretation. This task becomes easier to achieve if the writer attempts to record one requirement per statement or paragraph with one verb.

Another good tradition to follow is consistently to use the word "shall" rather than mix "must," "will," "might," and "may" to indicate priority or create semantic confusion. Here is an example of a bad requirement for the readers to analyze and attempt to rewrite properly:

> *Product SKUs entered by the customer will be validated against the SKU master list if possible and the results will be presented in the tabular format to the user.*

Some of the issues a good requirements expert will notice about this statement are

- Usage of "will" instead of "shall"
- "will be validated"—validated by whom or what?
- "if possible"—and what happens if it is "impossible"?
- "results"—what kind of "results"?
- "tabular format"—imposing solution
- No unique identifiers
- Usage of "customer" instead of "user"

A possible improved version of the same requirement may look something that shown in Table 7.3.

Table 7.3   SKU Validation Feature

FR NAME	SKU VALIDATION
FR ID	FR 1.1
Precondition	User has navigated to the "Search" page and initiated a search based on one or multiple SKUs
Primary Actors	User, system
FR Description	The ABC system shall validate Product SKUs entered by the user against the SKU master list • If the SKU entered can be located in the SKU master list, the ABC system shall communicate to the user that the product was found and prompt the user to add the product to the shopping basket • If the SKU entered cannot be located in the SKU master list, the ABC system shall communicate to the customer that the product was not found
Priority	Must have
Related NFRs	See NFRs 1.1 and 1.2

It is also important to point out that the criteria for good requirements outlined in Chapter 6 are still applicable in the case of functional and nonfunctional requirements in the IT sector (see Table 7.4).

Words to Avoid

Table 6.8 provides a list of potentially troublesome words and phrases that tend to appear frequently in project management documentation

Table 7.4 Criteria for Good Requirements

CRITERIA	EXPLANATION
Necessary	Will the product or service being created meet the prioritized, real needs of the project without this particular requirement? If yes, the requirement is not necessary. Example: A stereo in a Formula One car.
Verifiable	Can one test that the requirement is met in the final product or service? If not, the requirement should be removed or revised. Example: "Safe baby bottle" versus "A baby bottle that meets the Food and Drug Administration's safety requirements."
Attainable	Can the requirement be met in the product or service under development? If not, the requirement should be removed or revised.
Unambiguous	Can the requirement be interpreted in more than one way? If yes, the requirement should be revised. Example: "Sustainable building" versus "A building that is capable of generating at least 50% of its own energy needs."
Complete	Are all conditions under which the requirement applies stated (e.g., all possible scenarios, alternatives, and exceptions)? Example: "The system shall scan the passport and extract the traveler's name." What happens if the system can't scan the passport?
Consistent	Can the requirement be met without conflicting with other requirements? If not, the requirement should be removed or revised.
Traceable and Uniquely Identified	Has the requirement been uniquely identified? Is the origin of the requirement known? Examples: • Feature 6.0 Energy Efficiency o R 6.1 The building shall be built from sustainably harvested wood. o R 6.2 The insulation materials used shall range from R-20 to R-30 in the walls and from R-50 to R-70 in the ceilings.
Concise	Is the requirement stated simply and clearly so that an average person without special technical knowledge can understand it?
Design Free	Is the requirement stating what must be done without indicating how (unless mandated by the situation)?
Standard Constructs	Requirements are stated as imperative needs using "shall."
Prioritized	Has the requirement been assigned a priority relative to other requirements in the document?

Source: Adapted and amended from Wiegers, K.E. *Software Requirements*, (2nd ed.), Redmond, WA: Microsoft Press, 2003.

in basically all the industries and types of organizations. Unfortunately for project professionals, these terms remain the "bread and butter" of the executive, sales, and marketing professionals' lexicon, and all attempts to eliminate them from their lingo remains fairly futile, to the best of my knowledge.

However, allowing words like these to sneak into project management (and especially requirements) documentation can cause serious problems in the future and play the role of a time bomb waiting to explode. One example of this happened during the construction of a new building on a university campus in Western Canada. The project had several key stakeholders, including the university itself as well as municipal and provincial governments that happened to finance parts of the project.

The college executives, apparently in attempt to appear socially responsible, claimed at the very beginning of the project that the building would be "sustainable." The project manager, who was appointed at a later point, missed this word and allowed it to sneak into the project documentation. The problems started at the end of the planning stage of the project when the engineers, architects, and energy consultants were working on the final design of the building. It turned out that, considering the allocated budget, the building could generate only 10%–15% of the energy needed to operate it. However, the government officials claimed that, in their minds, the commitment to make the building sustainable implied that at least 75% of the energy should be self-generated.

As a result, it took a lot of time and negotiations to arrive at the point that was "comfortable" for all the stakeholders. However, the project still went several million dollars over the budget and was six months late (the lion's share of that time was spent trying to arrive at the consensus regarding the sustainability issue).

This topic is strongly correlated with the measurability issue discussed in Chapter 6. Typically, every time an ambiguous term is encountered in the project management documentation, it requires the requirements analyst or a project manager to embark on the "let us impose some measurability on that statement" journey, where vague words have to be replaced with concrete numbers or percentages.

Requirements versus Design Discussion Revisited

One of the key issues that is witnessed on numerous IT and software development projects is overeagerness of the project stakeholders (both technical team members and customers) to delve into the discussion of the granular design aspects of the final product well before all the functional and nonfunctional requirements have been defined. The remarks of more experienced team members that the location and the color of the "Submit" button should be postponed until later were very frequently met with the following comment:

"Well, we know this now; why postpone the discussion until later?"

There are two main reasons for separating functionality and design discussions. The first one is that defining the functionality of any software product is a complicated and cumbersome process that has not been fully grasped by many IT and software development professionals. Adding the design-related discussions into the mix complicates things even more and distracts both team members and customers from more important aspects.

Second, one should always remember that technical team members (e.g., developers, architects, etc.) typically have a much better understanding of various design options available to the team. Thus, it is only logical to expect that developers, architects, and user interface designers will be able to come up with more efficient and innovative solutions. Furthermore, in many cases these solutions could be the ones that the customer did not even know were possible.

Before we explore this topic further, let us look at the respective definitions of the requirements and technical design.

Requirements describe what the customer wants; they communicate business capabilities required to solve business problems or achieve business objectives.

Technical design describes how the requirements will be satisfied and which system components will deliver the new capability.

How can one distinguish between a functional requirement and a design-level solution? One of the easiest ways to weed out design elements in the specification document is to look for phrases such as

"The system (or customer) shall do X by ..."

Table 7.5   Design versus Requirements

THE SYSTEM (OR CUSTOMER) SHALL DO X BY …	QUESTION
… choosing an option from a drop-down menu	Why does it have to be a drop-down menu necessarily?
… pushing a "Submit" button	Can it be a "Proceed to Checkout" button instead?
… clicking in the checkbox	Why not a radio button?

See Table 7.5 for several examples of design sneaking into requirements.

Parking Lots

What frequently happens during the requirements discussion meetings is that great, cool, and incredibly innovative design solutions unexpectedly pop up all over conference rooms. The obvious question at that point is, "If we are not venturing into design issues right now, what do we do with these cool ideas?"

The solution is to create a "parking lot" to capture these "too early to discuss" items so they can be revisited at a proper time of the project. A parking lot can take several forms depending on the complexity and the formality of the project. For example, more Agile project teams may decide to use whiteboards or flip charts to capture design ideas.

On the other hand, it is recommended that more sophisticated projects capture this info in the special section of the system requirements specifications (SRS) document.

Nonfunctional Requirements

A Look at Nonfunctional Requirements

Although functional requirements define what a system is supposed to do, nonfunctional requirements define how a system is supposed to be. Nonfunctional requirements (NFRs) are often called "qualities of a system." It appears sometimes that nonfunctional requirements are taken somewhat less seriously than their functional cousins. As one customer put it, "Isn't it obvious that the system should be fast, reliable, robust, and user friendly? Why even document that?"

The appropriate response is that properly documented and implemented nonfunctional requirements can make or break the overall success of the product. The example that I like to use is typically delivered in a form of a brainteaser type question:

> This product was a runaway success. There were dozens of competing products on the market with practically identical functionality; however, this device outperformed its opponents when it came down to cool design (look and feel), ease of use (usability), and great battery life (performance). What product is being described?

The answer is, of course, iPod by Apple. Although there were a lot of MP3 players available on the store shelves, the iPod was winning the battle. Why did the overwhelming majority of people pick Apple's offering and ignore other products? There probably were other factors that played a role in iPod's dominance of the market, but the obvious gap in the "nonfunctional requirements" area cannot be completely ignored. Table 7.6 provides the reader with some of the more popular

Table 7.6 Nonfunctional Requirements

TYPE OF NFR	EXPLANATION	EXAMPLE	
		BAD REQUIREMENT	BETTER REQUIREMENT
Look and Feel	Describes the intended spirit, the mood, or the style of product's appearance. Specify the intention of the appearance and not a detailed design of an interface.	*"The product shall appear attractive."* *"The product shall have an expensive appearance."*	*"The product shall comply with corporate branding standards."* *"90% of users shall find the product attractive."*
Usability	Make the product conform to the user's (and not the developer's) abilities and expectations of the usage experience.	*"The product shall be easy to use."* *"The product shall be easy to use by users with English as a second language."*	*"75% of non-English speakers shall be able to find, order, and pay for the book 30 minutes after entering the site."*
Performance	These requirements are recorded when • The product needs to perform some tasks in a given amount of time • Some tasks need to be done to a specific level of accuracy • The product needs to have certain capacities	*"The page shall load with adequate speed."*	*"The product shall identify whether the aircraft is hostile or friendly in 0.25 seconds."* *"The precision of a ballistic missile shall be ± 10 meters."*

(continued)

Table 7.6 Nonfunctional Requirements (Continued)

TYPE OF NFR	EXPLANATION	EXAMPLE	
		BAD REQUIREMENT	BETTER REQUIREMENT
Availability	These requirements are recorded when • The product needs to be available and fully operational at prolonged lengths of time • Referred to as "Uptime"	*"The system shall be available at all times."* *"The system shall be available when needed."*	*"The system shall be at least 99.5% available between 9:00 a.m. and 6:00 p.m. on weekdays."*
Robustness	Describes the degree to which a system continues to function properly when confronted with invalid inputs or defects in connected software or hardware components.	*"The product shall be hard to break."*	*"If the text editor fails before the user saves the file, the system shall be able to recover all the changes made since the last 'Save.'"*
Security	Confidentiality: Data stored or transferred by the product is protected from unauthorized access and disclosure.	*"The product shall provide adequate security."*	*"The system shall ensure that only authorized users have access to the data."* *"Customer credit card information shall be PGP encrypted by the system."*

quality attributes as well as the examples of improper and proper documentation of nonfunctional requirements.

One final thing to remember about nonfunctional requirements is that whereas implementation of some NFRs goes hand in hand, so to speak (e.g., maintainability and availability), it is fairly difficult to build a system that scores high on both, say, efficiency and robustness. Some other key pairings of quality attributes are presented in Table 7.7.

Table 7.7 Compatibility of Nonfunctional Requirements

	AVAILABILITY	EFFICIENCY	MAINTAINABILITY	RELIABILITY	ROBUSTNESS	USABILITY
Availability				+	+	
Efficiency				−	−	−
Maintainability	+	−		+		
Reliability	+	−	+		+	+
Robustness	+	−		+		+
Usability		−		+		

Note: + denotes positive correlation
− denotes negative correlation

Documenting IT and Software Development Requirements

Let us now delve into the creation of the system requirements specifications document for the "Airport Check-In Kiosk" project mentioned earlier in this book (see Chapters 3 and 5 from the project charter and high-level scope, respectively).

There are several disclaimers to be made before getting into the actual analysis of the system requirements specifications document at hand:

1. The document—especially the "System Features" section—has been simplified as much as possible when compared to the original. Many of the possible alternatives, exceptions, and additional functionality have been removed to make the scope simpler and more manageable.
2. The purpose of this chapter and the attached requirements specifications document was to demonstrate the proper spirit of the SRS rather than to attempt to create a "perfect" requirements document.

Introduction

Document Purpose   In this section, the purpose of the document is discussed. It could be a good idea to have a generic text prepared for each type of document and just insert the appropriate information as it changes from project to project, such as the project name, for example.

Here is an example of the "Document Purpose" paragraph from the "Airport Check-In Kiosk" project requirements specification:

> This document is the Software Requirements Specification for the "Airport Check-In Kiosk Software." It addresses intended audiences, scope, user classes and functional and nonfunctional requirements of the future product. The SRS document is a configuration item and must be placed under change control once agreed. Updates to the SRS must be reviewed and approved by the Project Manager, Business Analyst, and any relevant stakeholders for the section that is changed.

Please note that a complete version of the "Airport Check-In Kiosk" project requirements specification can be found on the Taylor & Francis Group/CRC Press website at http://www.crcpress.com/product/isbn/9781482259483.

Intended Audience   In the "Intended Audience" section, the project managers or requirements analysts (whoever authors the document) are also encouraged to use a prepared paragraph that can be reused from document to document and just modified whenever necessary. Below, one can see a "prefabricated" list of the stakeholders who must familiarize themselves with the requirements specifications document.

This document is intended for the following audiences:

- Project manager
- Business analyst
- Technical team members: developers, testers, architects, and so on
- Users of all categories
- Business stakeholders
- External customers

The list can obviously be easily modified and updated depending on the nature, size, and complexity of the project in question.

Project Scope   The "Project Scope" section should be synchronized with whatever is contained in the similar section in the project charter document. Sometimes, if the project charter was well written and validated, it is a matter of simple "cut-and-paste." In our case, we are assuming that the corresponding section in the "Airport Check-In Kiosk" project charter was properly documented and, most important, did not undergo any significant changes:

> ABC Software Systems shall study, configure, and implement the Airport Check-In Kiosk software system for XYZ Airlines by September of 2010.

References Section   In the "References" section, the requirements analyst should list the documents that could have any relevance to the current requirements document. In the example shown in Table 7.8, the requirements analyst chose to reference the "XYZ Airlines User Interface Guide" because all the software system screens must abide by the corporate guidelines.

Table 7.8   References Table

DOCUMENT TITLE	URL LINK
"XYZ Airlines User Interface Guide"	Click here to access the document

Table 7.9 Airline Kiosk Features

FEATURE ID	FEATURE DESCRIPTION
F 1.0	Kiosk Menu
F 2.0	Traveler Identification
F 3.0	Traveler Reservation Search
F 4.0	Confirm or Change Seat
F 5.0	Pay for Luggage
F 6.0	Print Boarding Pass
F 7.0	Navigation

Product Description

Product Features   Once more, if the project charter was properly written and the project manager captured all the relevant high-level features of the future product or service, the requirements analyst only has to transfer the table (see Table 7.9) from the project charter into the requirements specifications document.

User Classes   "User Classes" is one of the most important sections of the document because here the analyst captures the key classes of people who will end up using the final product or service and hence the groups that must be interviewed in one form or another to capture their requirements with respect to the new system. If one or more of the groups are omitted during this process, then it is very likely that they will be ignored in the future and their requirements will not be collected, which can cause unpleasant surprises later in the project life.

   In the particular example shown in Table 7.10, the analyst identified only two groups of users on the project: the travelers who will use the kiosks to obtain boarding passes and the XYZ Airlines IT personnel who will support and maintain the system.

Table 7.10   User Classes

USER CLASS	CHARACTERISTICS	FAVORED?
Travelers	XYZ Airlines customers who will be using the kiosks to check in for their flights and obtain their boarding passes	*Yes*
IT employees	XYZ Airlines employees who will be responsible for system maintenance and updates	

Operating Environment   This section typically describes the operating environment in which the new product will be deployed. In more complicated settings, such as a large bank, insurance company, or a multinational retailer, this area could get very extensive with dozens if not hundreds of systems deployed on a multitude of servers. In some cases, it is easier and more descriptive to insert a system diagram that shows the major components of the overall system, subsystem interconnections, and external interfaces.

In our case, the analyst pointed out in the document that the new software will be deployed on the Windows 7 operating system:

> The "Airport Check-In Kiosk Software" shall be deployed on the existing kiosks running Windows 7 O/S.

System Features

"System Features" is by far the largest and the most complicated of the sections in the requirements specifications document. Here, the analyst in conjunction with her team must list all the functional and, depending on the layout of the document, the nonfunctional requirements of the new product.

Many project teams choose to insert a flowchart showing all the actions of the user and the system. Flowcharts can help all the stakeholders, especially the nontechnical ones, see whether the steps of a process are logical, uncover problems or miscommunications, define the boundaries of a process, and develop a common base of knowledge about a process.

When both technical and nontechnical teams get together and start a flowcharting exercise, they very frequently can uncover redundancies, dead ends, missing alternatives, and exceptions to the process. In general, the alternative and exception to the business process (and in the more general context of this book) are defined as follows:

- *Alternative:* An alternative way of getting to a successful completion of a process, which is different from the normal course of events. For example, if we define "passport authentication" as a normal course, identification using a frequent flyer card would be considered an alternative course. In other words, the path to success is different, but the user is still able to identify himself.

- *Exception:* A path of the business process that does not lead to a successful completion of the task. For example, if the user's passport is scanned but deemed to be a forgery, or if the user does not have either a passport, credit card, or a frequent flyer card, she will most likely not be issued a boarding pass by the system.

Figure 7.1 demonstrates just the first several steps dealing with the identification of the user before proceeding to the next steps,

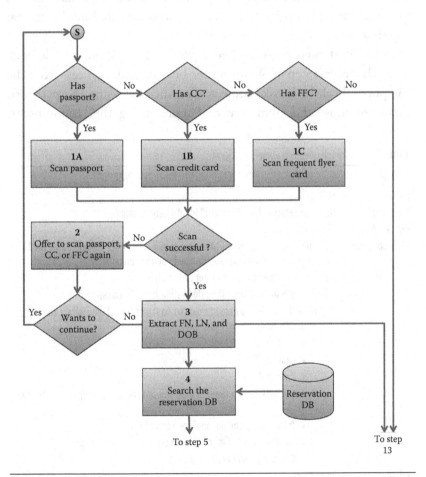

Figure 7.1   Airport check-in flow diagram, part 1.

eventually leading to the issuing of the boarding pass. For the complete set of flowcharts describing all the interactions between the user and the system, please see the "Airport Check-In Software" system requirements specifications under the Downloads tab on the Taylor & Francis Group/CRCPress website http://www.crcpress.com/product/isbn/9781482259483.

System Feature—Traveler Identification—Passport Functional requirements capture the intended behavior of the system. They describe step by step the interaction between the user and the system or between several systems. Best practices prescribe that functional requirements must contain an ID; a precondition; a list of primary actors; the description; the priority; and, if applicable, related nonfunctional requirements.

In our particular example (see Table 7.11) we decided to demonstrate the second step of obtaining the boarding pass process from the "Airport Check-In Kiosk" project: identification using the passport. First, we chose the tabular way of representing the requirements.

Table 7.11   Traveler Identification—Passport

FR NAME	TRAVELER IDENTIFICATION—PASSPORT
FR ID	FR 2.1
Precondition	User has selected the "Passport" identification option
Primary Actors	User, system
FR Description	1. The system shall prompt the user to scan his or her passport and shall conduct a tutorial explaining how to do that properly.
	2. The user shall scan his or her passport.
	3. The system shall read the information from the passport.
	A. If the system is able to read the passport info, it will extract the person's
	• First Name
	• Last Name
	• Date of Birth
	B. If the system is unable to read the passport, it shall prompt the user to.
	• Try scanning the passport one more time
	• Try other ways of identification (see FR 2.2 and 2.3) or
	• Proceed to the check-in counter
Priority	Must have
Related NFRs	See NFRs 7.1, 7.2, and 7.3

Although this depiction is by no means mandatory, it is highly recommended to the analysts because it

- Allows the clear separation of one requirement from another
- Acts as a checklist of all the components needed to describe the requirement completely

For all the other functional requirements, see the "Airport Check-In Kiosk" system requirements specification under the Downloads tab on the Taylor & Francis Group/CRCPress website http://www.crcpress.com/product/isbn/9781482259483.

External Interface Requirements

User Interfaces   In the "User Interfaces" section, the analyst is expected to describe the characteristics of each interface between the user and the system. In certain cases, the analyst may decide to choose wireframes, screen shots, or even mock-ups to demonstrate the key attributes of user interfaces in the requirements document. However, the best practices of software development recommend that the analyst reference a certain style guide that has already been developed at the company for all products in general or a specific product family in particular.

For example, in our project the requirements analyst referenced the "XYZ Airlines User Interface Guide" that had been developed at the airline earlier:

> The software user interface shall conform to the current corporate guidelines described in the "XYZ Airlines User Interface Guide" (see "References" section).

Hardware Interfaces   The document author is supposed to describe the logical and physical characteristics of each interface between the software product and the hardware components of the system. This may include the supported device types, the nature of the data, and control interactions between the software and the hardware.

In our document, this section was not really applicable to the context of the project at hand. Hence, the analyst kept the section header (to demonstrate that that particular topic had been considered) and marked it as "not applicable":

N/A

Software Interfaces In this section, the analyst is required to describe all the relevant connections between the product being developed and all other components, including

- Databases
- Operating systems
- Tools
- Libraries
- Others

Furthermore, a description of the incoming and outgoing messages, the nature of communications, and the data to be shared should also be described in this section of the document.

In our case, the document author pointed out that there would be a connection with the central ticket registration database:

> "Airport Check-In Kiosk Software" shall be communicating with the central registration database (for more information, see the "System Features" section of this document).

Communications Interfaces The document author must describe any communications functions between the new system and other entities, including

- E-mail
- Web browsers
- Network server communications protocols
- Electronic forms
- Others

Also, the analyst must describe or reference either functional or nonfunctional requirements that describe communication security or encryption issues, data transfer rates, and synchronization mechanisms.

Once more in our document this section was not applicable to the context of the project at hand. Hence, the analyst kept the section header and marked it as "not applicable":

N/A

Table 7.12 Nonfunctional Requirement—Performance

NFR NAME	PERFORMANCE
NFR ID	7.3
Precondition	N/A
Primary Actors	N/A
FR Description	1. All transactions shall take less than one second.
Priority	Should have
Related NFRs	N/A

Nonfunctional Requirements

Performance Requirements Performance requirements typically describe how fast the system should perform its functions. In our case, the analyst, together with all the stakeholders, assumed that all the actions of the system should not take more than one second (see Table 7.12).

Security Requirements Security requirements deal with such topics as possible loss, damage, or harm that could result from the use of the product. The analyst must define the following prevention mechanisms to address these issues:

- Safeguards or actions
- Internal policies or regulations
- External policies or regulations
- Safety certifications
- Privacy policies
- Identity authentication requirements
- Others

In our document for simplicity we assumed that there were no explicit security requirements inherent in this project. Hence, the analyst marked this section with the "not applicable" comment:

N/A

Other Software Quality Attributes This section of the document traditionally includes all other nonfunctional requirements of the system that have not yet been mentioned in the document. These may include

- Adaptability
- Availability
- Correctness
- Flexibility
- Interoperability
- Maintainability
- Portability
- Reliability
- Reusability
- Robustness
- Testability
- Usability

In our scenario, only the Usability (see Table 7.13) and Availability (see Table 7.14) quality attributes were deemed to be necessary to document.

Table 7.13   Nonfunctional Requirement—Usability

NFR NAME	USABILITY
NFR ID	7.1
Precondition	N/A
Primary Actors	N/A
FR Description	1. The system interfaces shall conform to corporate GUI standards (click here to access the document).
Priority	Must have
Related NFRs	N/A

Table 7.14   Nonfunctional Requirement—Availability

NFR NAME	AVAILABILITY
NFR ID	7.2
Precondition	N/A
Primary Actors	N/A
FR Description	1. The system shall be at least 95% available between 5:00 a.m. and 1:00 a.m. seven days a week.
Priority	Must have
Related NFRs	N/A

Appendix Section

The "Appendix" section is created to allow the project team to track different issues or to include additional information not covered by all other subsections of the document. These may include but are not limited to

- Dictionaries (including data dictionaries)
- Meeting minutes
- Parking lots
- Issue logs

8

DOCUMENTING REQUIREMENTS

Engineering and Product Development Projects

Historical Perspective: Viking Longships

The Vikings were the Norse warriors, explorers, and merchants who raided, explored, and settled wide areas of England, Scotland, Ireland, Wales, Iceland, France, Spain, Africa, and Italy. They started their expansion by executing multiple raids of the English shores. According to *The Anglo-Saxon Chronicle*, Viking raiders struck England in 793 AD and raided Lindisfarne, the monastery that held Saint Cuthbert's relics. Their raids continued to increase in frequency and the number of participating troops, until in 865 AD the Great Heathen Army led by the brothers Ivar the Boneless, Halfdan, and Ubbe Ragnarsson arrived in East Anglia. They established their presence in Northern England until they were driven out by the English king Harold Godwinson in 1066. The archeologists and linguists recently came to the conclusion that all British towns that end with "by"—for example, Ashby, Corby, Crosby, and so on—were founded and named by the Viking invaders.

Interestingly enough, Harold lost the famous Battle of Hastings in the same year to another descendant of the Vikings (Normans) who settled in Northern France a hundred or so years prior to the events: future king William the Conqueror (or William the Bastard, as he was known before the battle).

According to the Russian *Primary Chronicle*, three Viking (or Varangian, as they were known in Russia) brothers Rurik, Truvor, and Sineus were the first kings of the Russian royal dynasty that spanned from the ninth until the sixteenth century. And, yes, famous (or infamous) Russian tsar Ivan the Terrible, who was a last ruling member of the Rurikid dynasty, can trace his roots directly to the

Norse warriors, who arrived in Russia almost seven centuries prior to his birth.

After establishing their foothold in Russia, many of the Vikings traveled south to the Caspian Sea and farther to the Byzantium Empire, where many of them enlisted in the much-feared Varangian Guard of the Byzantine Emperors.

In the eleventh century, a branch of the Norman royal family headed by Roger I conquered Sicily and ruled there for the next 200 years. Vikings also reached the shores of North America, where Erik Thorvaldsson and his son Leif Erikson established several colonies in what is today known as Newfoundland.

One of the main questions posed by the Viking Expansion is how a relatively small group of soldiers and explorers could reach lands so far away from their own country. Historians name many reasons for this phenomenon, but one of them they universally agree on is the Viking longship. These sturdy, light, and agile vessels carried Norsemen across the Baltic, Mediterranean, and Caspian seas; the Atlantic Ocean; and multiple rivers in continental Europe.

Let us try to examine the design of the Viking longship using modern project scope management techniques. Here is a possible list of business requirements that the first Viking warriors might have imposed on their ship builders (see Figure 8.1):

- The ships must be sturdy enough to withstand long journeys in rough seas.
- The ships need to be light, so that they can be carried over the river rapids whenever necessary.
- The ships must be maneuverable and agile to give advantage in sea battles.
- The ships need to be very fast to catch the prey or to escape from a stronger enemy.

The Norse engineers came up with several ingenious solutions to address these objectives (see Figure 8.2). First, they introduced (some argue for the first time in history) a keel to increase the robustness and the stability of their ships. Next came the ribs of the vessel, which were carefully selected from the naturally curved branches of the trees rather than created by bending more easily available straight boards.

Figure 8.1 Viking ships, business requirements.

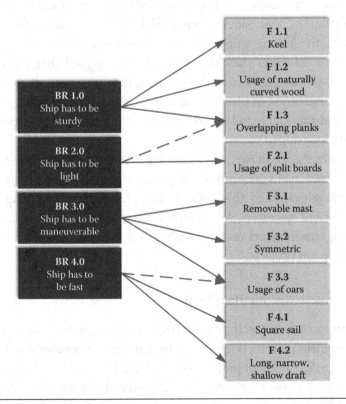

Figure 8.2 Viking ships, features.

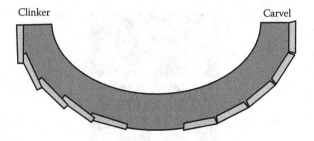

Figure 8.3   Viking boat, clinker versus carvel.

The Norse shipbuilders assumed that the naturally curved timber would inherently be stronger and less susceptible to breaking.

The next step was to use overlapping planks in the construction of the hull (see Figure 8.3). This clinker methodology served several purposes. First, it allowed the builders to use thinner boards without any negative effects on the structural integrity of the hull. This allowed decreasing the weight of the ships.

Second, this approach improved the flexibility of the boats, thus strengthening their sides to withstand the most violent storms.

Next, the Viking shipbuilders used split boards rather than sawn planks to construct their ships. Again, they argued that the boards usually split along their weakest points, thus increasing their sturdiness. Introduction of the removable mast, the symmetric design of the ship, and the square sail greatly improved the maneuverability of the Viking longships.

Finally, the use of oars, the square sail, and the long and narrow shape of the vessels had a great positive impact on the speed of the Viking boats.

Having examined this ancient example of the engineering ingenuity of our ancestors, let us now look at the general guidelines of writing requirements documentation in the engineering and product development projects.

Requirements Specifications Template

The requirements specifications template for engineering and product development projects is not very different from the one used in IT and software development projects (see Table 8.1).

In many cases nowadays we see a mix of engineering and software development projects especially in the areas of electronics:

Table 8.1 Outline of the Requirements Document for the Engineering Industry

---

- Introduction
  - o Document Purpose
  - o Intended Audience
  - o Project Scope
  - o References
- Product Description
  - o Product Features
  - o User Classes and Characteristics
  - o Product Environment
- Product Features and Requirements
  - o Feature X
    - Attribute Y
    - Function Z
- Appendix

TVs, media players, cars, medical devices, and the like. In those cases the product features and requirements section of the document may be expanded to include both engineering functions and attributes as well as functional and nonfunctional software requirements (see Table 8.2).

What Are the Requirements Writing Guidelines?

In general the requirements writing guidelines on engineering and product development projects are consistent with those for the requirements seen in Chapter 6. Again, as in the case with previous chapters, the requirements should be concise and written using the "shall" construct whenever possible. When recorded they also should contain at least the following components for engineering and product development requirements:

- Requirement title
- Requirement ID
- Requirement description
- Priority

Also, the requirements should adhere to the rules listed in Table 7.4, in Chapter 7 for IT/software development and multidisciplinary projects. Furthermore, the language the requirements are written in

Table 8.2   Outline of the Requirements Document for the Mixed Projects

- Introduction
  - o Document Purpose
  - o Intended Audience
  - o Project Scope
  - o References
- Product Description
  - o Product Features
  - o User Classes and Characteristics
  - o Product Environment
- Product Features and Requirements
  - o Feature 1.0 (IT or Software Development)
    - Functional Requirement 1.1
    - Functional Requirement 1.2
    - Functional Requirement 1.x
    - Nonfunctional Requirement 1.1
    - Nonfunctional Requirement 1.2
    - Nonfunctional Requirement 1.x
  - o Feature 2.0 (Engineering or Construction)
    - Function 2.1
    - Function 2.2
    - Function 2.x
    - Attribute 2.1
    - Attribute 2.2
    - Attribute 1.x
- Appendix

should abstain from the "ambiguity words" listed in Table 6.8. For a full discussion of this topic, please see Chapter 6.

Finally, the concept of design-free requirements whenever possible is still applicable in the case of multidisciplinary specification documentation. For more information on the topic, please see the section "Requirements versus Design" in Chapter 5. By the same token, usage of "parking lots" to preserve interesting and useful design ideas is encouraged on multidisciplinary projects.

Let us consider a real-life example of an ambiguous requirement presented by the customer to the project team and attempt to identify all the deficiencies and imperfections:

> ABC Construction has to build an energy efficient house proto-type that conforms to the modern sustainability criteria.

Does the reader see any issues with this requirement? Try to identify them by using the criteria listed earlier in this chapter. Here is a list of potential questions the experienced requirements analyst may ask:

- What is an "energy efficient home"?
- What are the "modern sustainability criteria"?
- Which criteria are to be used on this project?
- Where is the requirement ID?
- What about requirement priority?

Table 4.3, Feature 6.0—Energy Efficiency Requirements shows what a better written requirement for the energy efficient home may look like.

Now that we have defined the best practices of documenting engineering and product development requirements, let us look at a couple of real-life examples of requirements specifications. These include:

- The "Port Upgrade" project at a North American port authority
- The "West Coast Style Energy Efficient Home" project at a design and construction company

Note: Please see the Taylor & Francis Group/CRC Press website http://www.crcpress.com/product/isbn/9781482259483 for the full versions of the requirements specifications for the "Port Upgrade" and the "West Coast Style Energy Efficient Home" projects under the Downloads tab.

Just as in Chapter 7, before we move into the analysis of actual samples, there are several disclaimers one needs to make:

1. The documents, especially the "Product Features and Requirements" section, have been simplified as much as possible when compared to the originals. Many of the extra attributes and additional functionality have been removed to make the scope simpler and more manageable.
2. The purpose of this chapter and the attached requirements specifications documents was to demonstrate the proper spirit of the requirements rather than to attempt to create a "perfect" requirements document.

Documenting the Multidisciplinary Requirements

Introduction

Document Purpose   The introduction section of the requirements document for the multidisciplinary projects is very similar to those in IT documents. The overall purpose and the high-level overview of the document should be described in this section. It is usually a good idea to have this paragraph prepared ahead as part of the template replacing only the name of the project.

In our case the "Purpose" paragraph for the "Port Upgrade" project looks like this:

> This document is the Requirements Specification for the "Port Upgrade" project. It addresses intended audiences, scope, user classes, and detailed requirements of the future product. The Requirements Specification document is a configuration item and must be placed under change control once agreed. Updates to the Requirements Specification must be reviewed and approved by the Project Manager and any relevant stakeholders for the section that is changed.

Intended Audience   The "Intended Audience" section should include all the stakeholders who should familiarize themselves with the requirements document before the project moves into the Execution stage. These may include but are not limited to the project team, project sponsors, customers (both internal and external), and representatives of various departments from within the organization.

For example, on our "Port Upgrade" project, the group of key stakeholders was represented by the following:

- Project manager
- IT team
- Engineering team
- Marketing team
- PR team
- Legal team
- Planning team
- Logistics team
- Security team
- Construction contractors

- Executive management
- External stakeholders

Project Scope Again, as described in the previous chapter, project scope described in this section of the document should correspond (unless there were authorized changes) to the similar section in the project charter document. For example, the "Energy Efficient House" project had the following project scope:

> The scope of the project is the design and construction of a five-bedroom, four-bathroom West Coast style energy efficient (ENERGY STAR certified) home.

References Section The "References" section should list all the relevant documents that may be of interest to the project stakeholders. For example, in the "Energy Efficient House" project, requirements specifications the documents shown in Table 8.3 were listed in the references section.

Product Description

Product Features Just as in the case of the requirements specifications for software development projects, the easiest way to fill out this section of the document is to "transfer" the features list directly from the project charter, assuming, of course, that it has not been changed since the document has been signed off. An example of the features list from the "Port Upgrade" project is shown in Table 8.4.

In this particular case the employees of the company decided to break down their project scope based on the departmental domains, which is very typical for multidisciplinary projects in general.

User Classes and Characteristics As mentioned in the previous chapter, the user classes section is one of the most important sections of the

Table 8.3 References

DOCUMENT TITLE	URL LINK
"Effective Insulation"	Click here to access the document
"High-Performance Windows"	Click here to access the document
"Efficient Heating and Cooling Equipment"	Click here to access the document
"Lighting and Appliances"	Click here to access the document
"Third-Party Verification"	Click here to access the document

Table 8.4 Port Upgrade High-Level Features

FEATURE ID	FEATURE DESCRIPTION
F 1.0	Land acquisition
F 2.0	Legal aspects
F 3.0	Public relations (including federal, state, and municipal governments)
F 4.0	Marketing (including Chinese, Japanese, Indian, and Korean markets)
F 5.0	Planning—Building Design
F 6.0	Construction
F 7.0	Engineering
F 8.0	IT components
F 9.0	Logistics (including building a road and bus connection)
F 10.0	Security

Table 8.5 References Table

USER CLASS	CHARACTERISTICS	FAVORED?
Buyers	External customers who will end up purchasing the house	Yes
Sales and Marketing	Internal customers who will use the house in their marketing and PR campaigns	

documents because omitting individuals or groups of stakeholders can lead to missed requirements.

Therefore, in the case of the "Energy Efficient House" project we managed to identify the following two groups: the future buyers of the energy efficient homes and the ABC Construction sales and marketing teams. In this particular case, the prospective buyers of the house were considered to be preferred users, and the sales and marketing teams were deemed to be secondary users. This implies that if, for example, a certain feature is desired by the buyers, but sales and marketing people do not want it, the decision will be made in the favor of the buyers (see Table 8.5).

Product Environment This section is supposed to describe the environment in which the product of the project will be deployed and used. The author of the document can outline the geographic location, temperatures, humidity levels, winds, rain, snow, or any other external criterion that may be relevant to the performance of the product.

For example, in the case of the "Energy Efficient House" project, the requirements analyst included the following description:

- Initially, the final product should be mobile and ready to be transported, assembled, and exhibited at the Home Design Expo in April 2013.
- After the Expo, the house design should allow for a fairly quick deployment in climate with temperatures as high as +40°C and as low as –20°C and a rainfall of up to 2,000 millimeters.

Here is another interesting example of product environment description from the "Port Upgrade" endeavor:

- The new facility shall be located to the east of the existing Port Authority territory (see Figure 8.4).

Product Features and Requirements

The "Features and Requirements" section is by far the largest part of the requirements specifications document. It contains all the requirements, functions, and attributes pertinent to the project. Ideally, all the deliverables of the endeavor, tangible and intangible, should be listed in this section of the document in accordance with the best practices of requirements documentation.

For analysis purposes, let us examine two examples from the two requirements documents appended at the end of this book.

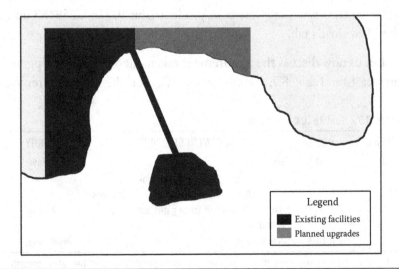

Figure 8.4   Port map.

Table 8.6   Feature 1.0—West Coast Style Home

FEATURE ID	REQ ID	REQUIREMENT DESCRIPTION	PRIORITY
F 1.0	R 1.1	Post and beam construction	See note below
	R 1.2	Exposed timber structural members	
	R 1.3	Extensive glazing and skylights	
	R 1.4	Open floor plans	
	R 1.5	Integration of interior and exterior spaces	
	R 1.6	Wood finishes on both interior and exterior (stained)	
	R 1.7	Flat or minimally canted roofs	
	R 1.8	Orientation to views or natural features	
	R 1.9	Integrated with natural setting, extensive use of native trees and landscaping	

Note: At least six of the above nine requirements must be satisfied.

The first set of requirements is taken from the "Energy Efficient House" project (see Table 8.6, F 1.0—West Coast Style Home).

The project team has employed a very interesting and rather unique requirements documentation trick. First, they managed to identify in a fairly unambiguous way what constitutes a West Coast style home (see requirements 1.1–1.9). However, to provide the designers with some flexibility, the requirements analyst added a note stating that at least six of the nine requirements must be satisfied.

Note: For the full set of the requirements for the "Energy Efficient House" project, please see the Taylor & Francis Group/CRC Press website http://www.crcpress.com/product/isbn/9781482259483 under the Downloads tab.

Let us now discuss the requirement taken out of the "Port Upgrade" project (see Table 8.7, F10.0—Security). For the full requirements

Table 8.7   Feature 10.0—Security

FEATURE ID	REQ ID	REQUIREMENT DESCRIPTION	PRIORITY
F10.0[a]	R 10.1	Fencing	Must Have
		R 10.1.1 1.8-m high chain link fence topped with three strands of barbed wire	
	R 10.2	Road and pedestrian fence gates, manually operated	Must Have
	R 10.3	Security cameras	Must Have

[a] *Note:* The security requirements will be designed and operated to meet the latest security standards in the *International Ship and Port-facility Security (ISPS) Code*.

specifications document, please see the Taylor & Francis Group/CRC Press website http://www.crcpress.com/product/isbn/9781482259483 under the Downloads tab.

This particular feature describes the security attributes of the new port facility. As can be seen from this example, requirement 10.1 represents a classic example of a justified intrusion into the design aspects during the requirements stage of the project.

The rules of requirements engineering tell us that phrases such as "1.8 m high chain link fence topped with three strands of barbed wire" should be avoided at all costs because it is up to the design team to decide what kind of fence—the specific height and the presence or the absence of the barbed wire—is to be constructed. However, on the other hand, the project team was already familiar with the *International Ship and Port-facility Security (ISPS) Code* issued by the International Maritime Organization that specifically mandated all the port facilities in the world conform to the above-mentioned design-level requirement.

Appendix Section

The "Appendix" section is created to allow the project team to track different issues or to include additional information not covered by all other subsections of the document. These may include but are not limited to

- Dictionaries (including data dictionaries)
- Meeting minutes
- Parking lots
- Issue logs

In both of the requirements documents, the "Appendix" section is left unfilled to simplify the specifications and focus on more pertinent issues.

9

Documenting Requirements

Multidisciplinary Projects

Historical Perspective: The Palm Jumeirah Project

The Palm Jumeirah project was conceived by the upper echelons of the UAE government sometime in the late 1990s. The reasoning behind the decision to start the project had one major root cause. The ruling al Maktoum family realized at a certain point that oil, the major source of Dubai's revenues, was expected to run out by 2016. To address this issue, a strategic decision was made to convert the city into an international hub of business and tourism.

The Dubai rulers estimated they needed to boost annual tourism levels from approximately 5 million tourists to 15 million tourists per year. But there was another seemingly insurmountable problem with that goal: The coastline of Dubai was roughly 44 miles at the time. This implied that housing and entertaining 15 million additional people could present a bit of a challenge.

Hence, the decision was made to create a giant palm tree–shaped artificial island (see Figure 9.1) off the coast of Dubai to increase its coastline. The requirements imposed from the very beginning were quite original. One of them called for "natural" construction, which meant the contractors were not allowed to use concrete blocks to build the foundation of the island, a normal methodology employed by construction companies worldwide. As a matter of fact, the Burj Al Arab hotel was built in Dubai several years earlier using the same approach. The new island was expected to add an extra 34 miles to the Dubai coastline. Another key demand was that the new structure have zero impact on the environment.

And so the project was started. ... An interesting aspect of this endeavor was that most people viewed it as an amazing construction

Figure 9.1   Palm Jumeirah.

project, but in my opinion, it is much, much more than just a construction venture. Let us try once more to reverse engineer some of the key features of this project.

First and foremost, there was the construction of the actual island. It required 94 million cubic meters of sand and 5.5 million cubic meters of rock (see Figure 9.2). By the way, that is enough rock either to build two of the largest Egyptian pyramids or construct a 2.5-meter wall around the world.

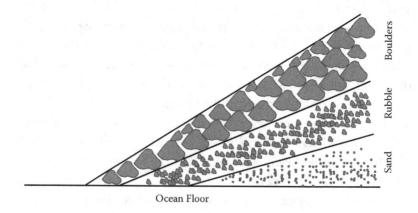

Figure 9.2   Palm Jumeirah island profile.

Planned or not, there was also a public relations aspect to this project. September 11, 2001, came soon after the project was initiated. And this event brought along a whole bunch of concerns, both strategic and tactical. On the strategic end, tourist travel to the Middle East plummeted as affluent Western Europeans and North Americans no longer viewed that part of the word as a vacation destination. On a more tactical end, the developers had to convince prospective buyers that owning a villa on Palm Jumeirah still was a value proposition. Directly connected to the 9/11 issues was the problem of providing the 1,200 Western specialists with the necessary security.

Logistics was also one of the key requirements on the project, as the rock had to be blasted and transferred from far away in the desert to the shores of Dubai. That implied hiring hundreds of trucks to deliver the boulders as the island was gradually being built.

In addition, special boats and barges had to be deployed to gather the sand from the bottom of the Persian Gulf, transport it to the site of future Palm Jumeirah, and disperse it off the coast of the city. Consider the task of bringing close to 40,000 workers on buses on a daily basis, and the sheer complexity of the logistics undertaking becomes apparent.

Also, as was mentioned earlier, the environmental impact of the construction had to be considered. A very sophisticated computer model determined that the water near the island would quickly become stagnant because the entire structure was initially designed to be "closed off" by the breakwater surrounding the "palm." This discovery led to the creation of two openings in the surrounding breakwater crescent island (see Figure 9.1).

After the island was built, it was time to install the infrastructure, including gas pipes, an electricity grid, water pipes, sewage, roads, and even a monorail. Then came the time to erect the actual buildings, including hundreds of high-end luxury villas.

Finally, it was up to the Nakheel's (the parent company in charge of the entire project) sales and marketing team to "do its magic" and sell these properties to affluent buyers around the world. The marketing campaign was so successful that all the properties on the artificial island sold out in less than 72 hours! Many celebrities, including David Beckham and some other members of the English soccer team, ended up owning the luxury villas on Palm Jumeirah. It is even rumored that Hamid Karzai, the president of Afghanistan, has a house opposite Kieron Dyer, the West Ham midfielder!

Why is this story being told at the beginning of the "Documenting Requirements: Multidisciplinary Projects" chapter? The problem is that if one stops 100 people on the street and, assuming they had heard about the Palm Jumeirah project, asks them, "What kind of project was that?" almost all of them would probably claim that it was a great example of a construction project. But is this really, especially in the light of what has just been discussed, just a construction project?

After all, it involved creation of the island, infrastructure building, environmental components, sales, marketing, public relations, security, rock blasting, sand collection, and logistics. Would the actual construction of the island and the villas have been successful without all the other components? Hence, in my opinion, the Palm Jumeirah project is one of the perfect and most famous examples of multidisciplinary endeavors that we are starting to see more and more of in our professional lives.

Requirements Specifications Template

The requirements specifications template for multidisciplinary projects is very similar to the one for engineering, construction, and product development ventures (see Table 9.1). There is, however, one distinction: Because multidisciplinary projects by definition can

Table 9.1   Outline of Requirements Document for Multidisciplinary Projects

- Introduction
  - Document Purpose
  - Intended Audience
  - Project Scope
  - References
- Product Description
  - Product Features
  - User Classes and Characteristics
  - Product Environment
- Product Features and Requirements
  - Feature X
- Appendix

Table 9.2 Outline of Requirements Document for Multidisciplinary Projects—Expanded

- Introduction
  - o Document Purpose
  - o Intended Audience
  - o Project Scope
  - o References
- Product Description
  - o Product Features
  - o User Classes and Characteristics
  - o Product Environment
- Product Features and Requirements
  - o Feature 1.0 (General)
    - Requirement 1.1
    - Requirement 1.2
    - Requirement 1.x
  - o Feature 2.0 (IT or Software Development)
    - Functional Requirement 1.1
    - Functional Requirement 1.2
    - Functional Requirement 1.x
    - Nonfunctional Requirement 1.1
    - Nonfunctional Requirement 1.2
    - Nonfunctional Requirement 1.x
  - o Feature 3.0 (Engineering or Construction)
    - Function 1.1
    - Function 1.2
    - Function 1.x
    - Attribute 1.1
    - Attribute 1.2
    - Attribute 1.x
- Appendix

include requirements from different areas, it is possible that some of the higher-level requirements will have to be broken down into functional and nonfunctional requirements (or use cases, user stories, etc.) for the IT component of the project. Similarly, some of the features may have to be described using functions and attributes for the engineering components of the venture, if there are any (see Table 9.2).

What Are the Requirements Writing Guidelines?

In general, the requirements writing guidelines on multidisciplinary projects are consistent with those for the engineering and construction requirements we saw in Chapter 6. Again, as in the case with previous chapters, the requirements should be concise and written using the "shall" construct whenever possible. Also when recorded they should contain at least the following components for general and engineering/construction requirements:

- Requirement title
- Requirement ID
- Requirement description
- Priority

In the case of software requirements, they should be recorded following the rules outlined in Chapter 7. Also, the requirements should adhere to the rules listed in Table 7.4 in Chapter 7 for IT/software development and engineering/construction projects.

Furthermore, the language the requirements are written in should abstain from the "ambiguity words" listed in Table 6.8. For a full discussion of this topic, please see Chapter 6.

Finally, the concept of design-free requirements whenever possible is still applicable in the case of multidisciplinary specification documentation. For more information on the topic, please see the section "Requirements versus Design" in Chapter 5. By the same token, usage of "parking lots" to preserve interesting and useful design ideas is encouraged on multidisciplinary projects.

As in the previous two chapters, let us consider a real example of a deficient requirement taken from a real-life requirements document for a multidisciplinary project, attempt to identify all the imperfections, and rewrite the requirement in the proper format:

> The Marketing department's standard operating procedures as well as those of all other affected departments should be updated, and adequate training must be provided to all necessary employees from the above-mentioned departments to ensure the seamless transformation after the ABC project deployment.

What are the issues with this requirement? This is a list of potential problems with the above-mentioned scope component:

- Who are the "other affected departments"?
- What is meant by "adequate training"?

Table 9.3 Feature 4.0—Standard Operation Procedures (SOP) Updates

FEATURE ID	REQ ID	REQUIREMENT DESCRIPTION	PRIORITY
	R 4.1	SOP Updates—Marketing Department	Must Have
	R 4.2	SOP Updates—Customer Relationship Department	Must Have
F4.0	R 4.3	SOP Updates—IT Department	Should Have
	R 4.4	SOP Updates—Corporate Sales Department	Must Have
	R 4.5	SOP Updates—Personal Sales Department	Should Have

- Who are the "necessary employees"?
- What is a "seamless transformation"?
- Several separate requirements are combined.
- What about requirement IDs?
- What about requirement priorities?

Tables 9.3 and 9.4 show how a better-written requirement may look.

Now that we have defined the best practices of documenting multi-disciplinary requirements, let us look at a couple of real-life examples of requirements specifications. These include the following:

- The "Mobile Number Portability" project at a wireless communications company
- The "CRM System Implementation" project at a large insurance company

But before we move into the analysis of actual samples, just as in the previous chapters, there are several disclaimers one needs to make:

1. The documents—especially the "Product Features and Requirements" section—have been simplified as much as possible when compared to the originals. Many of the extra attributes and additional functionality have been removed to make the scope simpler and more manageable.

Table 9.4 Feature 5.0—SOP Changes Training

FEATURE ID	REQ ID	REQUIREMENT DESCRIPTION	PRIORITY
F5.0	R 5.1	New SOP Training—Marketing Department	Must Have
	R 5.2	New SOP Training—Customer Relationship Department	Must Have
	R 5.3	New SOP Training—IT Department	Should Have
	R 5.4	New SOP Training—Corporate Sales Department	Must Have
	R 5.5	New SOP Training—Personal Sales Department	Should Have

2. The purpose of this chapter and the attached requirements specifications documents was to demonstrate the proper spirit of the requirements rather than attempt to create a "perfect" requirements document.

Documenting Multidisciplinary Requirements

Introduction

Document Purpose   The introduction section of the requirements document for multidisciplinary projects is very similar to those in IT and engineering documents. The overall purpose and the high-level overview of the document should be described in this section. It is usually a good idea to have this paragraph prepared ahead as a part of the template replacing only the name of the project.

In our case, the "Purpose" paragraph for the "Mobile Number Portability" project looks like this:

> This document is the Requirements Specification for the "Mobile Number Portability" project. It addresses intended audiences, scope, user classes, and detailed requirements of the future product. The RS document is a configuration item and must be placed under change control once agreed. Updates to the RS must be reviewed and approved by the Project Manager and any relevant stakeholders for the section that is changed.

Intended Audience   Typically, the multidisciplinary projects—mostly due to their size and complexity—have a lot of stakeholders involved. These may include but are not limited to the project team, project sponsors, customers (both internal and external), and representatives of various departments from within the organization.

For example, on our "Mobile Number Portability" project, the group of key stakeholders consisted of the following:

- Project manager
- Project team
- IT team
- Networks team
- Value-added services team

- Sales and marketing team
- Customer care team
- Executive management

Project Scope Again, as described in the two previous chapters, project scope described in this section of the document should correspond (unless there were authorized changes) with the similar section in the project charter document. For example, the "CRM System Implementation" project had the following project scope:

> The scope of the project involves the configuration and implementation of the XYZ CRM system at the ABC Financial Services.

References Section The "References" section should list all the relevant documents that may be of interest to the project stakeholders, for example, in the "CRM System Implementation" project requirements specifications the "XYZ CRM System Overview" and the "XYZ CRM System User Manual" documents (see Table 9.5).

Product Description

Product Features The easiest way to fill out this section of the document is to "transfer" the features list directly from the project charter (or business case), assuming, of course, that it has not been changed since the document was signed off. An example of the features list from the "Mobile Number Portability" project can be found in Table 9.6.

Just as in the case of the "Port Upgrade" discussed in the previous chapter, the employees of the company decided to break down their project scope based on the departmental domains, which is very typical for multidisciplinary projects in general.

User Classes and Characteristics As mentioned in the previous two chapters, the user classes section is one of the most important

Table 9.5 References

DOCUMENT TITLE	URL LINK
"XYZ CRM System Overview"	Click here to access the document
"XYZ CRM System User Manual"	Click here to access the document

Table 9.6   Mobile Number Portability High-Level Features

FEATURE ID	FEATURE DESCRIPTION
F 1.0	Infrastructure Upgrades—IT
F 2.0	Infrastructure Upgrades—Networks
F 3.0	Infrastructure Upgrades—Value-Added Services
F 4.0	Changes to Contract Management
F 5.0	Tariff Changes and Risk Analysis
F 6.0	Changes to Standard Operating Procedures
F 7.0	Training of Personnel
F 8.0	Call Center Capacity Extension
F 9.0	Market Research and Campaigns
F 10.0	Software Changes—IT

sections of the documents because omitting individuals or groups of stakeholders can lead to missed requirements. So, in the case of the "CRM System Implementation" project, we managed to identify the following groups: business intelligence department, marketing department, actuary department, IT department, and data warehouse team (see Table 9.7). The business intelligence, marketing, and actuary teams received "preferred treatment" on this project because they were supposed to be the primary users of the new system, whereas IT and data warehouse people were supposed to play the supporting role.

Table 9.7   User Classes

USER CLASS	CHARACTERISTICS	FAVORED?
Business Intelligence	Employees of the business intelligence department and users of the business intelligence module of the CRM system	Yes
Marketing	Employees of the marketing department and users of the campaign management and direct marketing modules of the CRM system	Yes
Actuaries	Employees of the actuary department; can use any module of the CRM software	Yes
IT	Employees of the IT department responsible for the support and maintenance of the system	
Data Warehouse	Employees of the data warehouse department responsible for the support and maintenance of the data warehouse	

Product Environment   This section is intended to describe the environment in which the product of the project will be deployed and used. The author of the document can outline the geographic location, temperatures, humidity levels, winds, rain, snow, or any other external criterion that may be relevant to the performance of the product. For instance, in the case of the "Mobile Number Portability" project, the requirements analyst included the following description:

- Expected changes to the internal corporate standards, processes, and environments
- Expected changes to the external market environment: stiffer competition, decreased consumer loyalty, and so on

Here is another example of a product environment description from the "CRM System Implementation" endeavor:

- The XYZ CRM system shall be deployed on the existing ABC Financial Services network and servers.
- The XYZ CRM system needs to be fully integrated with the existing data warehouse.
- The users shall access the system via a web interface.

Product Features and Requirements

The "Features and Requirements" section is by far the largest part of the requirements specifications document. It contains all the requirements, functions, and attributes pertinent to the project. Ideally, all the deliverables of the endeavor, tangible and intangible, should be listed in this section of the document in accordance with the best practices of requirements documentation. For analysis purposes, let us examine two examples from the two requirements documents appended at the end of this chapter.

The first set of requirements is taken from the "Mobile Number Portability" project at a mobile phone company (see Table 9.8).

Note: For the full set of the requirements for the "Mobile Number Portability" project, please see the Taylor & Francis Group/ CRC Press website http://www.taylorandfrancis.com/product/ isbn/9781482259483 under the Downloads tab.

Table 9.8   Feature 2.0—Infrastructure Upgrades, Networks

FEATURE ID	REQ ID	REQUIREMENT DESCRIPTION	PRIORITY
	R 2.1	New Ericsson Server for Networks	Must Have
F2.0	R 2.2	Upgrades to Existing Equipment	Should Have
	R 2.3	Modifications to Signaling Protocols	Must Have

In the case of "Feature 2.0—Infrastructure Upgrades, Networks" the employees of the network department defined their requirements as follows:

- New Ericsson server
- Several upgrades to the existing equipment
- Modifications to signaling protocols

This requirement is interesting from several aspects. First, requirement 2.1 seems to delve into design right away: It lists a specific server (Ericsson) in the requirements document. This seems to be a classic case of going into design at the time when the requirements are being discussed and documented. However, in this particular case the venture into design has been perfectly justified. It turned out that the company had a policy of buying their network equipment from only Ericsson, so it was perfectly justified to list that particular server on a requirements document.

Requirement 2.2 appears to be somewhat vague, inasmuch as it mentions "several upgrades" instead of outlining the specific changes to be implemented. This is a perfect example of a requirement that needs further analysis and clarification. It was actually pointed out to the project team that this particular scope component needed further explanation.

Finally, the third component, "Modifications to signaling protocols," implies a series of changes to the software code, which implies that requirement 2.3 would have to be broken down into a series of functional and nonfunctional requirements before the document is signed off and baselined.

Let us now discuss the requirement taken out of the "CRM System Implementation" project. For the full requirements specifications document, please see the Taylor & Francis Group/CRC Press website http://www.crcpress.com/product/isbn/9781482259483 under the Downloads tab.

Table 9.9 Feature 1.0—Call Center Module

FEATURE ID	REQ ID	REQUIREMENT DESCRIPTION	PRIORITY
	R 1.1	"Single view of the customer" functionality	Must Have
	R 1.2	"Drill-down/drill through" functionality	Must Have
	R 1.3	"Search" functionality	Must Have
F 1.0	R 1.4	"Internal redirection" functionality	Must Have
	R 1.5	"Statistics on customer behavior"	Must Have
	R 1.6	"Customer web navigation" help (online)	Should Have
	R 1.7	"Customer satisfaction survey" functionality	Should Have
	R 1.8	"Automated mailing" functionality	Should Have

F 1.0—Call Center Module   Feature 1.0—Call Center Module is supposed to describe the customization that needs to be implemented on the off-the-shelf customer relationship management system. The team, after studying the software system, identified the following components that needed to be fine-tuned (see Table 9.9).

Again, as in the previous example, practically each one of the above requirements needed to be expanded into functional and nonfunctional requirements (or use cases, user stories, and user scenarios).

Appendix Section

The "Appendix" section is created to allow the project team to track different issues or to include additional information not covered by all other subsections of the document. These may include but are not limited to

- Dictionaries (including data dictionaries)
- Meeting minutes
- Parking lots
- Issue logs

In both of the requirements documents, the "Appendix" section is left unfilled to simplify the specifications and focus on more pertinent issues.

10

CREATING THE REQUIREMENTS MANAGEMENT PLAN AND REQUIREMENTS TRACEABILITY MATRIX

Introduction

When Does One Write the RMP and the RTM?

The requirements management plan (RMP) is a document that describes how requirements will be analyzed, documented, and managed throughout the project. It is frequently published in conjunction with the requirements traceability matrix (RTM). Both the RMP and RTM are supposed to be created along with the requirements specifications, and all three documents act as key inputs in the creation of the project plan document.

On smaller and medium-size projects, a shortened RMP can be incorporated either into the requirements specifications document or into the project plan. The RTM is usually included in the appendix of the requirements documentation. Having said that, on larger, more sophisticated ventures, it is a good idea to have these documents as separate, stand-alone artifacts.

RMP Benefits

There are several benefits of the RMP. First, it outlines how the requirements were collected and what methodologies have been used to elicit requirements from the users, customers, documentation, and all other potential sources. Second, it describes the requirements tracking and reporting methodologies, explaining how the requirements will be managed and how the changes to them will be communicated to all the project stakeholders. Third, it outlines the key steps in initiating the changes, assessing the impact of the requested changes, and the mechanism for either accepting or rejecting the changes.

What Is Traceability?

Requirements tracing is the process of documenting the links between the user requirements for the product or service you're building and the work components developed to implement and verify those requirements (see Figure 10.1). Those products may include business problems or requirements, features, or technical requirements (i.e., detailed, functional, and nonfunctional requirements as well as functions and attributes).

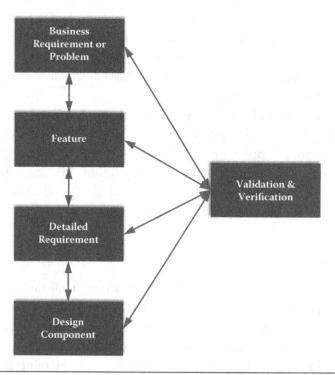

Figure 10.1   Requirements traceability.

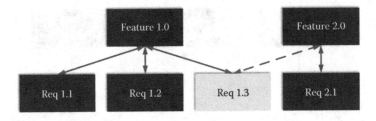

Figure 10.2 Requirements interdependency.

What Are the RTM Benefits?

There are many benefits to creating the RTM. One of those moments arrives when a change request is made and the technical team needs to identify the primary requirement (or feature, or design component) that needs to be changed. However, what frequently happens is that one scope component might have multiple relationships with either its "children" (i.e., design components) or its "parents" (i.e., features in our case) and changing one requirement could affect several features (see Figure 10.2).

Imagine the following simplified scenario. A company is designing a new baby stroller. Among multiple other scope components, the product scope contains the following features:

- F 3.0 Stroller Weight
    - Req 3.1 The new stroller weight shall be less than 35 pounds (≈16 kilogram).

- F4.0 Child Weight
    - Req 4.1 The new stroller shall support the child weighing up to 40 pounds (≈18 kilogram).

- F 5.0 Stroller Price
    - Req 5.1 The retail price of the stroller shall be less than $450.

All the features and requirements listed above appear to be unrelated, at least in the way they were documented. Let us assume that all these requirements were possible, but at some point the marketing department, after additional focus group studies, requested to decrease the weight of the stroller from 35 pounds to, say 25 pounds.

There are generally speaking two possible approaches to accommodating this change. One would be to use lighter components in

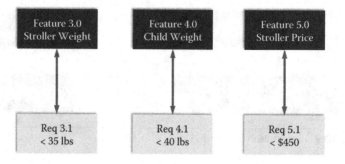

Figure 10.3   Stroller requirements: before.

the construction of the stroller, for example, tubes with thinner walls, or tubes of smaller diameter. This will most likely affect the stroller weight problem, but there is no guarantee the device will support the weight of 40 pounds. In other words, the change to requirement 3.1 will also affect requirement 4.1.

Another way of addressing this issue would be to use more durable materials in the construction of the stroller. For example, the aluminum parts can be replaced by titanium components. But this modification will most likely increase the price of the stroller to more than the $450 outlined in requirement 5.1.

Therefore, although it was assumed that the initial requirements structure looked like that shown in Figure 10.3, the actual RTM looks like that shown in Figure 10.4. The RTM can also be used to track the current status of the requirements on the project and find missing scope components. Project managers can also use traceability

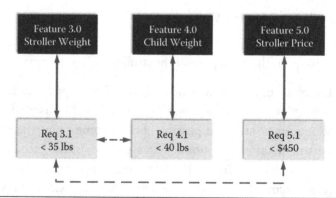

Figure 10.4   Stroller requirements: after.

to help them in assessing the progress of the project. As requirements are traced to design components and later to verification and validation tasks, management can estimate the project completion status based on how many requirements have been traced to artifacts created later in the planning.

Furthermore, the RTM provides the project team with an improved process visibility. The project manager or an analyst can determine where a requirement came from, its importance, how it was implemented, and how it was tested.

There are five RMP and RTM documents on the Taylor & Francis Group/CRC Press website http://www.crcpress.com/product/isbn/9781482259483 under the Downloads tab. In this chapter, we analyze several excerpts from a couple of them, but readers of the book are encouraged to study and analyze them all.

RMP and RTM Analysis

Introduction

Purpose The "Purpose" section is supposed to describe to the readers the purpose of the document and provide the project stakeholder with a high-level list of topics to be covered in this document. It could be a good idea for the author of such documents to have a well-written standard paragraph that can be reused from project to project. In our case, we started all our RMP and RTM documents with the following:

> The purpose of this plan is to establish and document a systematic approach to organizing and documenting the requirements of the product. This plan also establishes the process to maintain agreement between the customer and the project team on the evolving and changing requirements of the product.

Scope Again, as in the previous section, it could be a good idea to have a prepared "static" statement that can be reused from document to document:

> This plan provides guidelines for the management of requirements for a typical multidisciplinary project at ABC Port Authority.

Table 10.1   Glossary

TERM	EXPLANATION
Product Feature	A product feature is a capability or characteristic of a system that directly fulfills a stakeholder need, which is documented in a project's Vision document. A feature is a summary of an entire set of behaviors but does not describe those behaviors.
Stakeholder	A stakeholder is defined as anyone who is materially affected by the outcome of the project. Effectively solving any complex problem involves satisfying the needs of a diverse group of stakeholders. Stakeholders will typically have different perspectives on the problem and different needs that must be addressed by the solution.
Stakeholder Need	The stakeholder need is a business or operational problem (or opportunity) that must be fulfilled to justify purchase or use. This is the highest level of requirement, also known as a "need."
Baseline	The baseline is a reviewed and approved release of artifacts that constitutes an agreed basis for further evolution or development and that can be changed only through a formal procedure, such as change management and configuration control.

Definitions, Acronyms, and Abbreviations   This section should contain a glossary of all technical terms, acronyms, and abbreviations used in the document. It may be a good idea to organize these terms in a tabular form for ease of use and understanding, as shown in Table 10.1.

References Section   The references part of the document should list all the relevant project documentation that contains the information discussed in the RMP. The "usual suspects" in this case are the requirements specifications document and the project plan. But it is up to the project manager or a requirements analyst (whoever happens to author this document) as to which other references to include here.

Applicable references are

• "Energy Efficient House" Project Plan
• "Energy Efficient House" Requirements Specification

Overview   This is yet another section of the document where a prefabricated statement could be useful and can be transferred from one RMP to another. In our "Port Upgrade" project, the "Overview" paragraph looked like this:

This document contains specific details and strategies for managing the requirements of design and multidisciplinary projects at ABC Port Authority. The document details how requirements are organized and administrated within a project. It also describes how requirements will be identified, assigned attributes, traced, and modified.

The document also describes the change management processes for requirements, including the workflows and activities associated with maintaining control of project requirements.

Requirements

Requirements Planning   The requirements planning section is one of the most important in the document. Here, the author should outline the methodology that was used to collect the requirements in the first place as well as identify the key requirements providers. For example, in the case of the "Energy Efficient House" project, the project manager listed the following facts:

> The requirements elicitation was conducted by analyzing "Effective Insulation," "High-Performance Windows," "Efficient Heating and Cooling Equipment," "Lighting and Appliances," and "Third-Party Verification" published by ENERGY STAR (a joint program of the US Environmental Protection Agency and the US Department of Energy). Also, marketing surveys and focus group studies were conducted to obtain size, square footage, and the style of the house to be built.
>
> Please refer to the "Energy Efficient House" Requirements Specification for more information.

Requirements Tracking   In the requirements tracking part of the document, the author should mention the methodology that will be used to track the requirements as the project evolves from the planning to the closeout phases. Here are a couple of examples from the "Port Upgrade" and the "Energy Efficient House" projects, respectively:

> Requirements are and will be tracked using XYZ requirements management software by the project manager.
>
> Requirements are and will be tracked manually by the project manager. No special software shall be used.

Requirements Reporting   In the requirements reporting section, the project manager or the analyst should describe the ways of updating the stakeholders about the changes and progress of the requirements on the project. It is also possible to direct the reader to a specific section of another project management or requirements document:

> Any significant changes to the requirements shall be communicated to the project stakeholders via weekly Status Reports. For more information, please see the "Communications Management" section of the Project Plan.

Configuration Management

Change Initiation   This is also a very important section of the document that describes how the changes will be handled on the project. In my experience, this is a very important "conversation" to initiate with all the project stakeholders to prevent the potential dreaded scope creep that has contributed to the failure of many projects.

It is generally a good idea to state that once the requirements documentation and the project plan have been baselined, all future changes would have to go through the change control process, and each one of them would have to be thoroughly assessed from all possible angles, including, obviously, its impact on the cost and the duration of the project.

> After the Requirements Specifications and the Project Plan are baselined, all scope changes must go through the change management process (see Figure 10.5).

Change Impact Analysis   The change impact analysis is another important section of the document that describes what factors will be considered when assessing the potential changes on the project.

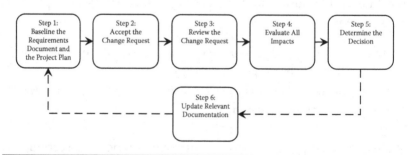

Figure 10.5   How to manage requirements.

In many cases, having a standard paragraph that can be reused from project to project can be quite helpful and make the life of the project manager or an analyst a little bit easier. In our sample documents, we reused the same statement that looked something like this:

> The following factors shall be considered and analyzed when assessing the change requests:
>
> - Impact on blueprints, bills of materials, technical drawings, design documents, project documents
> - Technical work to be done by engineers, construction crew, developers, architects, and so on
> - Management work to be done (project manager's time)
> - Documentation to be updated
> - Meetings you need to conduct (everyone involved)
> - Impacts on the sequence, dependencies, effort, and duration of all the tasks in the project plan
> - Impact on budget
> - Impacts on areas such as marketing, public relations, customer support, and training, among others
> - Impacts on all other areas of project management, including quality, communications, and the like
> - Cost of assessing the change request (will be charged to the customer regardless of whether the change request has been approved or rejected)

Change Tracing, Tracking, and Reporting   In this section, the author of the document should indicate how and what media will be used to communicate all the updates to the project stakeholders:

> All change requests shall be communicated to the project stakeholders via weekly Status Reports. For more information, please see the "Communications Management" section of the Project Plan.
> Also, all affected documents, including Requirements Specification and the Project Plan, shall be updated accordingly.

Change Authorization Levels   The change authorization levels are yet another very important section of the document that lists all the senior stakeholders whose approval is needed for the implementation of the changes on the project:

All change requests have to be approved by the directors of the departments whose requirements are affected by the requested modifications.

- Guy Ruggeri—Federal Government, Representative
- Christian Goranson—State Government, Representative
- Darryl Lass—Municipal Government, Representative
- Allan Minier—President and CEO
- Clayton Tilford— Director, Engineering
- Chris Agan— Director, IT
- Erik Baldon— Director, Logistics
- Roxie Manhart— Director, Legal
- Louisa Basquez— Director, PR
- Karina McMasters— Director, Sales and Marketing

Requirements Prioritization Process

Here, the author of the document needs to describe the mechanism that was used to generate the requirements priorities. In most cases, it is recommended to go with a "Must Have," "Should Have," and "Nice to Have" model for the requirements prioritization because it is fairly easy, straightforward, and easily understood by the stakeholders:

All requirements have been prioritized based on the following model:

- *Must Have:* Means that failure to implement the requirement will result in the failure of the entire project
- *Should Have:* Important requirements, but failure to implement the requirement does not automatically imply failure of the project
- *Nice to Have:* A desirable but not extremely important requirement

Requirements Traceability Matrix

Finally, we arrive at the last section of the document, the RTM. As mentioned earlier, the RTM is supposed to show the relationship between all the high-level features, requirements (i.e., detailed requirements, functional and nonfunctional requirements, functions, and attributes), and the related scope components.

One of the ways of showing these relationships is graphical, similar to that depicted in Figure 10.4. It is more user friendly and easier to read and understand. However, maintenance of a separate Vision file and constant copying and pasting of an updated diagram as the requirements change and evolve could become a cumbersome task.

Hence, the easier way of creating the RTM is the tabular approach, where all the features and related requirements are listed in one table to show all the "parent–child" relationships (see Table 10.2 for an example for the RTM from the "Port Upgrade" project).

Table 10.2 Sample Requirements Traceability Matrix

FEATURE ID	REQ ID
F 1.0	R 1.1
	R 1.2
F 2.0	R 2.1
	R 2.2
	R 2.3
	R 2.4
F 3.0	R 3.1
	R 3.2
	R 3.3
	R 3.4
	R 3.5
	R 3.6
	R 3.7
F 4.0	R 4.1
	R 4.2
	R 4.3
	R 4.4
F 5.0	R 5.1
	R 5.2
	R 5.3
	R 5.4
	R 5.5
F 6.0	R 5.1–5.5
	R 7.1
	R 9.1–9.3
	R 10.1–10.3
F 7.0	R 7.1

(continued)

Table 10.2   Sample Requirements Traceability Matrix (Continued)

FEATURE ID	REQ ID
F 8.0	R 8.1
	R 8.2
	R 8.3
	R 8.4
F 9.0	R 9.1
	R 9.2
	R 9.3
F 10.0	R 10.1
	R 10.2
	R 10.3

11

FINAL PRODUCT DESIGN

Historical Perspective: The Katana Sword

Katanas—or, as we also know them, samurai swords—emerged in Japan sometime between the twelfth and the fourteenth centuries during the Kamakura Period. Historians believe that the katana replaced the longer and heavier predecessor *tachi* because it could be drawn faster, thus allowing the samurai to draw the sword and strike down the enemy in a single motion.

Katanas were extremely sharp; the sword was designed to cut through iron-plated armor. Legend has it that the best katanas forged by Japanese blacksmiths could cut through four to five individuals standing next to each other in one single stroke! Another legend claims that katanas were responsible for saving the Japanese from the Mongol invasion in 1274, when badly outnumbered Japanese warriors were able to hold off an invading army of Kublai Khan until the Mongolian fleet was destroyed by a typhoon.

Modern weapons experts consider katanas to be the best cutting tools ever made by humans because they combine two previously unheard of attributes: a razor-sharp and yet resilient blade that could withstand considerable blows. The eternal problem that blacksmiths had to deal with for thousands of years before was the fact that the hard steel was very fit to be sharpened, but the tempering process (i.e., heating followed by fast cooling) left the steel very brittle and susceptible to breaking from blows. On the other hand, steel that has undergone a slow cooling process remains relatively soft and is thus better able to withstand strikes without breaking, but it loses the ability to maintain a sharp edge. Thus, the Japanese weapon makers had to deal with the eternal and seemingly unsolvable issue: How do we make the sword blade hard enough not to lose its edge when sharpened and yet soft enough not to break when struck by other weapons?

They came up with an ingenious solution to address this centuries-old problem. The first step involved selecting the best samples of low-carbon soft steel and high-carbon hard steel available. Then, each piece was repeatedly forged by heating and folding it numerous times to create a layered structure and work out all the impurities. Later, a high-carbon band of steel was heated again and bent into a U shape, whereas the soft, low-carbon piece was inserted into the center (see Figure 11.1).

The next stage involved taking the untempered blade and covering its top part with a secret mixture including clay and ash (see Figure 11.2). Then, the blade was reheated and quickly dipped into cold water. Several things happened simultaneously:

- The top clay-covered section of the blade cooled more slowly. Because the cooling process is slower, the blade retained some softness and flexibility.
- The bottom, exposed part cooled faster, thus hardening in the process.
- Because the two parts of the sword cooled at different rates, the blade bent, creating a natural curve that improves the cutting ability of the weapon (see Figure 11.2).

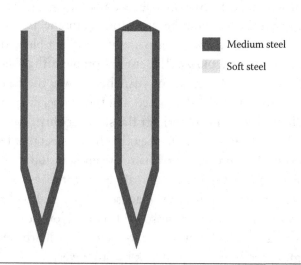

Medium steel

Soft steel

Figure 11.1 Katana cross-sections: initial.

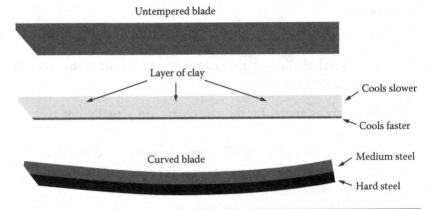

Figure 11.2 Katana design.

The end result of this procedure is a curved blade with a softer, more flexible core and a very hard and sharp cutting edge. Figure 11.3 shows two of the many available types of swords produced by Japanese craftsmen, the Honsanmai and the Shihozume.

The story of the Japanese katanas demonstrates how the proper approach to the design of the product—proper problem formulation, identification of key objectives, and finding creative ways to address these issues—can enable the project teams to come up with ingenious products.

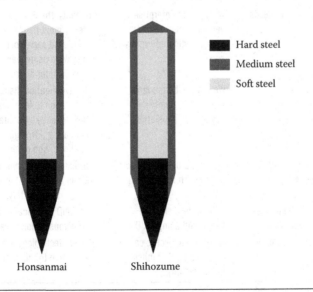

Figure 11.3 Katana cross-sections: final.

Design Process

Design Process Challenges

There are several challenges that can potentially hinder the smooth progress of the design process:

- The needs as stated by the customers are actually not their real needs.
- The problems stated by the customers are ill defined and vague, and all the constraints are unknown or the possible context is poorly understood.
- The problems presented by the customers are loaded with inconsistencies.
- Formulation of the problem is solution dependent; that is, the solution is inherent in the formulation.
- There is no solution to the problem presented by the customer.

Let us now look at some examples of the above-mentioned challenges (see Table 11.1).

Table 11.1   Design Challenges

CHALLENGE	EXAMPLE	EXPLANATION
Stated needs ≠ Real needs	"We need an Enterprise version of SAS software with a dedicated expensive server."	In reality, the Statistics Department needed a simple dedicated server because the one they were using was overloaded (see Chapter 5 for the full story).
Ill-defined problem	"We have to be prepared for the 'Mobile Number Portability' legislation."	The investigation discovered that, in addition to technical features, this project also contained marketing, PR, legal, customer relations, and other features.
Problem is loaded with inconsistencies	"We need a powerful gaming laptop with long-lasting battery."	Currently, the technology allows for either a powerful laptop or a long-lasting battery.
Formulation of the problem is solution dependent	"System data shall be backed up using RAID[a]."	Why RAID specifically? There are numerous options available.
There is no solution to the problem	"We need an electric car that can travel 1,000 miles before recharge."	Current technology does not have a solution to this problem.

[a] Redundant array of independent disks

How Complicated Can the Design Process Get?

The design process can become very complicated indeed, especially on modern, large multidisciplinary projects. One of the best examples of such complexity is the Chemical Industrial Park initiative undertaken in one of the developing countries to attract foreign investments and technology. The high-level idea was to build a technology park including several industrial buildings and to invite foreign investors who would bring their equipment and know-how to the country.

Initially, this project was viewed as a "construction" endeavor that would include the erection of several buildings, but very quickly after only the initial analysis it was discovered that the project in question included the features shown in Table 11.2. It should be noted that each of the features listed in the table represents a fairly complicated subproject in the overall Chemical Industrial Park program.

Let us consider another example that is very familiar to practically all readers who at least once in their lives have used an ATM

Table 11.2   Chemical Industrial Park

FEATURES	COMMENTS

Construction
  Ten manufacturing buildings
  Business center
  Training center
  Fence around the property
  Landscaping
  Sewer system
	The project included a large construction component including several manufacturing buildings for the foreign companies to move into, as well as business and training centers, a fence, landscaping, and the new sewer system.

Logistics
  Paved roads
  Railway
	The project required a new road leading to the complex from the main highway and a railway to deliver raw materials and off-load finished products.

IT and Telecom
  IT infrastructure of all buildings
  Telecom infrastructure
	Each building in the complex needed a modern IT and telecom infrastructure.

Marketing Marketing and PR program abroad	The marketing team had to create brochures, video clips, and other types of presentations to target foreign investors. In addition, the team had to identify the proper ways of determining their target markets and ways of communicating to them.

Legal
  Adjustments to local tax and
  customs laws
	Considerable amendments to the local tax and custom laws had to be introduced to the country's parliament to provide the potential investors with tax and customs exemptions.

to withdraw money, deposit checks, or pay their bills. Here is a very provocative question: Does the reader (especially one who is not familiar with application development) think that the creation of the ATM software is an easy or a very complicated project? Typically, the answer (just as in the case with the "Airport Check-In Kiosk") is that this project shouldn't be too complicated. One inserts his card into the slot, enters his PIN, and gets the money. These are seemingly simple tasks that we have done numerous times, but let us examine them step by step (see Table 11.3).

Even a superficial examination of the alternatives and exceptions as well as the business logic of a seemingly "simple" system once again reveals to us the sheer complexity that can be

Table 11.3   Partial List of Questions for ATM Project

IDENTIFY YOURSELF

- Is it one card per account, or can the user have several accounts linked to one card?
- o If yes, then who will create and administer this mechanism?
- What happens if the PIN entered is incorrect?
- o How many incorrect tries do we grant per user?
- o What happens if the user takes back the card after two attempts and then reinserts the card again? Do the first two wrong tries still count?
- o If the user exceeds the maximum allowed number of wrong attempts, do we take his card away or just prevent him from using the machine again?

Options for the user

- With what options shall the ATM provide the user?
- o For example, "Withdraw Money," "Deposit Money," "Transfer Funds," Make a Payment," and so on.
- Will the user be able to withdraw the money from the credit card account using his personal debit card?
- Will the user be able to withdraw money from the business account using his personal debit card?
- Should the default withdrawal amounts be presented to the user?
- o What default withdrawal amounts should be presented to the user?
- Should the ATM provide an option for a custom amount?
- What happens if the amount entered cannot be dispensed (i.e., not a multiple of 10 or 20)?
- What currencies shall the ATM dispense?
- o If the ATM is to dispense several currencies, what exchange rates should be used?
- Can users who are not customers of the bank withdraw money?
- o What procedures should apply in this scenario?
- Others

encountered by the designers. In addition to the examples above, it is worthwhile to examine several other potential challenges encountered by the project managers and their teams during the design stage of the projects.

By definition, the design problems are typically ill structured because the solution usually cannot be found by applying formulas or predetermined "recipes." Furthermore, design problems are often open ended because they typically have several acceptable solutions. To confirm this statement, one just needs to examine all the competing products or services in the market in one particular domain, for example, the number of TV sets available for sale at the local electronics store or the number of office desk models available at a furniture store.

Because of these two challenges, in a lot of cases creating the design of the product or service is akin to solving an equation with multiple unknown variables. For example, imagine that our goal is to design a chair. The reader can see at least five different types of chairs in Figure 11.4: a director's folding chair, household chair with leg support, dining chair, lawn chair, and school desk chair.

If our mission is to design a chair, we can't really start the process until we determine what type of chair is to be created, and to answer

Figure 11.4 Types of chairs.

that question we need to identify the primary use of the chair. In other words, how and by whom will it be used?

And even if we identify the answer to that question (for the sake of argument, let us assume that we are to build a lawn chair), a large number of other variables pop up:

- Should the chair be made from plastic, wood, aluminum, cloth, or some combination of these materials?
- What is the target price of the chair?
- Which design of the lawn chair would be the best?
- What exactly is meant by "best design"? Are we talking about attractiveness, value, sturdiness, reliability, resistance to humidity, or what?

This fairly simple example amply demonstrates how uncertain the design of even a simple chair can get. Once these challenges are extrapolated to more complex projects, such as building a chemical industrial park or deploying a new core system at the bank, we can start appreciating how much these challenges are amplified.

Design Process Detailed

The classical design process consists of eight distinct steps (see Figure 11.5). The first step, "Define Problems and Objectives," includes clarifying objectives, establishing relevant metrics, and identifying constraints. These steps typically happen in the initiation stage of the

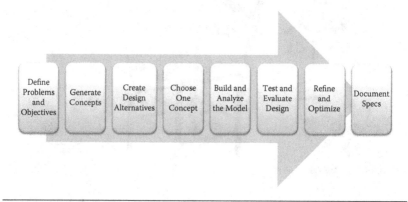

Figure 11.5   The design process.

project and are best captured in the project charter (see Chapter 3 for a detailed description of the project charters).

High-level conceptual design is the next stage of the design process. Here, the project team must determine key functions and attributes (or functional and nonfunctional requirements) of the product or service and generate several design alternatives. These actions typically take place during the planning stage of the project before the final version of the project plan can be baselined.

Once the execution phase of the project starts, the project team must select one optimal design and engage in the detailed analysis, modeling, and testing of the chosen concept. If needed, the model needs to be refined and optimized until the desired balance of features and constraints has been reached.

In the final stage of the design process that also takes place during the execution stage, the final scope must be documented and communicated to the project team and the customers (see Chapter 14 for the detailed description of technical inspections, customer walk-throughs, and peer reviews).

Clarifying Client's Objectives

Just as in the case of understanding the client's problems, business requirements (i.e., objectives), and high-level features, understanding and clarifying the client's objectives remains one of the integral parts of the design process. The project manager running this phase of the project must ensure good communications among the clients, users, and designers. Performing the design process implies translating the client's objectives into the kinds of words, pictures, numbers, rules, and so on that are needed to characterize and describe both the object being designed and its behavior.

One of the main tools of achieving this, again as in the case of features and requirements elicitation, is asking the right questions. In the design stage, the questions that should be asked are very similar to the questions asked before, only they become more pointed, deeper, and more detail oriented. For example, if the design team was tasked with the creation of a new "safe and sturdy" chair, the questions might look something like those shown in Table 11.4.

Table 11.4 Types of Questions

TYPES OF QUESTIONS	QUESTIONS
General	• Why do you need another product?
	• How will you use it?
	• How much can you spend?
	• How much should it cost?
Clarifying	• What does "safe" mean?
	• What does "sturdy" mean?
	• How much money are you willing to spend?
Identifying the Constraints	• Where will it be used?
Establishing Functions and Attributes	• How much weight should the chair support?
Design Requirements	• Should it be a padded chair?
	• Should the chair swivel?
	• Should the chair roll?
Design Alternatives	• Should the upholstery of the chair be manufactured from leather? cloth? artificial leather? vinyl?
Design Model and Analysis	• Should the chair conform to certain safety regulations?
Refining and Optimization	• Is there any way to save on upholstery?
	• Do we have to make the chair frame out of aluminum?
Physical Constraints	• What are the dimensions of the chair?
	• Would it be acceptable if they are: $L: 2' < L < 2.5'$ $W: 2' < L < 2.5'$ $H: 3.5' < H < 4'$?

Formal Methods of Design Process

There are several detailed design approaches available to project teams:

- Morphological charts
- Objectives tree method
- Pairwise comparisons
- Three-point voting

In this particular section of the chapter, we examine each of these methods in detail and supply the readers with relevant examples of their usage.

Morphological Charts

We start building the morphological charts by identifying the key features of the product or service or, if the project team was able to dig deeper into the requirements of the product, by outlining main functions and attributes (or functional and nonfunctional requirements for IT and software development projects). For example, if our goal was to design a new laptop bag for a business traveler, our key functions and attributes may end up looking like this:

- Bag size
- Color
- Contain laptop and accessories
- Contain documents and smaller items (business cards, USB)
- Provide access to items inside
- Material for the laptop bag
- Options for carrying
- External pockets

Once the key features have been determined, the team can generate several options or means by which these features can be achieved. For example, in our case (see Table 11.5) the team listed several options for the bag size expressed in terms of the laptop monitor dimensions:

- 12–13"
- 14–15"

Table 11.5 Sample Morphological Chart—Before

FUNCTIONS AND ATTRIBUTES	DESIGN COMPONENTS				
Bag size	12–13"	14–15"	16–17"	18"+	X
Color	Brown	Black	Green	Pink	White
Contain laptop and accessories	One main section	Two main sections	Three main sections	Four main sections	X
Contain documents and smaller items (business cards, USB)	No internal compartments	One internal compartment	Two internal compartments	X	X
Provide access to items inside	Flap	Zipper	X	X	X
Material for the laptop bag	Genuine leather	Artificial leather	Cotton	Nylon	X
Options for carrying	Shoulder strap	Grip	Shoulder strap and grip	X	X
External pockets	None	One	Two	Three	Four

- 16–17"
- 18"+

The options for the bag color were:

- Brown
- Black
- Green
- Pink
- White

Furthermore, there were several alternatives available for the number of the main sections in the bag that were supposed to hold the laptop and the accessories, including the power cord and the mouse:

- One main section
- Two main sections
- Three main sections
- Four main sections

The feature requiring the bag to have smaller internal compartments to hold items such as USB drives, business cards, pens, and so on resulted in the following design choices:

- No internal compartments
- One internal compartment
- Two internal compartments

Also, the team was able to generate two alternatives for the feature requiring the secure containment of the items in the bag:

- Flap
- Zipper

By the same token, there were several choices available for the material from which the bag could be manufactured:

- Genuine leather
- Artificial leather
- Cotton
- Nylon

Table 11.6 Sample Morphological Chart—After

FUNCTIONS AND ATTRIBUTES	DESIGN COMPONENTS				
Bag size	12–13"	14–15"	16–17"	18"+	X
Color	Brown	Black	Green	Pink	White
Contain laptop and accessories	One main section	Two main sections	Three main sections	Four main sections	X
Contain documents and smaller items	No internal compartments	One internal compartment	Two internal compartments	X	X
Provide access to items inside	Flap	Zipper	X	X	X
Material for the laptop bag	Genuine leather	Artificial leather	Cotton	Nylon	X
Options for carrying	Shoulder strap	Grip	Shoulder strap and grip	X	X
External pockets	None	One	Two	Three	Four

Options for carrying the laptop bag included

- Shoulder strap
- Grip (handle)
- Shoulder strap and grip

And finally, the feature requiring the bag to have external pockets was broken down into the following design components:

- None
- One pocket
- Two pockets
- Three pockets
- Four pockets

Once all these design options had been systemized and presented in one easy-to-understand table, the team could fairly easily make several important decisions regarding the final design of the bag (see Table 11.6). The final design of the bag consisted of:

- Bag size: 18"+ inches
- Color: brown
- Number of main sections: two

- Number of internal compartments: two
- Cover: flap
- Material: genuine leather
- Options for carrying: shoulder strap and grip
- External pockets: two

Objectives Tree Method

On real-life projects, the customers, users, and other requirements owners rarely provide their objectives in a systematic fashion. In other words, they typically do not provide the problems first, followed by the business requirements designed to address these problems, followed by technical requirements including functions and attributes or functional and nonfunctional requirements.

What usually happens, even if the customers and users come prepared to talk to the project team, is that they just "unload" all their objectives with no particular system in mind. Let us consider an example of such a project taken from real life:

Client: We need your team to design a new office chair for us. It has to have a futuristic design, be very comfortable, and have casters so that it can be easily rolled around the office without damaging the floors. By the way, it would be really nice if we can target a retail price of less than $200.

Project Manager: OK, let us start with the comfortable part. What exactly do you mean by this?

Client: Well, it has to be ergonomic … you know, adjustable seat, armrests, back, height, and back support.

Project Manager: Understood. Why do you want the price to be less than $200?

Client: You see, there is a lot of competition on the market, so we thought we should make the price very attractive in order to make the product marketable.

Project Manager: Have you considered anything else to enhance the product marketability?

Client: Yes, I have already mentioned the futuristic design… And our sales team thinks that we can sell more of our products if we improve the durability of our product…

Project Manager: What do you mean by "improve durability"?

Client: If we could provide the customer with at least a three-year warranty, it would really help our guys in sales.

Project Manager: OK, let us write down all your objectives:

- Futuristic design
- Comfortable
- Portable
- Rubber-coated casters
- Price <$200
- Ergonomic
- Adjustable seat
- Adjustable armrests
- Adjustable height
- Adjustable back support
- Adjustable back
- Marketable
- Three-year warranty

Client: Yes, I think you managed to capture all of them.

Project Manager: Now, let us try to group them:

- Ergonomic/comfortable
  - Adjustable seat
  - Adjustable armrests
  - Adjustable height
  - Adjustable back support
  - Adjustable back

- Marketable
  - Futuristic design
  - Price <$200
  - Three-year warranty

- Portable
  - Rubber-coated casters

Project Manager: And now let us try to show them graphically (see Figure 11.6).

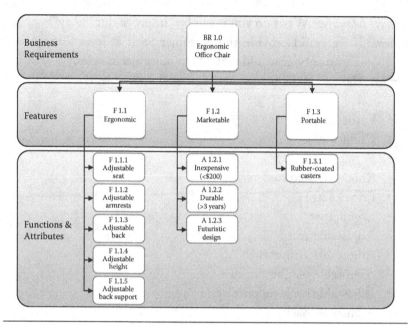

Figure 11.6   The objectives tree example: ergonomic office chair.

Pairwise Comparisons

Sometimes we get really lucky on the projects and our customers come to us not only with very specific and well thought-through objectives in mind, but also with well-defined priorities "attached" to their requirements. However, more often than not, the clients and users will have a very vague appreciation for the relative importance of various features and requirements.

This is when the simple and straightforward "pairwise comparison" method comes in handy. Suppose we were designing some kind of packaging product, a juice box, and the four high-level features mentioned by our customers were

- Low cost
- Small size
- Ease of use
- Robustness

The next step implies writing down combinations of all possible pairs of features and asking the client to determine which feature in each pairing is more important. The more important feature in each

Table 11.7 Sample Pairwise Comparisons

BUSINESS REQUIREMENTS	LOW COST	SMALL SIZE	EASE OF USE	ROBUSTNESS	TOTAL SCORE
Low Cost	X	0	0	1	1
Small Size	1	X	1	1	3
Ease of Use	1	0	X	1	2
Robustness	0	0	0	X	0

pair is awarded one point and the less important one, zero points. The results of this exercise are shown in Table 11.7. In this particular case, the results were

- Low cost < Small size
- Low cost < Ease of use
- Low cost > Robustness
- Small size > Ease of use
- Small size > Robustness
- Ease of use > Robustness

Note: The ">" sign denotes "more important than," and "<" denotes "less important than."

Thus "Low cost" received 1 point in total, "Small size" 3 points, "Ease of use" 2 points, and "Robustness" 0 points.

The pairwise comparison is a fairly straightforward and simple method of determining the relative importance of the product objectives, especially if the number of features to assess is fairly small. Keep in mind that the number of pairings is calculated as

$$Number\ of\ possible\ pairings = \frac{m!}{2!(m-2)!}$$

where

m = total number of objectives to be compared.

Thus, for example, if we had seven features to rank, the number of resulting pairings would be

$$Number\ of\ possible\ pairings =$$

$$\frac{7!}{2!(7-2)!} = \frac{1 \times 2 \times 3 \times 4 \times 5 \times 6 \times 7}{1 \times 2 \times 1 \times 2 \times 3 \times 4 \times 5} = 21$$

- Low cost
- Small Size
- Ease of Use
- Robustness

Figure 11.7   Three-point voting: before.

Three-Point Voting

I have used the "three-point" or the "three-checkmarks" voting system on numerous occasions to both prioritize requirements and design components. The procedure involves the following steps:

- Once all the attributes of the product or service have been identified (via brainstorming, analysis of customer requirements, or some other technique) they are written in a point form on a whiteboard or a flip chart, (see Figure 11.7). Usually, a dark color marker (e.g., black or blue) is used.
- The facilitator (typically the project manager) initiates a discussion where all participants are expected to provide their opinions about the importance of any of the attributes being discussed.
- Once the discussion is over, the facilitator hands the red marker to the first person in the room and announces the following rules:
  - Rule # 1: Each participant gets three checkmarks.
  - Rule # 2: Each participant must award all three checkmarks to the attributes listed on the board.
  - Rule # 3: If the participant feels that just one of the attributes is of utmost importance, then he or she should award all three checkmarks to that attribute.
  - Rule # 4: If the participant feels that only two of the attributes are important (e.g., A and B), but attribute A is more important than attribute B, then attribute A should get two checkmarks and attribute B one checkmark.
  - Rule # 5: If the participant thinks that any three of the attributes listed are important, then the checkmarks are equally distributed between three attributes.
  - Rule # 6: The number of checkmarks per participant must equal three.

- Low cost ✓ ✓ ✓
- Small Size ✓ ✓ ✓ ✓ ✓ ✓
- Ease of Use ✓ ✓ ✓ ✓
- Robustness ✓ ✓

Figure 11.8 Three-point voting: after.

- Rule # 7: After the first person awards her checkmarks, the red marker is passed on to the next person in the room until all the meeting participants have voted on the subject.
- Rule # 8: The facilitator then counts checkmarks awarded to each attribute, and the relative priorities are determined (see Figure 11.8).

This methodology can also be used to prioritize the high-level features as well as the requirements earlier in the project life cycle.

Design Presentation

Throughout the course of the project, and sometimes even before the official initiation, the team needs to make presentations to clients, users, and the technical team members. Sometimes these design-related presentations need to take place in order to demonstrate to the clients that the project team has a proper understanding of their needs and objectives.

On other occasions, right at the end of the planning stage, just as the best practices of project management recommend, the project team needs to verify the detailed scope with customers (customer walk-throughs) and the actual project team (technical team inspections). For more on this topic, please see Chapter 14. And yet on other occasions, the project manager may decide to provide the customers with the status updates on the project progress via such design presentations.

One of the major rules of preparing presentations is knowing your audience. There are several possible approaches to this problem. If the presentation is being made to the technical people, internal or external, then the presenter is expected to drill deeper into the more technical details. However, if the target audience consists of the CXO, marketing, sales, human resources, and other nontechnical representatives, then the focus of the presentation should be more on the business aspects of the project rather than on technical details (see Table 11.8).

Table 11.8   Design Presentation Guidelines

SECTION	DESCRIPTION
Title Slide	Identify the client, the project, the project team, and organization responsible for the work presented.
Executive Summary	Provide a high-level description of the presentation and the direction it will take.
Problems	Identify the key problems experienced by the customer that led to the inception of the current project.
Business Requirements and Features	Describe customer's business requirements resulting from the above-mentioned problems and the key high-level features needed to fulfill these requirements.
Alternatives	If applicable, provide the possible alternatives for achieving the desired solution, including time, budget, and quality implications.
Selected Design	Indicate which design has been selected and why.
Functions and Attributes or FR and NFR	If presenting to a fairly technical group or a group of actual users, describe the functions, attributes, or functional and nonfunctional requirements.
Testing	Share the results (if applicable) of the proof-of-concept testing with the meeting participants, especially the technical and the user groups.
Prototypes	Demonstrate the prototypes (if applicable). Videos, photos, architecture diagrams, design drawings, process flows, and 3D computer models are also useful in the presentation context.
Conclusions	Describe the work completed so far and the tasks yet outstanding.
Suggestions	Ask your audience members to provide their feedback and suggestions.

Prototypes, Models, and Proofs of Concept

The prototypes, models, and proofs of concepts mentioned earlier still create a lot of confusion among the members of the project teams, so we thought it would be a good idea to provide an explanation of each of these approaches.

- *Prototype:* First full-scale and usually functional representation of a new type or design of a construction. For example, most car companies usually produce a fully functioning prototype of their new models to test them for safety, usability, attractiveness, and the like.

- *Model:* Miniature representation of something. It can be built from paper, wood, plastic or metal or even designed on a computer.
- *Proof of Concept:* Model of some part of a design that is used specifically to test whether a particular concept would work as proposed.

Chapter Summary

We started this chapter with an example of an effective katana design by Japanese blacksmiths, where they managed to achieve a combination of a harder cutting edge with an overall flexibility of the blade.

In addition, we described the key formal methods of the design process, including the morphological charts, the objectives tree method, pairwise comparisons, and three-point voting.

Finally, we provided an outline of the "best-practices" design presentation and an overview of the prototypes, models, and proofs of concept.

12

CREATING WORK BREAKDOWN STRUCTURES AND WBS DICTIONARIES

Historical Perspective: The Great Pyramid

Let us revisit the story of the Egyptian pyramids mentioned in Chapter 2 by examining the story of the building of the Great Pyramid of Giza. The pyramid was built as a tomb for the fourth-dynasty Egyptian pharaoh, Khufu. The construction started in 2580 BC and concluded around 2560 BC. It is rumored that Khufu's vizier (the title equivalent to prime minister in modern times), Hemon, himself, acted as a project manager of this project.

The pyramid itself is 147 meters (480 feet) tall with a base of approximately 230 meters (750 feet) and contains around 2,300,000 individual blocks of stones weighing on average 2.5 tons (see Figure 12.1). Some of the stones reach 16 tons, and the granite slabs in Khufu's chamber weigh between 50 and 70 tons. The outer mantle consists of 144,000 casing stones weighing on average 15 tons each and polished to the accuracy of 0.25 millimeters (1/100th of an inch).

If we translate this endeavor into project management terms, the project would look like this:

- Project Size: 2,300,000 blocks of stone
- Project Duration: 20 years
- Project Cost: 4,800,000 person-months
  - At today's rates: $14,400,000,000 (assuming a modest salary of $500 per month)
- Excluding materials, tools, food, housing, and so on

Historians have found documentation for this project that, among other things, contains the names of all the craftsmen, overseers,

Figure 12.1 Egyptian pyramids.

inspectors, and other resources (25 titles in total). The entire work-force had been divided into two groups: elite skilled workers including quarry workers, haulers, and masons (about 4,000 people) and secondary workers including ramp builders, toolmakers, mortar mixers, and those providing backup services such as supplying food, clothing, and fuel (approximately 16,000).

Hemon had various project and functional managers reporting to him on this particular project; some of the titles included "overseer of the side of the pyramid," "director of the draftsmen," "overseer of masonry," "director of workers," and the "inspector of the craftsmen."

It is not known yet if the Egyptians actually used anything resembling a work breakdown structure, but as can be seen from this narrative, 20,000 people were separated into efficient, easily monitored units with specific tasks allocated to them.

The reason this historical case study is being mentioned at the beginning of the chapter dedicated to the work breakdown structures is that even several thousand years ago our ancestors came to the conclusion that success on large and complex projects cannot be achieved unless a lot of effort is invested in the project scope definition.

What Is a Work Breakdown Structure?

A *work breakdown structure* (WBS) is defined as deliverable oriented decomposition of a project into smaller components. It defines and groups a project's discrete work elements in a way that helps organize and define the total work scope of the project.

Work packages are defined as deliverable or project work components at the lowest level of each branch of the WBS that include the activities required to complete the work package deliverable.

In essence, WBSs are similar in concept to hierarchies or pyramids as shown in Figure 12.2. WBSs perform a very important role on any project, acting among other things as a linking mechanism between the elicited and documented project requirements and the detailed estimation activities that belong to the project time and project cost management domains.

WBS Components

The main idea behind the creation of the WBS is to list all the work required to be performed to complete the project successfully and break

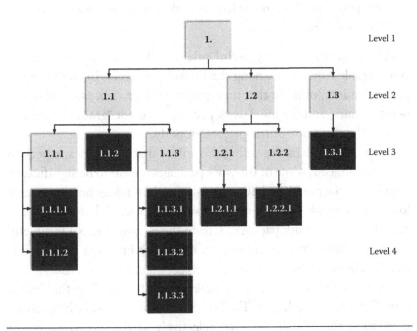

Figure 12.2   Generic vertical project WBS.

it down into manageable and assignable pieces: the work packages. This is done so that the project manager and the project team can estimate with an acceptable degree of accuracy all the "smaller" components of work, both in terms of effort and duration, and to roll up the individual estimates to obtain the overall estimate for the entire project.

Let us examine the key components of the WBS. Each box in the WBS is known as a "work element." Traditionally, a *parent* work element, for example, 1.1, is composed of *child* work elements, in our case 1.1.1, 1.1.2, and 1.1.3 (see Figure 12.2). The lowest level of work elements for any branch of the WBS tree is called a *work package*. In our example (see Figure 12.2) the work packages are highlighted in dark gray; they include work elements 1.1.1.1, 1.1.1.2, 1.1.2, 1.1.3.1, 1.1.3.2, 1.1.3.3, 1.2.1.1, 1.2.2.1, and 1.3.1.

Rules of WBS Creation

Traditionally, project managers obey the following rule when drilling into the WBS elements:

> Continue breaking down the work required to provide the deliverable of the project until the lowest level of work elements reaches the size of 80 person-hours.

Although this is a very useful rule to follow, it sometimes causes considerable confusion among the project managers. In certain cases, project leaders point out that their projects are smaller, say, 200 or 300 person-hours, and 80-hour work packages are not "granular" enough to describe the scope of the project properly.

Another complaint regarding this rule is that sometimes, especially on larger projects, some of the work packages appear to be significantly larger than the prescribed 80 person-hours, but it does not make sense logically to break them down into smaller "pieces." For example, in certain cases the work package "Create the Requirements Document" can reach 200–300 person-hours of effort, but breaking it down into smaller chunks does not make any project management sense.

Hence, we need to clarify a couple of points regarding the desired size of the work packages. The 80 person-hour rule is only a recommendation that should be used selectively at the discretion of the project manager and the project team. For example, in certain cases, especially on smaller projects, the teams have agreed to establish the size of the work package at one person-day (i.e., 8 person-hours). In other cases, involving very large projects, a decision was made to accept work packages larger than 80 person-hours in order not to jeopardize the logical uniformity of certain tasks, for example, the task of the "Create the Requirements Document" discussed earlier.

The numbering system of the work elements reflects the WBS level to which the element belongs. For example, work element 1.2.1 (see Figure 12.2) consists of three digits. Hence, we can easily conclude that belongs to the third level of the WBS. Again, traditionally, the highest level in the WBS is the project itself and is denoted as "1. The XYZ Project."

In certain cases, the project at hand is actually part of the larger program consisting of several projects. In this case for clarity purposes, it is recommended that all the work elements of the project should be marked with a prefix. For example, if we have a program XYZ consisting of, say, two projects, ABC and DEF, then the WBS elements of the ABC project would be marked with a prefix "ABC" followed by the element number (see Figure 12.3).

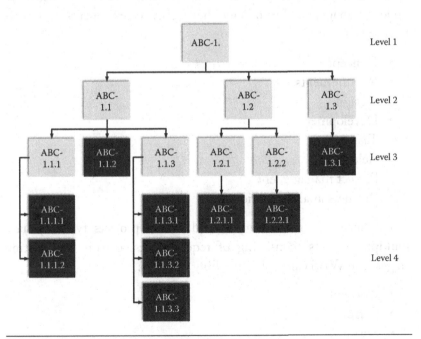

Figure 12.3   Generic vertical project WBS, with prefixes.

Many project managers, including even very experienced ones, frequently experience challenges with decomposition at the second level of the WBS. The most commonly voiced concern sounds something like, "OK, I have set level one as the project; what subcomponents should I break it into at the next level?"

There are several ways of approaching this challenge. The first option is to break the scope of the project into the traditional project management phases:

- Initiation
- Planning
- Execution
- Control
- Closeout
- Project management

Please note that although the "Project Management" subcomponent is not officially a part of the project phases, it is an absolutely essential part of the WBS. We discuss this matter in more detail later in the chapter.

In the IT, software development, and engineering sectors, some project managers prefer to name the level two components in the following fashion:

- Concept
- Requirements
- Design
- Development
- Testing
- Release
- Project management
- Business analysis (optional)

Furthermore, in the Agile world, where projects typically have multiple "sprints" consisting of requirements, design, and testing stages, the WBS can look something like this:

- Concept
- Sprint 1
- Sprint 2

- Sprint 3
- ...
- Sprint X
- System testing
- Closeout
- Project management

where

- Sprint 1
  - Requirements Elicitation 1
  - Design 1
  - Development 1
- Unit Testing 1

Despite the fact that the vertical WBSs are more appealing and are easier to absorb visually, drawing them in this format for larger projects can become a very cumbersome task. Thus, usually the project managers (and pretty much all project management software packages) create an inverted or indented WBS (see Figures 12.4 and 12.5). All other rules of project WBS creation, however, still apply to the indented WBSs.

Finally, it is very important to point out one of the most important rules of WBS creation. The work package level components (i.e., the lowest possible levels for any given WBS tree) should always start

```
→  1.
    →  1.1
        →  1.1.1
            →  1.1.1.1
            →  1.1.1.2
        →  1.1.2
        →  1.1.3
            →  1.1.3.1
            →  1.1.3.2
            →  1.1.3.3
    →  1.2
        →  1.2.1
            →  1.2.1.1
        →  1.2.2
            →  1.2.2.1
    →  1.3
        →  1.3.1
```

Figure 12.4 Generic indented project WBS.

→　ABC - 1.
　　→　ABC - 1.1
　　　　→　ABC - 1.1.1
　　　　　　→　ABC - 1.1.1.1
　　　　　　→　ABC - 1.1.1.2
　　　　→　ABC - 1.1.2
　　　　→　ABC - 1.1.3
　　　　　　→　ABC - 1.1.3.1
　　　　　　→　ABC - 1.1.3.2
　　　　　　→　ABC - 1.1.3.3
　　→　ABC - 1.2
　　　　→　ABC - 1.2.1
　　　　　　→　ABC - 1.2.1.1
　　　　→　ABC - 1.2.2
　　　　　　→　ABC - 1.2.2.1
　→　ABC - 1.3
　　　　→　ABC - 1.3.1

Figure 12.5　Generic indented project WBS, with prefixes.

with an active verb rather than noun. Let us consider one real-life example that happened on a small "House Renovations" project.

The project manager created a WBS with one of the components titled "Room painting" (see Figure 12.6). What he actually meant by that is all the activities associated with painting the room, including selecting the appropriate color, purchasing all the supplies, room preparation, actual painting, and the room cleanup. However, due to the relatively large size of the project, this particular scope component went unnoticed by the project team, who assumed that the project manager actually meant the process of applying two coats of the paint to the room walls. Hence, the estimate generated by the team was around 10 person-hours of effort and 10 hours of duration (assuming one resource was assigned to this particular task).

Unfortunately, the discrepancy in understanding between the project manager and his team was "discovered" only at the time of the actual performance of the task, which led to a significant time and effort overrun on the task. When challenged by the project manager, the team stated that they assumed that the color of the paint, purchasing of all the equipment, and the room preparation and cleanup had been considered by the project manager in advance.

1.1 - Room painting

Figure 12.6　Room painting WBS: incorrect.

Therefore, all junior project managers are constantly nagged by their mentors to record the work packages in the "Verb + Noun" format to avoid all possible confusion when the team arrives at the point of estimating the duration and effort for all the relevant tasks.

A WBS Sample

Let us examine the proper "Room painting" WBS in a bit more detail (see Figure 12.7). The project manager broke down the project into the following second-level phases:

- Choose the color
- Purchasing
- Prepare the room
- Painting
- Room cleanup

The "Choose the color" task is sufficiently definitive to break it down further, so it was decided not to break it down further, thus effectively making it a work package.

1.1   Room painting
     1.1.1   Choose the color
     1.1.2   Purchasing
          1.1.2.1   Drive to the store
          1.1.2.2   Purchase painting supplies
          1.1.2.3   Purchase paint
          1.1.2.4   Purchase masking tape
          1.1.2.5   Return back
     1.1.3   Prepare the room
          1.1.3.1   Remove all the wall fixtures
          1.1.3.2   Remove all the furniture
          1.1.3.3   Cover the floor with tarp
          1.1.3.4   Apply the masking tape
     1.1.4   Painting
          1.1.4.1   Paint the room the first time
          1.1.4.2   Paint the room the second time
     1.1.5   Room cleanup
          1.1.5.1   Remove the masking tape
          1.1.5.2   Remove the tarp
          1.1.5.3   Vacuum the floor
          1.1.5.4   Install the furniture
          1.1.5.5   Install all the wall fixtures

Figure 12.7   Room painting WBS: detailed.

Purchasing, on the other hand, had to be broken down further into

- Drive to the store
- Purchase painting supplies
- Purchase paint
- Purchase masking tape
- Return back

Although we are not yet interested in the sequencing of the events when creating WBSs, as sequencing is the domain of project time management and is taken care of when constructing network diagrams, it is a worthwhile mental exercise to attempt to visualize this process.

In our case, one cannot commence the purchasing activities until the driving to the store has ended. On the other hand, purchasing the painting supplies, paint, and masking tape, even if the tasks are being performed by one resource, can be done concurrently. After all, it is highly unlikely that the resource will go through the entire store, buy the painting supplies, then start from the very beginning to look for paint, and so on. However, only when all the shopping is completed can the resource get into her car and drive back to the house.

The next second-level scope component also presents us with several interesting observations. The project manager divided the "Prepare the room" work element into the following work packages:

- Remove all the wall fixtures
- Remove all the furniture
- Cover the floor with tarp
- Apply the masking tape

Again, despite the fact that when constructing WBSs we do not usually concentrate on the sequencing of the activities, it is still interesting to assess how the series of tasks will change depending on the number of resources assigned to them. In our case, if we had only one resource assigned to this part of the project, the situation is straightforward: Remove the fixtures, remove the furniture, put the tarp on the floor, and apply the masking tape. Some of these tasks can be interchanged (e.g., the worker may decide to get rid of the furniture first and then remove all the fixtures) but it is highly unlikely that he would be able to accomplish any of the tasks simultaneously.

Another interesting aspect that can be observed in this situation is that before starting to paint the room for the second time the worker will have to wait for the paint to dry. Such intervals where no activities happen between the tasks are called lags.

Furthermore, if the requirements were properly captured according to the best practices outlined in the previous chapters, it is fairly easy to convert these deliverables into the WBS work packages, as was demonstrated in the above example where the "Room painting" requirement was broken down into a series of work elements all starting with an active verb.

One final comment to make regarding the WBSs: Only the work package–level tasks are included in the network diagrams that directly deal with the proper sequencing of project events and the calculation of the critical path.

Note: For a full WBS for a real-life "Mobile Number Portability" project, please see the Taylor & Francis Group/CRC Press website http://www.crcpress.com/product/isbn/9781482259483 under the Downloads tab.

Generic WBS: Project Management Tasks

As promised earlier, let us return to the project management tasks in the WBS. Many inexperienced project managers have trouble comprehending the amount of time and effort invested in the management and general administration of an average project. Industry studies suggest that just the project manager's effort alone can account for 10%–15% of the total project effort. This implies that if one has a project at hand estimated to be, say, 1,000 person-days of effort, the work of the project manager can amount to 100–150 person-days of additional work.

By the same token, many project managers assume they can get away with just including a work package called "Project Management and Administration" and automatically assign around 20% (to account for meetings) of the total work effort on top of the project work. This technique will most surely backfire on most of the projects, because the majority of stakeholders have a very difficult time "visualizing" the amount of project management work that is invested in any given project.

Hence, it is a good idea to break down the project management work to a finer level of granularity to account for all aspects of

1.6   Project Management and Administration
    1.6.1   Initiation
        1.6.1.1   Contract negotiations
        1.6.1.2   Preliminary estimates
        1.6.1.3   Project charter
        1.6.1.4   Kick off meetings
    1.6.2   Planning
        1.6.2.1   Requirements specifications
        1.6.2.2   Project plan
    1.6.3   Execution/control
        1.6.3.1   Project reviews
        1.6.3.2   Action item tracking
        1.6.3.3   Time sheets
        1.6.3.4   Status reports
        1.6.3.5   Project meetings
        1.6.3.6   Corrective actions
        1.6.3.7   Work-arounds
        1.6.3.8   Subcontract management
        1.6.3.9   Change management
    1.6.4   Closeout
        1.6.4.1   Project completion
        1.6.4.2   Closeout meetings
        1.6.4.3   Lessons learned
        1.6.4.4   Contract closeout

Figure 12.8   WBS: project management tasks.

project administration and management. Figure 12.8 presents a typical breakdown of the project management–related work elements that can be broken down further if needed depending on the complexity and the size of the project or according to the individual preference of the project manager.

Generic WBS: Starting Phases

The starting phases of the project can also present certain troubles for junior project managers who have trouble generating work packages for the first two phases of the project: the initiation and the planning stages. Fortunately, these two stages, unlike the subsequent ones, can be somewhat standardized; that is, the same work packages can be reused, more or less, on many projects. Figure 12.9 presents the readers of this book with a standardized list of the work elements that can be used on almost every project.

1.1 Initiation
    1.1.1   Identify stakeholders
    1.1.2   Conduct meetings with the stakeholders
    1.1.3   Write the Project Charter
    1.1.4   Review the Project Charter with the stakeholders
    1.1.5   Update and incorporate stakeholder feedback
    1.1.6   Obtain sign-off on the Project Charter
1.2 Planning
    1.2.1   Identify all users and customers
    1.2.2   Conduct requirements elicitation meetings
    1.2.3   Conduct other requirements elicitation activities
    1.2.4   Analyze requirements
    1.2.5   Document requirements
    1.2.6   Conduct Requirements Specifications customer walk-throughs
    1.2.7   Conduct Requirements Specifications technical team inspections
    1.2.8   Conduct Requirements Specifications peer reviews
    1.2.9   Update and incorporate feedback
    1.2.10 Obtain sign-off on the Requirements Specifications
    1.2.11 Create Project Plan
        1.2.11.1   Create scope management plan
        1.2.11.2   Create time management plan
        1.2.11.3   Create cost management plan
        1.2.11.4   Create HR management plan
        1.2.11.5   Create communications management plan
        1.2.11.6   Create risk management plan
        1.2.11.7   Create quality management plan
        1.2.11.8   Create procurement management plan
    1.2.12 Conduct Project Plan customer walk-throughs
    1.2.13 Conduct Project Plan technical team inspections
    1.2.14 Conduct Project Plan peer reviews
    1.2.15 Update and incorporate feedback
    1.2.16 Obtain sign-off on the Project Plan
1.3 Execution
    1.3.1   Create final product design
    1.3.2   Conduct final product design customer walk-throughs
    1.3.3   Conduct final product design technical team inspections
    1.3.4   Update and incorporate feedback

Figure 12.9 Generic WBS template, initial phases.

WBS Dictionary

WBS dictionaries (see Table 12.1) are usually created on larger, more complex projects and are designed to provide all the relevant project stakeholders with detailed information about the work package, including the following:

- Project Name
- Contract Number

Table 12.1 Sample Work Breakdown Structure Dictionary

WORK BREAKDOWN STRUCTURE DICTIONARY	
Project Name:	5298 Main Street - Office Renovations
Contract Number:	ABC - 123456
Date:	22-Sep-2012
WBS Level:	1.1.5
Element Title:	Room cleanup
Element Description:	Room cleanup after painting has been complete
Element Objective:	To have the room ready for use
Element Effort:	Three person-hours
WBS Level:	1.1.5.1 Remove the masking tape
	1.1.5.2 Remove the tarp
	1.1.5.3 Vacuum the floor
	1.1.5.4 Install the furniture
	1.1.5.5 Install all the wall fixtures

- Date
- WBS Level
- Element Title
- Element Description
- Element Objective
- Element Effort
- WBS Level

Estimation Using WBS

Introduction: How to Improve Your Estimates

Although the majority of the estimation tasks fall into the domain of project cost and project time management, the relationship between the WBSs and the assessment of the total effort (and the total cost) is so strong that it would be worthwhile to discuss in this book.

One of the most frequently asked questions, both by senior executives and junior project team members alike, is, "How can we improve the accuracy of our estimates?" The response to this question is based on three pillars:

- Detailed understanding of the scope of the work with all the relevant constraints and priorities
- Access to good-quality, reliable historical data
- Active involvement of your team in the estimate generation

Access to good historical data is also an issue because very few companies actually capture key project information. In my personal experience, I have heard many excuses from senior managers of various companies about why they do not want to capture historical performance data. Some mention lack of understanding of the financial feasibility of such investments. Others claim lack of understanding of the benefits historical data can "bring to the table." And yet another group of fairly significant size mentions the political issues arising from comparing imposed targets and actual results.

Furthermore, although project managers are encouraged to be proactive and start gathering historical information on their own projects, it usually takes several years of working at the same company and on fairly similar projects before one project manager can accumulate an historical database of sufficient size to make any informed and reliable decisions.

In general, (at least) the following historical data should be collected by companies and project managers alike:

- Total budget
- Total schedule
- Total effort
- Team size
- Scope of software delivered
  - Lines of code
  - Design elements
  - Features
  - Requirements

- Type of software being developed
- Type of project and so on

These methods and their drawbacks lead us to the final estimation improvement technique: a combination of Wide-Band Delphi estimation coupled with the PERT methodology.

Improving Your Estimate Accuracy with Wide-Band Delphi and PERT

Wide-Band Delphi Wide-Band Delphi was created in the early 1940s by the Rand Corporation involved in the atomic bomb creation (the Manhattan Project). This methodology was later refined by Barry Boehm, a prominent figure in the software development industry, for technology project purposes. The "industrial strength" version of the Wide-Band Delphi technique consists of the following steps:

1. The coordinator presents each estimator with requirements or a design document and an estimation form.
2. Estimators discuss task or requirement complexity issues with each other (but not the estimate itself).
3. Estimators fill out forms anonymously (important).
4. The coordinator prepares a summary of the estimates on an iteration form (similar to an estimation form).
5. The coordinator has estimators discuss variation in estimates examining range, average, and extreme values.
6. Estimators fill out forms again, anonymously, and repeat steps 4–6 as many times as needed.

Notice several peculiarities in the above process. First, estimators are free to discuss a task or requirement and the complexity associated with implementing it, but no one is allowed to say something along the lines of "I think task A should take no more than 12 days" or "The Execution stage will cost us $150,000."

Furthermore, the estimation forms must be filled out anonymously with one person not knowing what estimates are being input by his neighbor. These steps are undertaken to ensure that vocal and strongly opinionated people on the team do not influence the quiet and shy team members who may and frequently do possess more accurate information.

For example, after collecting all the estimation forms, the project manager writes all the estimates on the whiteboard:

5 days
4 days
6 days
4 days
6 days
5 days
20 days
4 days
5 days

We can see right away that almost all the estimates are fairly similar and range between 4 and 6 days, with one exception: the 20-day estimate provided by one of the project team members. Rather than asking whoever came up with the larger estimate to stand up and explain her reasoning in front of the rest of the team, the project manager is expected to ask something along the following lines: "And why do you think some of us may believe that this task may take 20 days?"

It could happen that most of the team members in the room may think that the creation of a query or form should take no more than, say, four days. And yet there is one member of the team, a database expert, who knows for a fact that considerable parts of the database would have to be rewritten for this new query or form to work properly, thus increasing the task duration to 20 days. The potential problem in this situation is that the only person who knows the true duration (of effort) of the task may be overwhelmed by the opinions voiced by more vocal team members.

The appropriate attitude is that no one knows the right answer and team members are not allowed to discuss the actual durations or efforts of the tasks among themselves.

Wide-Band Delphi "Light"   Wide-Band Delphi "Light," on the other hand, dispenses with all the formalities typically unnecessary on the majority of the projects. For example, estimation forms can be replaced with small pieces of paper and estimates are recorded on a whiteboard or flip chart. Furthermore, this technique can be applied only to the most volatile and "controversial" tasks.

Program Evaluation and Review Technique (PERT)   The Program Evaluation and Review Technique was invented in the late 1950s by Booz Allen Hamilton, Inc. under contract to the DoD's US Navy Special Projects Office in 1958. The endeavor they were working on was the Polaris mobile submarine-launched ballistic missile project.

Let us pretend that we are working on a fairly simple and straightforward website development project and we have identified the following work packages:

- Initiation (i.e., write the project charter)
- Document requirements

- Design web pages
- Conduct development and unit testing
- Conduct system testing
- Conduct user acceptance testing
- Release of software
- Training
- Project management
- Project meetings

In the next step, we conduct one or several Wide-Band Delphi exercises with the entire technical team and generate the optimistic, most likely, and pessimistic duration estimates for each task (see "OPT," "ML," and "PESS" columns in Table 12.2).

People frequently ask, "Although we understand the concept of most likely estimates, how does one come up with optimistic and pessimistic ones?" The suggestion is to think of an optimistic estimate in the following manner: "If everything that can go right will go right on this task, how long will it take (how much will it cost, how many person-days will it require)?"

Coming up with a pessimistic estimate, on the other hand, implies answering the question: "If everything that can go wrong will go wrong on this task, how long will it take (how much will it cost, how many person-days will it require)?"

Table 12.2 Sample PERT Calculation

	OPT	ML	PESS	PERT MEAN	PERT ST. DEV	PERT VAR
Initiation	5	7	10	7.17	0.83	0.69
Document Requirements	30	50	90	53.33	10.00	100.00
Design Pages	10	14	18	14.00	1.33	1.78
Development and Unit Testing	100	150	225	154.17	20.83	434.03
System Testing and Bug Fixing	45	60	75	60.00	5.00	25.00
User Acceptance Testing	5	7	12	7.50	1.17	1.36
Release	2	4	6	4.00	0.67	0.44
Training	3	3	3	3.00	0.00	0.00
Project Management (15% of total)	30	44.3	65.9	45.48	5.98	35.70
Project Meetings (5% of total)	10	14.8	22	15.16	1.99	3.97
TOTAL FOR THE PROJECT				**363.88**	**24.56**	602.97

The mean duration, the standard deviation, and the variance for each task are calculated based on the following formulas (see "PERT MEAN," "PERT ST. DEV," and "PERT VAR" columns in Table 12.2):

$$Mean_{Task} = \frac{(Pess + 4ML + Opt)}{6}$$

$$St.dev_{Task} = \frac{(Pess - Opt)}{6}$$

$$Var_{Task} = St.dev^2 = \frac{(Pess - Opt)^2}{36}$$

The standard deviation of the entire project has to be calculated in a different way. First, all the task variances have to be added together to obtain the project variance (i.e., 602.97 in our example). Taking the square root of the project variance yields the project standard deviation (i.e., 24.56):

$$St.dev_{Project} = \sqrt{Var_{Project}}$$

These two numbers can be utilized by the project manager to establish a link between various effort targets and resulting probabilities of success. The science of statistics tells us that 68.3% of the normally distributed population is located within one standard deviation from the population's mean (see Figure 12.10). Translated from science-talk

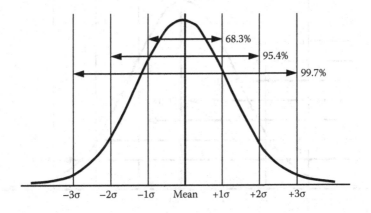

Figure 12.10   Normal distribution: two-sided estimates.

into plain English, this implies that the above-mentioned project has a 68.3% chance of requiring an effort of between 339 (363.88 − 24.56 = 339.32) and 389 (363.88 + 24.56 = 388.44) person-days.

By the same token, knowing that 95.4% of the population is located within two standard deviations, we can conclude that there is a 95.4% chance of the project finishing between 315 (363.88 − 2 × 24.56 = 314.76) and 413 (363.88 + 2 × 24.56 = 413) person-days.

Finally, increasing the range to between 290 (363.88 − 3 × 24.56 = 290.20) and 437 (363.88 + 3 × 24.56 = 437.56) person-days will yield a confidence level of 99.7%.

However, managers and customers alike are typically not very interested in hearing about the ranges; the typical human being thinks in terms of, "Is it possible to deliver the project with these resources?" For those scenarios, Figure 12.11 can be particularly useful. Again, using the mean and standard deviation from our sample project, we can make the following statements:

- There is a 0.3% chance of successful completion of the project if 290 person-days are invested.
- There is a 0.3% chance of successful completion of the project if 315 person-days are invested.
- There is a 16% chance of successful completion of the project if 339 person-days are invested.
- There is an 84% chance of successful completion of the project if 389 person-days are invested.

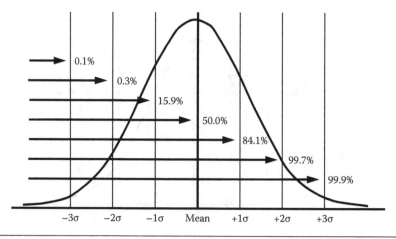

Figure 12.11 Normal distribution: one-sided estimates.

Table 12.3 Common Estimation Oversights

TYPICAL OMISSIONS	TOTAL PROJECT EFFORT (%)
Did we include sick and vacation days?	10–12
Did we include Project Management tasks?	5–15
Did we include Project Meetings?	5–15
Did we include Documentation tasks?	5–10
Did we include Testing tasks?	20–30
Did we include Requirements Elicitation tasks?	10–15

- There is a 99.7% chance of successful completion of the project if 413 person-days are invested.
- There is a 99.9% chance of successful completion of the project if 437 person-days are invested.

The first two statements are especially interesting. Wouldn't it be really cool to demonstrate using science and proven statistical laws that the probability of finishing the above project with 290 person-days invested is 0.3%?

Common Estimation Oversights What are some common tasks that frequently get overlooked by project managers, business analysts, and other technical team members? Table 12.3 is a list of questions to ask the team in order to catch all the "popular" omissions during the estimation exercises and the approximate guidelines of the percentages of the total project effort that should be allocated to them.

Chapter Summary

We started this chapter by defining the WBS and examining its key components. Then, we talked about the rules that should be followed when creating the WBSs and examined a sample WBS. Next, we looked at the key components of the WBS dictionary followed by a discussion about estimation. We talked about the Wide-Band Delphi methodology and the usage of PERT to improve the estimates generated by the project team.

13

TROUBLESHOOTING SCOPE PROBLEMS

Historical Perspective: General Hadik's Crucial Mistake

Sometime in 1757, an extraordinary event took place at the royal palace in Vienna. A general of the Austrian army, András Hadik de Futak was mercilessly slapped across the face with a pair of leather gloves by the Empress Maria Theresa.

A fascinating sequence of events preceded this dramatic occasion. Austria and Germany, along with almost all other European powers, had been engaged in a Seven Years' War. At one point, General Hadik, who had been leading a light cavalry brigade consisting of about 5,000 hussars, found himself in close proximity to the forces of his enemy, Prussian King Frederick. For some unexplained reasons, instead of attacking the Prussians, the Austrian general turned his brigade around and redirected them toward the Prussian capital of Berlin.

At the time, the city of Berlin was guarded by a small force of 500 soldiers, of whom 200 were raw recruits and the rest represented by a local militia. As a result, Hadik's forces were able to gain control of Berlin with hardly any shots fired. Prussian defenders literally dispersed in the city once they realized they were dealing with an enemy force that was 10 times bigger than their own contingent consisting of amateurs.

Hadik advanced to the city magistrate and proceeded to conduct a very hurried negotiation with the Berlin officials. The hastiness of the process was very well justified because his reconnaissance had informed him that the Prussian forces under the command of General Friedrich von Seydlitz had been observed in the vicinity of the city. The expected reaction of the German general to the news that his own capital had been occupied by a relatively small enemy force was easy to forecast; he would immediately rush to the aid of his compatriots.

The nature of the negotiations, on the other hand, took a very typical course by eighteenth-century standards. Hadik demanded a contribution of 600,000 thalers in exchange for his peaceful retreat from the city. The Berlin magistrate, citing financial difficulties, countered with an offer of 50,000. Hadik, while appealing to their patriotism and concerns for the well-being of Berlin, lowered his demands to 500,000. City officials, knowing that von Seydlitz was somewhere in the vicinity, raised the offer to 100,000 thalers. Eventually, both sides agreed on a contribution of 200,000, of which 15,000 thalers were requisitioned for the "personal use" of the general.

Both sides of the heated discussion were about to bid *adieu* to each other and part ways, when Hadik remembered something else: At the time, the Berlin leather manufacturers were famous throughout the world for the quality of their leather gloves. So, Hadik demanded that the officials supply him with two dozen pairs of ladies' gloves, stamped with the city coat of arms so that he could present them as a symbolic gift of the Prussian surrender to the Austrian Empress Maria Theresa.

The Berliners readily obliged, adding a hefty package of gloves to the bags of coins delivered earlier to Hadik's troops. The Austrian either did not think at all about checking the package contents or was too busy trying to escape from the city. What he did instead was proceed to Vienna, await the summons to the royal palace, where he described in color the heroic siege of Berlin, his strategic talents, and the heroism of his troops. As a final gesture, he offered a package of leather gloves to the Empress as a token of Austrian chivalry and Prussian humiliation. But, unfortunately, there was a small problem with the gloves packed by the shrewd Berliners: As it turned out, they gained a little revenge on the greedy general by making sure that all the empress's gloves were for the left hand!

What conclusions can we draw from this story? Hadik should have conducted a scope validation exercise upon the delivery of the package to ensure that the final product was indeed delivered according to his specifications. This small mistake represents a great multitude of the serious problems that could erode the scope definition efforts on projects. Therefore, this chapter of the book is dedicated to potential issues one may encounter during the scope definition process and the ways to address them.

Introduction

This chapter was not written as a depository of new developments in project scope management but rather as a handy troubleshooting guide for the potential scope-related issues that may surface at different stages of the project. As such, readers should expect to find the list of potential problems subdivided into categories, including scope elicitation, skills, project management, documentation, and scope management issues, with potential solutions tied to each problem.

Another interesting aspect to keep in mind is what database developers and analysts call a "many-to-many" relationship between the problems listed and their potential solutions. In other words, one problem can and usually does have several potential solutions that should be deployed at different stages of the project. However, upon finishing this chapter, I have discovered that one potential solution can also address several problems.

Scope Elicitation Issues

Lack of Communication between Project Team and Customers

Lack of communication is a very broad problem domain that can include a multitude of factors. Sometimes it can be caused by the stakeholders who have initiated the project but are "too busy" to spend time with the requirements analysts to iron out all the details of the scope. In addition, in many cases, as mentioned several times earlier in this book, the stakeholders are simply not prepared to assess the sheer complexity of the projects they are initiating.

Lack of Access to Higher Authority

There is by itself nothing wrong when the project is initiated by a representative of the executive team, and hence, at least the initial high-level requirements are conceived in the heads of the senior management. There is, however, one inherent issue with this situation that rears its ugly head almost every time at the initiation or the planning stages of the project.

Let us consider a very generic situation. A CEO of a company had a brilliant idea for a new product (or service) while watching TV a day earlier. He enters his company headquarters the next day, finds his executive vice president of marketing, and shares this idea with her. They both agree that this is indeed a great idea and decide to initiate a new project that would be mandated with creating the new product.

As a result of this brief conversation, the vice president calls the director of product management and asks him to initiate the new project as soon as possible. The director of product management, while having a very vague idea about what this project is about, invites the manager of the PMO and orders him to assign a project manager to the project and start working on the new initiative.

In his turn, the PMO manager summons one of his project managers and orders her to take this project on. Now, what should any good project manager do once she hears the words, "You have been assigned to work on project A?" She should start by asking a lot of questions, including the following:

- What are the key features of this new product?
- How will it be different from other products we have in our portfolio?
- How different will it be from the ones produced by our competitors?
- What is the deadline for this project?
- How many resources would you be able to assign to my team?
- Are we going to get the investment required to accomplish this initiative?

Do you think that in this particular scenario the manager of project management would be able to provide clear and coherent answers to the project manager's questions? Probably not. In that case, who is the only person in the company who can actually provide some—not necessarily clear or coherent—answers to these inquiries? It is the CEO of the organization.

And now the final question to the project management and other professionals reading this book: In how many cases in the situation described above would the project manager be allowed to sit down with the CEO of the company and, at least, attempt to get the answers to her legitimate questions?

Inability to See the Entire Project

This is another issue that has been discussed in this book several times. Very frequently, the project stakeholders, including the project team, fail to see that the scope of the project they are about to start working on is, sometimes by orders-of-magnitude, larger than what they perceive it to be. This is especially true for large corporations undertaking large internal endeavors such as rebranding, regulatory, and technology projects, to name a few.

For example, very frequently an enterprise resource planning software implementation is still viewed by many as "just an IT department's initiative" that could be safely ignored by the rest of organization's departments. And, yet after several months of running the project under that presumption, the stakeholders discover that the initiative in question has enormous impacts on the sales, marketing, human resources, finance, accounting, and operations departments.

Absence of Requirements Prioritization

Very frequently, the features and requirements included in the project scope are not prioritized. What is the potential impact of not prioritizing the requirements or, something that many executives like to do, claiming that they are all "equally important"? Let us consider an example of a project involving building a family home for a customer. The requirements list for such an initiative would be very long but could probably include components such as

- Flooring in the kitchen
- Flooring in the rooms
- Gas pipes
- Water pipes
- Curtain rods
- Electrical outlets

Now, imagine that all these requirements either have not been prioritized or were all stamped with a "Must Have" priority. As the project is nearing its deadline, the project manager realizes that she is not able to complete the entire scope of work and decides to cut some of the features. Because all of them are of equal importance, she resolves to postpone the installation of the gas pipes but chooses to make sure that all the curtain rods have been installed properly. An even worse scenario would be if she decides to spend less time on the gas pipe installation, forgoing, for example, the quality control, thus exposing the entire structure to a possibility of a gas leak.

This scenario, although ridiculous, is presented to demonstrate the following point: On a project with hundreds or even thousands of requirements where the project manager does not possess an expert-level knowledge on every technical domain (think about large enterprise projects), it is very difficult to decide which requirements are really important and which can be postponed or cut from the project scope.

What Can Be Done?

There are certain steps a company can undertake to address the scope elicitation issues mentioned above. First, project managers must continue their efforts in educating all the project stakeholders, including the executives, about the potential issues with scope elicitation. This, in my experience, can take several forms:

- Project management/requirements courses for the executives and senior functional managers
- Project management/requirements presentations
- Lunch and learns
- One-on-one conversations with the stakeholders

Another important factor to consider is spreading the understanding of the concept of the enterprise project at the companies. Demonstrating to the stakeholders that it is very difficult in modern times to find a large, or even medium-sized, project that affects only one department at any given organization is practically impossible. Furthermore, training the project team in proper requirements elicitation and analysis practices is an essential step in improving project scope–related communications on any initiative.

Having a well-established project management methodology is yet another important aspect that instills the proper requirements management practices at any given company. The project management methodology should, among other documents, include a well-defined requirements document that is carefully fitted to the company needs. Existence of the properly governed project management methodology

Table 13.1   Scope Elicitation Issues and Possible Solutions

SCOPE ELICITATION ISSUES	WHAT CAN BE DONE?
Lack of Communication	• Executive education • Stakeholder education • Project team training
Scope Imposed by a Higher Authority	• Executive education • Empowerment of project managers
Inability to See the Big Picture	• Executive education • Customer walk-throughs • Technical inspections
Absence of Prioritization	• Executive education • Stakeholder education • Project team training • Peer reviews • Customer walk-throughs • Technical inspections

also provides project managers with sufficient empowerment to obtain access to the highest echelons of their companies and provides them with the ability to ask the right but difficult questions.

The combination of customer walk-throughs, technical team inspections, and peer reviews applied to the requirements documentation can vastly improve all the problems mentioned earlier. For more information on these techniques, see Chapter 14 of this book. For a summary of all potential solutions for the scope elicitation problems, see Table 13.1.

Lack of Skills Issues

Poorly Trained Requirements Professionals

This is one of the most widespread problems at many companies where the art and the science of requirements gathering, analysis, and documentation is basically an ad hoc process, where the executives just simply assume that all the project features are obvious and self-evident.

Unfortunately, this is not the case on all modern projects. As one of the famous IT experts on requirements once quipped, "I hate the term 'requirements gathering.' It implies that a project manager just goes to the field where requirements grow like mushrooms or flowers, and he just prances around picking them one after another and depositing them into his basket! That is absolutely not the case! The proper term that should be used is 'requirements elicitation' or even 'requirements extraction,' like the teeth in the dental office."

Technical Experts and Requirements Experts

Another very popular myth strongly tied to the topic discussed above is that any good technical expert—be it an architect, a mechanical engineer, an accountant, or a software developer—can automatically, without special training, become an effective requirements analyst.

Unfortunately, nothing can be further from the truth. The technical experts have been trained, starting from universities and throughout their respective careers, to receive a complete set of unequivocal, clear, and measurable requirements and convert them into specific designs. The main problem of their existence is that they continue to be bombarded with incomplete and ambiguous features that they do not know how to "translate" into an acceptable format.

Lack of Stakeholder Education

One of the major issues encountered by the project teams is that the project stakeholders usually do not appreciate the whole complexity of the requirement elicitation process. The inherent problem here is that our human psyche is trained to consider only normal or successful courses of events, be it obtaining the boarding pass for the flight or the installation of the new kitchen cabinets.

We typically do not consider the possibility that the passport scanner may not be able to read a specific type of passport or that the piping system could be nonstandard, thus preventing us from installing the new kitchen furniture successfully. For a more detailed discussion of this issue, please see the airport check-in kiosk and the ATM examples mentioned in this book.

What Can Be Done?

As mentioned earlier, training the technical project team members along with the project managers is the first essential step in improving the requirements management practices at the company. After all, if the key people who are responsible for collecting incomplete, vague, and unmeasurable requirements can't translate them into complete, clear, and measurable scope components, then the projects that such teams start are doomed for failure right from the very beginning.

The second step that is also very important in addressing the skills problems is executive and management education. The senior people at the company, the ones who make the budgeting and timing decisions on the projects, must have at least a general idea about concepts such as alternative courses, exceptions, enterprise requirements, and requirements quality. Understanding that a technical expert is not the same as a requirements expert is also a very important step in project scope management methodology development and advancement at any given organization.

A company must at some point seriously consider developing its own group of properly trained requirements analysts. There are usually two possible approaches to this task. In one model, the company hires, trains, and continually develops a designated group of employees whose sole responsibility is to elicit, analyze, document, and manage requirements. This approach is very popular in the information technology and software development industries where these professionals are typically called "business analysts" or "systems analysts." The second approach is to provide requirements training to the existing project managers without creating a separate pool of requirements professionals.

Finally, customer walk-throughs and technical team inspections, discussed in detail in Chapter 14, of the project documents in general and requirements documentation in particular can greatly assist in filling the gaps left by insufficient requirements skills levels at the organization. For a summary of all potential solutions for the skills problems, see Table 13.2.

Table 13.2   Lack of Skills Issues and Possible Solutions

SKILLS ISSUES	WHAT CAN BE DONE?
Poorly Trained Professionals	• Train technical team in requirements engineering
Technical Experts versus Scope Experts	• Understand that a technical expert is not the same as a scope expert
	• Train requirements analysts
Insufficient Stakeholder Education	• Executive education
	• Educate users and management about requirements
	• Customer walk-throughs
	• Technical inspections

Project Management Issues

Teams under Pressure

I am sure every project manager in the world has at least once in his life been in the situation when he was ordered to deliver a proverbial, "Ferrari tomorrow for the price of $500." Imposition of very large and complex projects with inadequate budgets, timelines, and human resources unfortunately happens all the time.

What happens when the executives or customers underestimate the size of the project or, alternatively, overestimate the abilities of their project teams? This case has a lot of potential development scenarios but, sadly, only two possible outcomes: Either the product of the project is not delivered at all, or something is indeed delivered but has serious quality issues. That is assuming, of course, that we are not contemplating the option of extending the project or throwing additional monetary or human resources at it.

Excess of Scope

The "too much scope" problem is tied to the "external pressure" issue discussed above. Again, generally the events can develop according to the following scenarios: Either the size and the complexity of the project scope was a well-known fact from the very inception of the project, or for whatever reasons it was assumed that the project scope is small and simple, and at a later point the stakeholders have discovered that it is much larger and more complex than was initially conceived.

Quick De-Scoping at the End of the Project

What happens sometimes closer to the end of many projects is that the senior stakeholders, typically executives or customers, realize that the project can't be delivered with all the current requirements and decide to cut the scope of the project. Unfortunately, the "quick" de-scoping of the project can represent a process way more painful than the initial addition of the features at the beginning of the venture.

Imagine a customer orders a custom-made car that, among others, includes the following features:

- Car stereo
- Power windows
- Heated seats

Sometime during the final phases of the project, she calls the car company and tells them that to save some money and time she decided to de-scope these three components. For simplicity, we can assume that the budget remains the same, although this is not a very likely scenario in real life. What issues would the car manufacturer face at this time? With respect to the car stereo, the following questions would have to be answered:

- Has the car stereo been ordered?
- Has it already been installed in the car?
- How long will it take to disconnect and remove the stereo from the car?
- Will the removal of the stereo affect any other car systems?
- How should we cover the open slot in the dashboard where the stereo was?
- Can we return the stereo to the manufacturer?
- Will we get a full refund?

When it comes to the power windows and the heated seats, the car producers will have to address the following issues:

- Is it possible to remove the heating elements (electronic power-windows mechanism) from the seats (car doors), or should all the seats (doors) be replaced?
- If all the seats and doors have to be replaced, who will pay for the acquisition of the new components?
- How long will the seat and door replacement take?
- Will the replacement affect any other car systems?
- Is it possible to return the seats and doors to their respective manufacturers and get full refunds?

It doesn't take a car manufacturing expert to understand that the removal of the above-mentioned features from the final product will most likely have a negative impact on both the duration of the project and its budget. Moreover, it is very likely that this action will introduce new technical risks that have a very serious possibility of affecting the overall quality of the product.

What Can Be Done?

There are many various options available for organizations to address the project management–related requirements issues. First, it should be understood by the executives and the customers that only the project teams responsible for the delivery of a given project should be responsible for the generation of project estimates. Although it is acceptable to use external professional expertise when generating time and budget forecasts, the project team should at the end of the day participate in the process and feel comfortable with them.

Second, both project management and requirements management processes and templates based on the industry best practices, but fine-tuned to the company needs, must be deployed to address the issues mentioned above. The chances of ad hoc management pressure applied to the project teams diminishes greatly if the project manager can refer the stakeholders to the approved processes that require a detailed study of the project requirements before any precise estimates can be generated.

Third, proper usage of the "Lessons Learned" documentation from previous similar projects can strengthen the project manager's position when discussing project estimates with the customers. At a basic level, the project leader can state something to the effect of, "While working on a similar project in the past, we needed 18 months and spent $750,000. What makes you think that we can accomplish this initiative in less than a year for $200,000?"

Also, educating the executives that a quick de-scoping of the project, especially during the late stages, can be as damaging as imposing too much scope at the beginning of the endeavor is also an essential step in addressing the project management–related requirements problems. For a summary of all potential solutions for the project management problems, see Table 13.3.

Table 13.3   Project Management Issues and Possible Solutions

PROJECT MANAGEMENT ISSUES	WHAT CAN BE DONE?
External Pressure	• Estimates should be generated by the project team only • Define project management process and templates • Define requirements process and templates • Base plans on requirements • Use Lessons Learned documentation
Too Much Scope	• Educate the executives that too much scope frequently implies no scope delivered at all or scope of poor quality • Analyze requirements feasibility • Use Lessons Learned documentation
Quick De-Scoping	• Educate executives and stakeholders that quick de-scoping can damage the final product

Documentation Issues

Undocumented Requirements

We have seen this phenomenon many times: The project manager has his requirements recorded in different formats. Some of the information is contained in e-mails, certain facts make it to his notebook, yet others are prominently displayed on the yellow Post-it notes attached to his screen monitor. There is probably nothing wrong with having the requirements recorded in different forms at the very beginning of the requirements elicitation process. However, once the requirements process nears its end, the project stakeholders discover that many of the features mentioned by the customers have been lost and did not make it to the final documentation. Actually, project teams can consider themselves lucky if they can discover all the missing scope by the end of the requirements elicitation process, that is, by the end of the planning stage of the project. Usually, these omissions are left undiscovered until the very end of the execution stage, when they rear their ugly heads and destroy the project deadlines and budgets so carefully prepared by the project managers.

Vague Scope and Lack of Measurability

In my consulting and training engagements around the world, I have repeated over and over again that the executives, sales, and marketing people speak their own languages full of words such as "sustainable," "flexible," "cutting-edge," and "efficient," just to name a few. This phenomenon is beyond the paradigm of bad or good. It is simply how they were trained to think and speak. Furthermore, it is very unlikely that anyone would be able to change this approach; at least, I haven't seen even one instance of this happening at the nearly 100 companies I have encountered in my career as a project manager or a project management consultant and a trainer.

The project managers, along with their team, should simply get used to the idea that the scope will be communicated to them in those terms. The only thing available to them is a multitude of questions to be directed at their customers in an attempt to better define what exactly those words mean in the context of their project.

What Can Be Done?

There several ways to address the inadequate documentation issues that are readily available for the management of any company. Having proper requirements (or scope) management processes along with good requirements documentation templates is probably one of the first steps a company should consider.

Also, organizations that already have several quality project documents left over from the previous projects can benefit greatly if they encourage their employees to reuse those documents when working on their new initiatives. Reuse of good project documentation can serve a dual purpose. It can act as a standard for all the project managers or requirements analysts to follow as a reference. Yet on the other hand, it could also, especially on similar projects, allow the project team members to copy and paste the blocks of requirements directly from the old documents.

Teaching the project team members to label each requirement uniquely and to attempt in every case to identify the source of the requirement by following the traditional Feature to Requirement to Design Component model would also boost the quality of the project documentation.

Finally, the implementation of the customer walk-throughs, technical team inspections, and peer reviews described in detail in Chapter 14 will also improve the quality of project documentation. For a summary of all potential solutions for documentation issues, see Table 13.4.

Table 13.4 Documentation Issues and Possible Solutions

DOCUMENTATION ISSUES	WHAT CAN BE DONE?
Undocumented Scope	• Reuse quality requirements
	• Identify sources of requirements
	• Uniquely label each requirement
	• Adopt RS template
Vague Scope and Lack of Measurability	• Implement peer reviews
	• Implement technical team inspections
	• Implement customer walk-throughs
	• Train requirements analysts
	• Identify sources of requirements

Scope Management Issues

Customers Have Direct Access to the Technical People

How many times has the reader witnessed the following scenario? Both the requirements document and the project plan have been finalized and the team has entered the execution stage of the project. The technical project team members are working hard on delivering the agreed-upon scope of the project when suddenly one of them receives a phone call from a high-ranking company manager or executive asking (in reality, ordering) him to add or tweak something in the project scope. Another request that typically follows the first one is that the change is so insignificant that the project manager does not really have to know about it.

The technical team member in question is so intimidated by this conversation with his superior that he quietly makes the requested change. The tweak goes unnoticed until the very end of the project, when the team discovers that the tinkering with the project scope that took place several weeks or even months ago has adversely affected other design components, thus creating a cascade of issues for the project team to address.

What happened in this, alas too frequently encountered, scenario is that the project manager who supposedly holds all the relevant project information was dropped from the communication lines. As a result, both the project manager and the rest of the team were not able to assess the proposed change and consider all potential impacts of the change and the risks associated with it, leading to serious problems closer to the end of the project.

Frequent Scope Creep

Another problem somewhat related to the one discussed earlier is the frequent changes to the project scope even if the project manager is informed about them. The proverbial "scope creep" is a function of several variables. The impact of changes to the project scope is dependent on frequency of changes, the size and the complexity of changes, and the timing of the changes.

The first one is fairly obvious; the more often the customer walks into the project manager's office and proclaims something along the lines of, "Oh, by the way, wouldn't it be really cool if we could add this great feature to the project?" the greater the impact on the overall project delivery.

The negative effect of size and the complexity of the change on the overall project success is also fairly self-evident. The request to install an energy-efficient heater in the home is not going to have the same impact on the overall project as the demand of the client to make the entire building energy efficient.

Finally, the impact of the change is a function of the timing. Imagine that a project team is working on the construction of a family home. The requirement document mandates the team to build a house, build a fence around the property, and conduct some landscaping work. Let us consider now two identical scenarios where the customer requests adding a swimming pool to the scope of the project. The only difference in the scenarios considered would be the timing of such a request: In the first case, the request arrives at the beginning of the execution stage and in the second one at the end of the construction.

In which scenario would this enhancement have a bigger negative impact on the project? Obviously, it will happen in the second case. All the landscaping will have to be removed, the water pipes already lying in the ground will have to be dug out, and the entire piping infrastructure will have to be redesigned.

What Can Be Done?

One of the most important techniques at the disposal of the project managers is their ability to manage stakeholder expectations by keeping the lines of communication open with their stakeholders throughout the entire project.

Table 13.5 Scope Management Issues and Possible Solutions

SCOPE MANAGEMENT ISSUES	WHAT CAN BE DONE?
Customers Communicate Directly with the Technical People	• Educate customers, executives, and the project team members about proper Change Control procedures
Scope Changes Frequently	• Manage your stakeholder expectations
	• Baseline and control requirements documents
	• Track requirements status
	• Establish Change Control procedures
	• Perform change impact analysis
	• Maintain change history
	• Use Lessons Learned

Baselining and controlling the requirements documents is yet another important ingredient in keeping the project scope under control. Usually, this job falls on the shoulders of the requirements analyst in the industries where such a position exists (typically, IT and software development domains), and in all other fields this becomes the responsibility of the project manager.

Establishing a clear and stringent change control policy as part of the overall project management process is also a very important factor to address the "scope creep" problems. A must-have part of the change control process is a mandatory comprehensive change impact analysis that should cover all potential risks associated with the enhancement requested.

Finally, another useful trick at the disposal of project managers is to keep track of all the change requests submitted by the stakeholders and document them in the "Lessons Learned." This enables the project manager to show the overall impact of all the changes on the flow of the project. For more information on managing project scope and proper change control processes, please see Chapter 15 of this book. For a summary of all potential solutions for the scope management problems, see Table 13.5.

Chapter Summary

As mentioned in this chapter's Introduction section, this chapter was conceived as cheat sheet of a sort for project managers and other project team members to use when encountering specific scope management problems. As such, the entire chapter has been divided into five general areas, including scope elicitation, skills, project management, documentation, and scope management issues. In the scope elicitation section, we looked at possible solutions for issues including lack of communication on the project; scope being imposed directly by higher authorities; inability of the companies to see a bigger, more comprehensive picture of the projects; and the absence of scope prioritization.

In the skills part of the chapter, we considered challenges including using poorly trained—from the requirements engineering perspective—project team members and insufficient stakeholder education regarding the complexity of the requirements elicitation process.

The project management issues included external pressure to lower the project estimates, having to deal with too much scope for a given time and budget, and the effects of quick de-scoping of the project close to the project closeout.

The documentation challenges section included a detailed discussion of the ways to address undocumented scope, vague scope, and the lack of measurability in the requirements documents.

Finally, we analyzed scope management problems, including customers and executives communicating directly with the technical project team members as well as the negative effects of uncontrolled "scope creep" on overall project results.

14
SCOPE VERIFICATION

Historical Perspective: The Admiral's Mistake

A couple of tragic incidents took place on a gloomy October day in 1707. First, an ordinary sailor was executed by the order of his commanding officer, and then approximately 1,500 people died in one of the most horrific disasters of the British Navy.

A British Navy convoy under the command of Admiral Sir Clowdisley Shovell was returning back to home base after a mission near the French coast. Unfortunately, during the voyage the ships encountered a patch of very heavy fog. The admiral decided to stop the fleet to convene a council of his naval officers in order to discuss the next steps, inasmuch as proceeding at full speed in such thick fog while they were somewhere near the English coast was extremely dangerous.

The officers took careful measurements using their nautical equipment and came back with an answer that the fleet was far enough from the land and that it was safe to proceed ahead at full speed. At this point, an ordinary sailor approached the admiral; asked for permission to address him; and, after being granted permission, told the officers that they had been mistaken. Apparently, he had taken his own measurements using his own nautical tools, and it turned out that the convoy was much closer to the British shores than the admiral expected. Hence, according to him, the entire fleet should slow down and proceed ahead with extreme caution.

Sir Shovell's response to his monologue was unconventional, to say the least. He ordered the sailor to be hanged as a mutineer! Several hours later, it turned out that the sailor was right, and all the naval officers in the convoy were dead wrong. The entire fleet consisting of four ships was smashed into the rocks near the Scilly Isles. Rumor has it that almost the entire crew perished in that accident, but the admiral was able to make it to shore. Unfortunately, he was murdered by a local woman who had taken a fancy to his emerald ring.

Interestingly enough, notwithstanding whether the admiral chose to listen to or ignore the sailor's warnings, he had to execute him because there was indeed a law in the British Navy that strictly prohibited anyone but the senior officers on the ship from owning any kind of nautical equipment. Their reasoning was very simple: Considering the harsh living conditions on the ship, including spoiled food, rats, and scurvy, there was always a clear and present danger of a real mutiny. Thus, argued the Admiralty executives, if the sailors were incapable of knowing their exact location on the seas, there would be way less incentive for them to rebel and kill their superiors.

This story demonstrating the occasional stubbornness of some military leaders is being mentioned for a reason at the beginning of the "scope verification" chapter. It serves as proof that any leader, especially the project manager in our case, should always listen to the stakeholders on his project regarding possible risks, mistakes, and omissions in the scope. Moreover, rather than just simply sit around and wait for them to come and inform him about potential issues, he should proactively seek their feedback on all key project aspects, including the project documents.

Value of Scope Verification

Why spend time and resources on scope verification before the actual hands-on work starts on the project? Numerous times throughout my project management career, I was greeted by suspicious stares of the functional managers when requesting several hours of their people's time to spend on reviews and walk-throughs. "You want them to waste time reading documents before they actually have to work on the project? I am sorry, but they are too busy on other tasks!" was the phrase I heard over and over again.

So, obviously, although most of the project managers are sold on the document review idea, other stakeholders still remain unconvinced regarding its value. How can one persuade project stakeholders that several dozen person-hours of effort invested at the end of the documentation stage, before the work actually starts, can save a lot of effort and time at the end of the project? There are many ways to accomplish this seemingly difficult task, but to save some time, let us focus on the simplest and the most powerful examples. One of the most command-ing statistics released in a study several years ago claimed the following:

Forty-five percent (45%) of project costs industrywide is rework.

Let us ponder this number for a while. This statistic implies that almost half of the efforts invested in any given project are wasted on correction of the errors and omissions rather than creation of anything of value. What it also implies is that in a perfect world, where all the project mistakes and omissions can be completely eliminated right in the first stages of the project, the total cost of the endeavor, both in terms of dollars and human resources, can be cut in half. Obviously, we all know that there is no such thing as a "perfect world"; however, it would be reasonable to assume that it is still plausible to cut the project costs by 10% or even 20%. Would any CEO in his right mind reject this offer?

Many people, upon looking at these numbers exclaim, "Well, we do spend a lot of time on rework, but the number seems a bit exagger-ated and counterintuitive." Let us examine this notion based on a very simple example. Imagine that a young family has just purchased an old condominium and is planning on renovating it. Their total budget is $10,000. Let us also assume that there are 10 potential risks or mis-takes that are hidden in the scope of the project. These "risks" include not being aware that the strata require a special extra-thick underlay to be installed under the hardwood floor, the nonstandard design of the drainpipes in the kitchen, and a lack of stable floors in the bathroom, just to name a few.

Let us also assume that discovery and discussion of each of these issues would cost the family $10 per issue at the beginning of the project, but the price would go up to $1,000 per mistake if discovered at the time of implementation. In other words, the late discovery of these mistakes would imply reinstallation of the floors and changing the underlay, reor-dering custom kitchen cabinets to address the unusual drainpipe design, and strengthening the bathroom floors to the point where they could support heavy ceramic tiles. The successful scenario where all the issues are discovered and addressed early in the project could look like this:

Total budget: $10,000

Additional cost of discovering the mistakes: 10 mistakes × $10/mistake = $100

Total project cost = $10,000 + $100 = $10,100

The unsuccessful scenario where all the issues are discovered at the end of the project could be as such:

Total budget: $10,000

Additional cost of fixing the mistakes: 10 mistakes × $1,000/mistake = $10,000

Total project cost = $10,000 + $10,000 = $20,000

Interestingly enough, these sample costs per mistake were not just invented but rather were based on a study mentioned as early as Chapter 1 of this book, where we discussed the concept of the "cost of mistakes" in project management (see Figure 1.6). Actually, in our example we preferred to err on the conservative side, setting the ratio of costs for mistakes detected early versus mistakes detected late at 1:10 rather than 1:1,000, as can happen on some endeavors.

Customer Walk-Throughs, Technical Inspections, and Peer Reviews

Review Process

The proper approach to the review process, be it customer walk-through, technical inspection, or peer review, should follow the five steps outlined in Figure 14.1.

Preparing and Running the Reviews

First, the project manager should allocate time and resources for the review of each document at the very beginning of the project when only high-level schedules and resource requirements are being drafted. In other words, rather than having just one task in the work breakdown structure:

Figure 14.1 Documentation validation process.

1. Write the Requirements Document.

He should include and justify to the stakeholders the following set of tasks:

1. Write the Requirements Document.
2. Conduct the Requirements Document customer walk-through.
3. Conduct the Requirements Document technical inspection.
4. Conduct the Requirements Document peer review.
5. Analyze and incorporate all the changes to the Requirements Document.
6. Obtain final approval.

This is a very important step because, as the experience shows, steps 2–4 and especially step 5 can consume a lot of time and resources.

The next step is the preparation for the customer walk-throughs, technical inspections, and peer reviews. The project manager must inform the respective audiences that the reviews are coming up; educate all the stakeholders about their purpose and, most important, the value of these reviews; and make all necessary arrangements for the meetings about to take place:

- Book a well-ventilated room of adequate size.
- Ensure that the room has a projector and a whiteboard with markers and flip charts.
- If possible, order food and drinks to "entice" all the necessary participants to attend the meetings.
- Send out the document to be reviewed to all participants and ask them to familiarize themselves with it in order to prepare their questions, comments, and critique.

The third step involves conducting the actual reviews. The sole purpose of the project manager and, where applicable, the requirements analyst should be the extraction of as many errors, omissions, and ambiguities in the documentation out of the stakeholders present at these meetings. One of the major "mottos" of these meetings should be, "We are trying very hard to catch the one-dollar mistakes before they blossom into one-thousand-dollar disasters."

After the reviews have been completed, the project team should get together and analyze all the changes that have been proposed by the stakeholders. Some of these corrections will be fairly superficial, whereas others may require a lot of offline work and additional consultations with customers, technical experts, and even senior managers. Once all the recommendations have been resolved, the project manager should update the documentation accordingly and present his corrections to the stakeholders for final approval.

Customer Walk-Throughs

The main purpose of customer walk-throughs is to show the pertinent documentation to all relevant customer representatives and ask them the key question, "Here is what we have been able to gather, analyze, and document so far. Did we catch all the necessary requirements or did we miss anything?" The project manager and the requirements analyst basically give the customers an opportunity to go through the entire document and answer two very important questions:

1. Did I forget to mention anything of importance in my conversations with the analysts?
2. Now that I heard and saw the requirements outlined by other stakeholders, do I see any conflicts or a need for additional/ revised requirements?

Let us use a very simple example to demonstrate how this works in practice. Imagine that a baby products company decides to outsource a design of a new baby feeding bottle to a subcontractor (JM Design). The first draft of the project charter written by the subcontractor contains an innocuous-looking phrase:

> JM Design shall create a prototype of an ergonomic baby bottle of suitable size that shall conform to all international health requirements.

Note that we are using just an excerpt from the project charter rather than a full requirements document example to simplify the understanding of the process.

The customer walk-through meeting that consists of only two parties—representatives of the baby products company and the subcontractor—may look at this paragraph, and one of the customer representatives may say something to the effect of, "Wait a second, nobody mentioned that a bottle should be safe? This is an absolutely essential requirement; it must be included in the project charter!"

So, this particular section of the project charter is revised to look like this:

> JM Design shall create a prototype of a safe and ergonomic baby bottle of suitable size that shall conform to all international health requirements.

Technical Inspections

The main purpose of the technical inspections is to present the documentation to the technical project team and invite them to answer the following questions:

- Are all the requirements technically feasible or doable with current technology?
- Are there any ambiguities in the document?
- Do they see any potential conflicts in the requirements requested by the customers?

Let us examine this process using our previous baby bottle example. Once the project charter is presented to the technical team, they may notice the following issue in the statement:

> What did you mean by saying, "conform to all international health requirements"? There are no uniform international standards for baby bottles. For example, in the USA, the Food and Drug Administration (FDA) regulates teats and the bottle materials, specifically Bisphenol A. Argentina, Brazil, and Ecuador also prohibit Bisphenol A usage in baby bottles, but they have no regulation on teats. Korea has an altogether different legislation on this; they have banned an additional four chemicals from all children's products, including baby bottles. ... So, which country is this baby bottle being designed for?

Let us pretend that the primary market for the product is the United States, and hence the customer agrees to revise the statement to look like this:

> JM Design shall create a prototype of a safe and ergonomic baby bottle of suitable size that shall conform to the Food and Drug Administration regulations on baby bottles.

Peer Reviews

The next valuable step in the scope verification process is the peer review. Peer review is a very interesting process. I once worked for a company that encouraged the following process for each key project document before its final approval: Each project manager was required to contact another project manager, preferably senior and experienced, and ask him or her to read the document that had already undergone a customer walk-through and a technical inspection. The project manager conducting the peer review was not expected to know anything about that specific project; moreover, he was not even expected to be from the same department of the company. In other words, the project at hand could have been from the IT department, whereas the reviewer may have come from the marketing or engineering team.

Because the reviewer had very little knowledge about the project, he was not expected to provide the current project manager with any thoughtful feedback on the design issues or potential alternatives or exceptions in the processes described in the documentation, although he could have ended up doing just that. The reviewer was expected to comb through the document and find deviations from the proper ways of documenting things. For example, the reviewer may be completely unaware about the size of the project budget but will most likely take an issue with project budget being presented as: "Project budget—$157,000."

Rather, he would advise the project manager to record the project budget with plus/minus qualifiers: "Project budget—$157,000 ± 50,000."

Another purpose of the peer reviews is to look for ambiguous words in the project documentation that can be misinterpreted by either the project team or other stakeholders.

Once more, let us try to imagine how an experienced project manager may react to the statement we examined earlier. A good project manager will most likely "target" three words in the paragraph: *safe, ergonomic,* and *suitable.* Why would those words raise red flags in the mind of any experienced professional? Because they are ambiguous by project management standards, and therefore the reviewer may say something to the effect of

> Are you sure you have an understanding of what exactly these words mean? In this context, does "safe" mean "not harmful to babies" or "no-spill type of bottle"? Or does it mean "having an anticolic design"? Also,

what does "ergonomic" mean? Having handles? Some kind of a specific shape? Furthermore, what is a bottle of an adequate size? Are there any common sizes typical in the industry?

As a result of these questions, the project manager running the project may have to go back to the customers and get clarifications on these issues, and the final version of the statement from the project charter may end up looking something like this:

JM Design shall create a prototype of a "no drip" and "no spill" 280-ml baby bottle with handles that shall conform to the Food and Drug Administration regulations on baby bottles.

Now, just to review the changes the statement underwent in the review process, one can compare the initial paragraph with the final version of the statement:

JM Design shall create a prototype of an ergonomic baby bottle of suitable size that shall conform to all international health requirements

versus

JM Design shall create a prototype of a "no drip" and "no spill" 280-ml baby bottle with handles that shall conform to the Food and Drug Administration regulations on baby bottles.

What could have gone wrong if the project team had kept the original phrase untouched? Well, the project team could have decided that "ergonomic" implies some kind of futuristic design rather than simple handles. They could have misunderstood the safety requirement to mean preventing air from getting into the baby's mouth. The suitable-size feature could have ended in a bottle that would have been too large or too small. And finally, the project team would have encountered some serious issues with trying to create a bottle that would have satisfied all international health requirements.

The end result of such a project would have almost certainly been cost and schedule overruns, low quality of product, low team morale, and customer dissatisfaction, just to name a few. Basically, what we have demonstrated here is that the team was able to catch the proverbial "one-dollar mistakes" before they blossomed into "one-thousand-dollar disasters."

Documents That Need Reviewing

Depending on the size and complexity of the project at hand, the numbers of documents that need reviewing may expand or contract. For example, on a project that involves building a massive cruise ship terminal, every major project document, including even change requests, would undergo a rigorous customer walk-through, technical team inspection, and peer review. On the other hand, a smaller, less-sophisticated endeavor may not require an in-depth team analysis of each and every document produced by the team.

Having said that, there are several usual suspects that should always be subjected to the detailed walk-throughs, inspections, and reviews. These include the project charter, project plan, requirements document, and design document. This book is dedicated to the topic of project scope management; therefore, we concentrate on the documentation directly related to this knowledge area (see Table 14.1).

Table 14.1 Potential Questions about Project Documents

QUESTIONS TO EXPECT	DOCUMENT	WHAT SHOULD THE PROJECT MANAGER DO?
"Why are your estimate ranges so wide?"	Project Charter	Explain that the appropriate ranges for the Initiation stage estimates are +75% to −25% for regular projects and +300% to −75% for high-risk ventures.
"Can you do the project faster/cheaper?"	Project Charter	Explain the concept of project management triangle (scope, time, budget) or pentagon (scope, time, budget, effort, and quality) and find out which areas can be manipulated to deliver the project faster or cheaper.
"We need to add another feature."	Project Charter	Try to assess which problem the requested feature will solve, and, if necessary, add to the meeting minutes. If required, schedule an "offline" meeting.
"Have you considered this risk?"	Project Charter	Quickly assess the risk and flag for incorporation into the documentation. Arrange for an offline meeting or follow up if necessary. Add to the meeting minutes in the document.

Table 14.1 Potential Questions about Project Documents (Continued)

QUESTIONS TO EXPECT	DOCUMENT	WHAT SHOULD THE PROJECT MANAGER DO?
"You need to communicate to person X from Department Y; he should be involved in this discussion."	Project Charter, Requirements Document, Design Document	Add to the meeting minutes and schedule a follow-up meeting with that person.
"Director of Department Z will have to assign resources to this project.	Project Charter, Requirements Document, Design Document	Add to the meeting minutes and schedule a follow-up meeting with that person.
"We have to add another requirement (alternative scenario or exception)."	Requirements Document, Design Document	Try to assess which problem the requested requirement (alternative scenario or exception) will solve, and, if necessary, add to the meeting minutes. If required, schedule an "offline" meeting.
"I think you have misinterpreted our stated needs."	Requirements Document	Briefly discuss the problem with the stakeholder. Add to the meeting minutes. Arrange for an offline meeting or follow up if necessary.
"You forgot to include this …"	Requirements Document	Briefly discuss the new scope item with the stakeholder. Add to the meeting minutes. Arrange for an offline meeting or follow up if necessary.
"There is conflict between these two (or more) requirements or features."	Requirements Document, Design Document	Add to the meeting minutes. Arrange for an offline meeting or follow up if necessary.
"We do not have the capability to make that happen."	Requirements Document, Design Document	Discuss why this can't be done and the alternative ways of reaching project objectives. Add to the meeting minutes. Arrange for an offline meeting or follow up if necessary.
"I can interpret this statement in several ways."	Requirements Document, Design Document	Rephrase the statement in a proper format to remove ambiguity.

Questions and Checklists

When conducting the reviews, one can facilitate the evaluation and feedback process by distributing the following cheat sheets to the meeting participants:

- "Questions to ask"
- "Dangerous words to avoid"

The "Questions to ask" list contains some of the key inquiries reviewers must keep in mind when analyzing the project documentation:

- Are all parts of the documents written at a consistent and appropriate level of detail?
  - Note: The answers to this question would most likely be provided by the experienced project manager during the peer review process.
- Did the team use a company-approved template to write the document?
- Are all features, requirements, and design components properly labeled (e.g., F1, R 1.1, DC 1.1.3, etc.)?
- Do we have priorities assigned to each feature, requirement, and design component?
- Did we cover all possible alternatives, exceptions, risks, and constraints?
  - Note: Based on experience, this is one of the most challenging tasks during the reviews. In all probability, the most valuable feedback will be provided during the customer walk-throughs and technical team inspections.
- Is there any information missing in the document? Are there any "TBDs" in the documents?
- Does the Requirements Document provide an adequate basis for design?
  - Note: The answer to this question would in all likelihood be provided during the technical inspection by the project team members.
- Is every requirement in scope?
  - Note: It is a responsibility of the project manager to ask this question during the discussion of each requirement at the customer walk-through. As was indicated earlier in the book, according to studies, up to 50% of the features can be cut from the project if this question is asked.
- Can all the scope items be implemented with all the known constraints?
  - Note: Again, the answer to this will most likely be provided during the technical inspection session.

- Do all the requirements have appropriate measurability attributes associated with them?
  - Note: These omissions will undoubtedly have the best chance of being caught during either the technical inspections or peer reviews.
- Do all the key statements in the document have only one possible meaning?
- Can they be misinterpreted by any of the stakeholders?

Another tool that can assist the project team and other stakeholders immensely in avoiding ambiguity and misinterpretation of the requirements is the "Dangerous Words to Avoid" table in Chapter 6 (see Table 6.8).

Chapter Summary

This chapter started with the discussion of the value of scope verification and severe issues that await the project team that chooses to ignore them. As a result, we revisited some key statistics from the industry, including the concept of the "cost of mistakes."

Then, we looked at the three major types of reviews available to project teams, including customer walk-throughs, technical team inspections, and peer reviews. We started by examining the typical flow of such reviews and learned about the step-by-step approach of running these processes.

We have also, by using a baby bottle design example, demonstrated the transformations one statement can undergo as it goes through a customer walk-through, technical inspection, and peer review.

Later, we looked at the major project documents that require reviews; they included at least a project charter, project plan, requirements document, and a design document. Finally, at the end of the chapter, we examined the questions that should be asked during each review and the "dangerous words" that should never appear in the project management documentation.

15

CONTROLLING PROJECT SCOPE

Historical Perspective: The Story of the *Magenta*

Something extraordinary took place on December 2, 1913, in France: The pride of the French Navy, the battleship *Hoche*, was disposed of by the French government by sinking it as a practice target during a naval exercise.

The surprising part of that story is that the *Hoche*, along with three of its sisters—*Marceau*, *Magenta* (see Figure 15.1), and *Neptune*—had been built in 1893, or only 20 years prior to their humiliating demise. Just for clarification purposes, navy ships are expected to have a much longer life cycle. As this chapter is being written, there are currently a considerable number of ships in the US Navy that were commissioned in the late 1960s or early 1970s, thus making their service close to 45 or even 50 years.

For the explanation, we would have to go back to the late nineteenth century and explore what exactly happened during the construction of these vessels. The *Conseils de Travaux*, charged with overseeing the construction, used a very innovative approach to the project in question. Rather than carefully planning the requirements and the resulting design of the battleships, the council apparently decided to say, "Let us start building something, and as we progress through the project, add new and cool features to the scope as soon as we can find them."

Just to illustrate how exactly this methodology was implemented, we can review the transformations the *Magenta* went through—after she was laid down—over the course of 12 (!) years of her creation:

- Initial design: The battleship was designed to possess an armament of three 13.4-inch (large) guns, a top speed of 14.5 knots, and a displacement of 9,800 tons.

Figure 15.1 Battleship *Magenta.*

- First change: Shortly after the ship was laid down, the designers decided that, although having a ship with three large guns was great, installing two large and two smaller (10.8-inch) guns would be even better.
- Second change: The engineers changed their minds again by deciding that it would be better yet if the *Magenta* had four large guns instead of two large and two small ones.
- Third change: By far the best change ever, the project team decided to lengthen and broaden the ship to increase its speed to 16 knots.
- Fourth change: The team decided to add military masts and a conning tower.
- Fifth change: Torpedo nets and searchlights were added.
- Sixth change: A battery of large-caliber machine guns was added to the ship.

What was the end result of this very long project? The *Magenta* ended up with the following attributes:

- It was 300 tons overweight and lost 30% of planned stability (examine Figure 15.1 to see how low the battleship sat in the water).
- The battleship had 60 guns of different calibers (imagine the logistics of transferring all that ammo around the ship during battles).

- It was calculated that if the *Magenta* trained all her guns to one side, she would have capsized and been lost.
- A foreign critic (he was English) described the *Magenta* as "a half-submerged whale with a number of laborer's cottages built on its back."

The lessons of this case study are fairly obvious: Good project results cannot be achieved if the project manager loses control over scope and fails to curb the expectations of the stakeholders.

Expectations Management

About Stakeholder Expectations Management

Before starting the discussion about the tools and techniques available to project managers to control the scope of the projects, we should probably touch upon one of the most intangible domains of project scope management: stakeholder expectations management. There are several reasons why the stakeholders frequently appear illogical and overly optimistic when it comes to their expectations regarding the final project outcomes.

First, they frequently are not aware that the concept of the project automatically implies an introduction of uncertainty and risk. No matter how many times the project team and customers conducted the documentation walk-throughs and inspections, there is always a considerable chance that a certain requirement has been missed, misinterpreted, or documented in the wrong fashion.

Second, there is also a possibility that the perceived state internal or external constraints either have been misconstrued or have changed during the project life cycle. For example, during the renovation project, the team may discover that the kitchen floors are not strong enough to support the new heavy ceramic tiles and need to be strengthened.

Third, stakeholders frequently do not understand fully the complexity of the project or the complexity of the technology used in the project. For example, let us consider the "Airport Check-In Kiosk" project again. Most airline systems nowadays give a customer an option during his check-in to order a kosher, halal, or vegetarian meal. Therefore, it is completely reasonable to expect that an airline ordering a new automated check-in system can request such a feature to be included in the project scope.

It is very likely that the business representatives of the airline, unfamiliar with current technology, could view this feature as a fairly simple procedure: The system asks a traveler if he wants to order a special meal, and if the answer to this question is "yes," then the kiosk should offer him a menu with the three above-mentioned options. The traveler then selects the meal of his choice and the update is sent to the airline catering company. The technology professional's view of this feature is completely different. Here is a partial list of questions that the project team will have to answer to implement the feature in question:

- How many types of kosher, halal, and vegetarian food are available?
- If there is more than one type of food available per category, do we need to show the choices to the traveler?
- How often are the dish selections updated?
- How will the dish selection be maintained?
- Does the catering company have a technology platform to receive the traveler food selection requests?
- If yes, how easy or difficult is it to integrate both?
- What happens if the traveler orders, say, a kosher meal and the catering company does not have any in their inventory?

What this case study demonstrates, as have many other examples in this book, is that the customers usually have a very vague idea about the technical and technological challenges encountered by the project teams when implementing their requirements.

Finally, stakeholders will not always be perfectly logical in their approach to the project problems. For an example of such a phenomenon, let us take a trip outside the world of project management and use an example from daily life.

A friend of mine once signed up for a frequent flyer program with a local airline. The promise made to her in the initial e-mails was that once she achieved a certain mileage per year, she would have access to the airline's and its partners' business lounges at airports around the world. Because she traveled a lot around the entire world on business, she considered the ability to get a normal meal, a comfortable seat, access to free wi-fi, and (who are we kidding?) a glass of wine or two an absolute necessity.

After a year of grueling travel, she finally accumulated, say, 30,000 miles that, according to the airline brochure, would have given her the eligibility to use the airport lounges. On her next trip, after going through the check-in and airport security, she proudly walked into the airline lounge, where she was stopped by the receptionist and the following conversation took place:

Receptionist: Can I please see your frequent flyer card?

Traveler: Yes, sure.

Receptionist: Oh, unfortunately, you are not eligible to use the lounge on this particular flight.

Traveler: Why not?

Receptionist: You have only 30,000 miles on your account, and according to our rules, at this point you would get access to the lounges only if you are flying on our airline.

Traveler: But I am flying on your airline! Here is my flight itinerary.

Receptionist: Yes, but you see, this particular flight is being operated by one of our European partner companies. This makes you ineligible.

Traveler: But here is a brochure that states, "Collect 30,000 miles and you can get access to all our lounges and partner lounges around the world!"

Receptionist: Did you read the fine print at the bottom? It states, "Only when traveling on the flights operated by our company!"

What happened in this particular case, and who is to blame for the misunderstanding that took place? Purely from a legal perspective, the airline was 100% right because it did state unequivocally that the travelers would get access to the lounge only if traveling on the flights operated by their company. The customer was supposed to read the entire document, including the fine print, and form her own conclusions and expectations about her experience at the airport.

However, from a higher, more strategic view, what did the company get as a result of its actions? They got a very displeased customer who had the potential to spend thousands of dollars every year on the flights operated by that particular organization.

Did the airline do a particularly great job of managing the customer's expectations? Probably not, inasmuch as the vast majority of people have a short attention span when it comes to marketing media and tend to ignore the small font at the bottom or on the reverse side of the promotional materials they get. One way of controlling customer or other stakeholder expectations is to include a section entitled "Scope Exclusions" to the project management or requirements documents to state explicitly the features that will be excluded from the project scope. For example, the "Scope Exclusions" section of the project charter for the energy efficient home project may look like this:

Scope Exclusions:
- Landscaping
- Fence around the property
- Car garage

About Scope Changes

Impact of the Changes

As mentioned earlier in this book, any change on the project has at least a three-dimensional impact on the project. The first and most obvious dimension is the sheer size and complexity of the change. The larger the modification requested to be implemented on a project, the more considerable effect it would have on the scope, timing, and the budget of the endeavor.

To illustrate this point, let us return to the "Airport Check-In Kiosk" example discussed multiple times in this book. Imagine that two additional features have been requested by the project clients sometime during the execution stage of the project:

- Feature X.0 Security Questions
- Feature Y.0 Traveler's Visa

The first one simply requires the system to ask the traveler several questions:

- Has anyone given you any packages to take with you?
- Did you pack your luggage yourself?
- Have you ever left your luggage unattended?

The logic accompanying these questions is also fairly straightforward: If the customer answers "Yes" to any of the questions, ask him or her to go directly to the check-in counter and talk to the airline representative.

The second feature is a bit more complicated. We want the system to

1. Understand which country has issued the traveler's passport.
2. Compare the visa requirements for that country's citizens with the traveler's final destination country.
3. If the travel visa is required, the system should ask the traveler if he or she has a visa to that country.
4. If the traveler answers "Yes" to the previous question, the system will ask him or her to scan the visa.
5. After the visa is scanned, the system shall determine its validity and compare the dates on the visa with the dates on the traveler's itinerary.

What potential challenges can the project team encounter when implementing this feature? First, the system should be designed in such a way that it can recognize and read all types of passports of all the countries in the world. There are currently about 200 world countries, each one producing roughly between four and six types of passports. This information implies that the system in question should be "smart" enough to recognize approximately 1,000 types of travel documents that are not standardized and subject to constant design changes.

When it comes to checking for visa requirements, the system should have up-to-date information on the visa requirements for each country for the remaining 200 states. In other words, it implies creating and constantly updating a 200 × 200 table with 40,000 fields. Add to this mix the fact that some countries require certain travelers to obtain transit visas when doing a layover at their airports and the picture gets even more complicated.

Furthermore, how many types of visas can each country issue? For example, the governments of the United States and Canada issue several dozen different types of visas, including Diplomatic, Business Travel, Tourist Travel/Pleasure, Alien in Transit, Air or Ship's Crew, Treaty Trader, or Investor or Student, among others, just to name a few. Based on the information provided, how many types of visas should be in the system so that it can recognize, validate, and read all of them?

We can continue the list of visa-related questions, but it is hoped that it is very obvious now that the feature requesting the visa validation is much more complicated than the one dealing with security questions. As a result, the visa feature will have a much bigger negative impact on the project budget and schedule.

Another fairly obvious aspect of the changes on the project is the frequency with which the customer asks for the changes to be implemented; in other words, the more often the stakeholders ask for changes, the more significant is the impact they have on the key project parameters. To illustrate that point, let us consider the French shipbuilding example mentioned at the very beginning of this chapter. Initially, the French Navy started with a design that included three larger caliber (13.4-inch) guns on their ship. Then, they decided that having two large and two smaller (10.8-inch) guns would be a better idea. And yet sometime later in the course of the project, they changed their minds again by deciding to change the project scope to four large guns and no small guns.

So, the question one needs to ask here is, "What would have had a less significant impact on the project?" Is it the scenario where the stakeholders decided to replace two large guns with four large guns or the one where, as we described above, they decided to go through the two modifications rather than one?

Finally, one of the most underrated dimensions of the project scope changes is the timing of the change. Let us again start with two real-life examples. In both cases, we are looking at the "Mobile Number Portability" project implemented by the government of a country. The project mandated all the mobile services providers to enable the customers to switch freely between the companies while keeping their phone numbers with the original prefixes. The technical scope of the project was well understood from the very beginning; it included certain changes to be implemented by the IT and the network teams.

However, as mentioned earlier in this book, the project also had a major grouping of components that were overlooked initially—namely, the preparation of the call center for the influx of the phone calls from people willing to switch; upgrades to the existing hardware; personnel training; and, most important, the preparation of the new and aggressive sales and marketing campaigns designed to prepare the organization for the so-called mobile number portability wars.

Now, let us consider two scenarios. In the first one, the realization about the major "upgrade" of the scope, including the sales and marketing aspect, happened right at the beginning of the project execution stage, whereas in the second scenario this awareness took place a couple of weeks before the project's "go live" date established by the local ministry of communications.

In which case, do you think, would this aforementioned change be costlier and riskier to implement? Obviously, it would be the second scenario, where the organization would not only have to scramble to implement the sales, marketing, and customer care components of the project, but also have to worry about the potential negative impacts the new features may have on the "old" IT and network-related requirements already implemented.

Furthermore, it should be pointed out that the "cost of mistake" concept described in Chapters 1 and 14 may be fully applied to the lateness of the change assessment (see Figure 1.6). In other words the change that would cost a company $1 to implement at the beginning of the execution stage can potentially balloon into a $1,000 modification at the end of the project.

Another interesting aspect of the potential change impact can be assessed from a purely mathematical standpoint. It is fairly easy to construct a model that would predict the overall impact of continuous scope creep on the overall final scope of the entire project (see Table 15.1).

In this particular table, we look at the following scenarios: What happens on one-, two-, and three-year projects where the monthly scope creep rates are 1%, 3%, 5%, and 7%? The results are mind blowing, to say the least. A monthly 1% growth rate on project requirements will amount to "only" 13%; however, the same rate of growth

Table 15.1 Impact of Scope Creep

RATE OF MONTHLY SCOPE CREEP	1.00%	3.00%	5.00%	7.00%
Overall scope growth on a 12-month project	12.68%	42.58%	79.59%	125.22%
Overall scope growth on a 24-month project	26.97%	103.28%	222.51%	407.24%
Overall scope growth on a 36-month project	43.08%	189.83%	479.18%	1,042.39%

will increase the project scope by 1.5 times on a three-year venture. Furthermore, allowing the project scope to grow at a monthly rate of 5% will increase the overall project scope to grow almost sixfold on a three-year endeavor!

Good versus Bad Changes

Let us face the hard reality: Project managers and their project teams do not like changes. It simply goes against the very nature of the human psyche. As one of the project management professionals told me, "We have just spent endless hours in our war rooms conducting grueling documentation inspections and walk-throughs where we tried very hard to identify the most miniscule deviations from the normal course and potential design flaws. Finally, we all agreed that the requirements document was perfect. Then, I spent another week or so working with my team to develop a schedule based on our scope, and suddenly, a stakeholder walks into our office and claims that an important feature has to be added to the project. … You feel absolutely disheartened by this!"

Unfortunately, project managers have to rise somewhat above the tactical view of their work and take on a more strategic approach to the changes that happen on projects (see Table 15.2). Sometimes, changes happen because the project scope is too large and too complex and the requirements experts simply can't "catch" all the features, requirements, and design components by the end of the planning stage of the project. Customer walk-throughs, technical team inspections, and peer reviews help immensely in this effort but do not provide project stakeholders with a 100% guarantee.

A poorly organized requirements elicitation, analysis, and documentation process will almost inevitably result in overlooked or ambiguous scope elements that would need further clarifications, modifications, and redesign. The only way to address this issue is to have a well-established and developed requirements engineering process at the organization.

There are also inevitable external changes that can affect any project, including shifts in business objectives, new legislation, and technology breakthroughs that can have an adverse effect on the project scope, causing it to grow, shrink, or be altered. There is not much a

Table 15.2 Reasons for Scope Changes

REASONS FOR CHANGE	EXPLANATION/EXAMPLE
The project scope is very large and complex.	The larger and the more complex the project, the higher is the probability of overlooking certain requirements. Example: • Consider the construction of the cargo ship terminal versus the construction of a three-bedroom, two-bathroom family home.
The requirements quality is low (i.e., poorly defined, lots of omissions, and ambiguity).	The requirements elicitation, analysis, and documentation process has not been conducted by the properly trained team of professionals. Example: • The scope of the ERP implementation project has been defined by a team of trained business and systems analysts versus by a team of untrained developers.
There are changes in business objectives and plans.	The project or a grouping of features on the project is no longer necessary due to a change in the business objectives of the company. Example: • A project for a new desktop computer with a floppy disk drive is no longer feasible due to the invention of CD-ROM drives.
There are technology changes.	Competition releases a product or service with new features, and the management of the company feels that their product must also include similar capabilities. Example: • Mobile company A has released a new aggressive data plan service, and mobile company B feels obliged to match the features of the new product.
There are changes in government and other regulatory bodies' laws, policies, and directives.	The government of any given country, as well as any international regulatory body, can implement a new law or policy, thus seriously affecting the scope of the project. Example: • The scope of several marketing and value-added services projects had to be seriously altered after the implementation of the Mobile Number Portability legislation.
Modifications are initiated by the customers and users.	Modifications are initiated by customers and users who either change their minds about things or learn new "cool" ways of doing things. Examples: • Midway through the project, the customer realizes that a house with a pool, a tennis court, and a four-car garage will better suit her needs than a house without all these features.

project manager can do in such situations but accept such changes while remembering to assess their impacts on the project timeline, budget, resource requirements, and risks.

Finally, there is the problem of the customers constantly changing their minds about what they want. Usually, the root cause of this problem is hidden in the lack of client involvement during the requirements elicitation phases of the project. In addition, educating the stakeholders that late additions to the project scope will most likely have an adverse impact on other corners of the project management triangle is also a useful approach in such situations.

Controlling and Managing Project Scope

What Is the Best Practices Approach?

Almost all the project management approaches agree on the following universal procedure for change implementation on a project (see Figure 10.5). First, at the end of the planning stage, the project team should baseline the requirements documentation and the project plan. It is important to point out that the word "baseline" is not synonymous with the word "finalize." This difference should also be explained to all the project stakeholders. "Finalized" implies that the documents are frozen and are not subject to changes, whereas "baselined" means that whatever commitments the team made with respect to the project timing and budget are fixed as long as the scope described in the requirements documentation remains unchanged. If the scope changes, then the other two corners of the project management triangle will most likely have to be modified.

The next step includes the formal acceptance of a written change request from the project stakeholder willing to initiate the change (more about change requests in the next section of this chapter). The change request should be reviewed by the project team to assess its impacts on the budget, duration, and resource requirements of the project. The team should also examine potential conflicts with other requirements and design components as well as the risks introduced by the proposed modification. The detailed evaluation process is described in the section "Assessing the Impacts of the Requested Change" in this chapter.

The team then should get back to the change requester, and possibly the change committee, to present their findings. At this point, the key question that must be asked should look something like this:

> We assessed the requested change, and we think that it will add X months to the project duration and Y dollars to the project budget and will require Z units of additional resources. Furthermore, due to the technical design of the product, the request will introduce risks A, B, and C. Do you still want to proceed with the change?

If the change is approved, the key project documents, including the requirements specifications, the detailed design document, and the project plan, should be updated accordingly, and the team should start working on the updated scope. If, on the other hand, the change does not receive the blessing of the senior stakeholders, the change request should be properly documented and posted with all the other project documentation. The time, money, and person-hours spent on the assessment of the change request should be incorporated into the project plan.

Utilizing Change Requests

There are a multitude of change request versions used by project management professionals in various industries across the world. What we decided to demonstrate here is a universal document that can be made more or less complicated depending on the intricacy of the project in which the project management professional is involved (see Table 15.3).

The change request can be roughly divided into three parts. The first part is supposed to be filled out by the change requester himself; it is strongly recommended that all project managers strictly enforce this practice. The main reason for this is very simple. Let us start with a very basic example of a typical conversation between the change initiator (CI) and the project manager (PM) that takes place when the change is instigated on the project:

CI: Hi, I have been talking to John in Sales, who just returned from the industry expo, and he told me that our competition has introduced this (probably very complex and not very essential) feature to their product.

Table 15.3   Change Request Template

Project:	*<Name>*
Week Ending:	*<DD-MM-YYYY >*
Distribution:	*<List all the recipients of the Change Request.>*
Prepared By:	*<Insert Preparer's name here.>*
Change Request Name:	*<Provide a short name for the Change Request.>*
Change Request Number:	*<Start at 001.>*

PART A—TO BE FILLED OUT BY THE SUBMITTER

Submitter:	*<Insert Requester's name and title.>*	Type of Change:	*<Scope: Correction or Enhancement, Budget, Time, Other>*
Date of Submission:	*<Insert the date of submission.>*	Recommended Priority:	*<High/Medium/Low>*
Description of Proposed Change:	*<Describe proposed change in detail. If necessary, refer to additional documentation.>*		
Reason for Proposed Change:	*<Describe the reason for proposed change in detail. If necessary, refer to additional documentation.>*		

PART B—TO BE FILLED OUT BY THE PROJECT MANAGER AND THE PROJECT TEAM/THIRD-PARTY CONTRACTORS

Estimated Impact on Schedule:	*<Describe potential estimated impact on schedule.>*
Estimated Impact on Budget:	*<Describe potential estimated impact on project cost.>*
Other Impacts:	*<Describe other potential impacts on quality, risks, etc.>*
Submitter's Resolution:	*<Approved/Rejected/Escalated to the appropriate signing authority>*
Signing Authority's Resolution:	*<If applicable. Refer to appropriate company documentation, if necessary, e.g., "Submissions A, B, C, or D.">*

PART C—SIGN-OFFS

Name and Title:	Project Role	Signature

PM: We have baselined our requirements document and the project plan several weeks ago, and the team is already working on the implementation. So, I will be sending a change request template your way.

CI: Why?

PM: Well, you think that the addition of this feature will benefit the final product greatly. Therefore, it would be logical if you describe these perceived benefits so that we can present them to the Change Committee. Don't worry, you will need only to describe the change in as much detail as possible and provide the reasons for this modification. It shouldn't take more than 30 minutes.

CI: OK, I will give it a try.

PM: If you encounter any problems with the document, give me a shout. I will gladly help you out! I will also include a couple of sample change requests from our past projects as a reference.

Interestingly enough, in many cases the project manager never hears from the change requester again after the above-mentioned conversation. Why does this happen? The economists would explain this phenomenon in the following terms: The total utility of implementing the change was lower than the cost of the 30-minute effort to fill out the change request. In other words, "This is a very important modification that can make or break the overall project success, but unfortunately it is not worth even half an hour of my time."

This approach, where the project manager has the right to insist that the change request is filled out and submitted by the change requester, acts as a very powerful filtering mechanism against the frivolous and arbitrary modifications of the project scope.

So, returning to the change request template, what is the key information that should be included by the submitter in the first part? There is certain administrative information that should be provided that includes the project name, the date, the name of the submitter, and the proposed title for the change request. However, the most important sections are

- Description of Proposed Change
- Reason for Proposed Change

In the first part, the submitter must provide at least a high-level description of the new feature. For example, on a project involving the design of a new baby bottle, she may add something to the effect of the following:

Feature X.0—No-spill capability: The baby bottle shall not spill any liquid, even if turned 180 degrees.

The description of the benefits of such an enhancement could look something like this:

> Our sales team reports that up to 80% of the baby bottles sold in the market have a no-spill capability. Therefore, adding this feature can increase our sales by up to 50%.

The second part of the change request is filled out by the project manager after careful consultations with his team. The main question that needs to be answered here is, "How much (in terms of money, resources, time, and additional) will this modification cost the organization?"

And finally, the third part contains the final resolution, a "go" or "no-go" decision, made either by the submitter or a change committee. The main question that needs to be answered here is, "Is the value of implementing the proposed change—adjusted for the resource, timing, and financial costs—higher or lower than the cost of not carrying it out?"

Assessing the Impacts of the Requested Change

As mentioned earlier, one of the most cumbersome parts of the change process is the assessment of the potential impacts of the requested modification of the project scope. It is useful to divide these impacts into three broad categories (see Table 15.4):

- Technical or scope impacts
- Resources, timing, and financial impacts
- Other impacts or risks

It is also very important to point out that the project managers and all the stakeholders should differentiate between the costs incurred to assess the change and the costs incurred as a result of the change implementation. All the project stakeholders, including external customers and executive management, should be educated that a change request, even if not implemented, consumes resources and may have a negative impact on the project timelines and budgets.

Updates to the Documentation

Again, the project documentation, especially the key documents such as the project requirements document, detailed design document, and the project plan, must always be kept updated when changes happen on the project. The project manager should implement and maintain the version control of the documentation. For example, before the document has been signed-off (baselined, approved, etc.),

Table 15.4 Assessing Impact of Change

TYPE OF QUESTIONS	SPECIFIC QUESTIONS
What are the technical (scope) impacts?	• What are the new requirements resulting from this change? • Will this change introduce any conflicts with other features or requirements? • What are the impacts on the requirements documentation, design documentation, blueprints, bills of materials, technical drawings, and so on? • What other documents will have to be updated?
What are the impacts on the project resources, timeline, and budget?	• What is the resource investment (measured in person-hours) in terms of technical work to be done by engineers, construction crew, developers, architects, and the like required to assess the change? • What is the duration of the work needed to assess the change in terms of technical work to be done by engineers, construction crew, developers, architects, and so on? • What is the additional budget required to assess the change? • How many person-hours would the project manager have to spend to assess and implement the change? • What project management documents will have to be updated or created (Project Plan, Change Request, etc.)? • How many person-hours of the customer's or stakeholder's time will have to be invested in the meetings one needs to conduct? • How will the change affect the sequence, dependencies, effort, and duration of all the tasks in the Project Plan?
Other impacts	• Is the requested change feasible with all known constraints and staff skills? • Will the change affect any indirect areas such as marketing, public relations, customer support, training, and the like? • What is the impact of the change on all other areas of project management, including quality, communications, and so on? • What are the risks introduced by this change?

the manager should assign version numbers in the following format 0.N:

- Version 0.1
- Version 0.2
- Version 0.3
- ...

Once the document has been signed-off or approved, he can switch the numbering system to 1.N:

- Version 1.0
- Version 1.1
- Version 1.2
- ...

In both cases, the version number increases by 0.1 every time the document owner makes a change. This helps a lot in avoiding confusion with various versions of the same document existing in various forms, such as attachments to old e-mails, documents saved on peoples' computers, hardcopies lying around on employee desks, and so on. This numbering system should be clearly communicated to all project team members and stakeholders, as well as the importance of verifying which version each party is looking at during communications with one another.

The project manager shouldn't assume that all stakeholders regularly check the project documentation folder on the shared drive and are aware of all the changes and updates made to documents. Therefore, it would typically be a good idea to send a broadcast e-mail to all the relevant parties every time any of the key project documents get updated. For example:

> Please note that the Requirements document for the Energy Efficient Home project has been updated. Requirements R 1.7, R 1.8, and R 1.9 have been added to Feature 1.0—West Coast Style (see Table 15.5).
> **Note:** At least six of the above nine requirements must be satisfied. The latest version of the Requirements document is now version 1.23.

Table 15.5 Reasons for Scope Changes

FEATURE ID	REQ ID	REQUIREMENT DESCRIPTION	PRIORITY
F 1.0	R 1.1	Post and beam construction	*See note below*
	R 1.2	Exposed timber structural members	
	R 1.3	Extensive glazing and skylights	
	R 1.4	Open floor plans	
	R 1.5	Integration of interior and exterior spaces	
	R 1.6	Wood finishes on both interior and exterior (stained)	
	R 1.7	Flat or minimally canted roofs	
	R 1.8	Orientation to views or natural features	
	R 1.9	Integrated with natural setting, extensive use of native trees and landscaping	

Note: At least six of the above nine requirements must be satisfied.

Chapter Summary

We started this chapter with an in-depth discussion of the stakeholder expectations management topic, where we examined the reasons to handle and direct actively the expectations of both internal and external project clients. Scope changes, although small and imperceptible at first glance, can quickly accumulate if left untreated and have a significant impact on the overall project scope, resulting in budget and time overruns.

Furthermore, the project managers should realize that not all changes are necessarily bad; sometimes the change is needed from a strategic point of view to make the product or service more competitive in the market. Having said that, there are a lot of instances where proposed changes constitute the proverbial "bells and whistles" that do not really add any value to the project but consume a lot of team resources.

The only way to control scope creep on projects is to institute a proper change control process that includes change request documents. These documents generally consist of three parts: the section about the nature and value of the proposed change filled out by the change initiator, the section where the project team describes all potential impacts of the proposed change, and the section where the change requester of the change committee records its "go" or "no-go" decision.

When assessing the impact of the change, the project team must keep in mind all the possible effects, including the impacts on other requirements, schedule, budget, human resource requirements, documentation, and other potential risks.

References and Additional Reading

Allen, D. *Economic Principles: Seven Ideas for Thinking ... About Almost Anything.* Boston: Pearson Custom, 2010.

Berkun, S. *The Art of Project Management.* Sebastopol, CA: O'Reilly, 2005.

Boehm, B. *Software Engineering Economics.* Englewood Cliffs, NJ: Prentice-Hall, 1981.

Bortolon, L. *The Life and Times of Leonardo.* Philadelphia: Curtis, 1967.

Brøgger, A.W. *The Viking Ships, Their Ancestry and Evolution.* Oslo: Dreyer, 1951.

Brøgger, A.W. and Shetelig, H. *The Viking Ships.* New York: Twayne, 1971.

Bustos, L. *10 Bizarre Things That Influence Customers Online.* Get Elastic Blog (October, 2011): http://www.getelastic.com/10-bizarre-things-that-influence-customers-online/

Capra, F. *The Science of Leonardo: Inside the Mind of the Genius of the Renaissance.* New York: Doubleday, 2007.

Ceccarelli, M. *Distinguished Figures in Mechanism and Machine Science: Their Contributions and Legacies.* New York: Springer, 2007.

Claridge, A. *Rome: An Oxford Archaeological Guide*, 1st ed. Oxford, UK: Oxford University Press, 1998.

Cross, N. *Engineering Design Methods: Strategies for Product Design*, 4th ed. New York: Wiley, 2008.

Dym, C.L. and Little, P. *Engineering Design: A Project Based Introduction.* New York: John Wiley & Sons, 2008.

Fitzhugh, W. and Ward, E. *Vikings: The North Atlantic Saga.* Washington, DC: Smithsonian Institution Press, 2000.

Gause, D.C. and Weinberg, G.M. *Exploring Requirements: Quality Before Design.* New York: Dorset House, 1989.

Gottesdiener, E. *Requirements by Collaboration: Workshops for Defining Needs.* Reading, MA: Addison-Wesley Professional, 2002.

Haig, M. *Brand Failures: The Truth About the 100 Biggest Branding Mistakes of All Time.* Philadelphia: Kogan Page, 2003.

Hayes, J.R. *The Genius of Arab Civilization: Source of Renaissance,* 2nd ed. Cambridge, MA: MIT Press, 1983.

Hooks, I. *Managing Requirements: Issues in NASA Program and Project Management.* NASA SP- 6101 (08), 1995.

Irvine, G. *Japanese Sword: Soul of the Samurai.* Boston: Weatherhill, 2000.

Jones, S. *Estimating Software Costs: Bringing Realism to Estimating.* New York: McGraw-Hill Osborne Media, 2007.

Kim, S. *Essence of Creativity: A Guide to Tackling Difficult Problems.* New York: Oxford University Press, 1990.

Kroll, E., Condoor, S.S., and Jansson, D.G. *Innovative Conceptual Design: Theory and Application of Parameter Analysis.* Cambridge, UK: Cambridge University Press, 2001.

Lehner, M. *The Complete Pyramids.* London: Thames and Hudson, 1997.

Mackay, C. *Extraordinary Popular Delusions and the Madness of Crowds.* Petersfield, UK: Harriman House Classics, 2003.

McConnell, S. *Software Estimation: Demystifying the Black Art.* Redmond, WA: Microsoft Press, 2006.

More, C. *Understanding the Industrial Revolution.* London: Routledge, 2000.

Olson, J.S. *Encyclopedia of the Industrial Revolution in America.* Westport, CT: Greenwood, 2001.

Project Management Institute®. *A Guide to the Project Management Body of Knowledge.* Newtown Square, PA: Project Management Institute, 2001.

Regan, G. *Brassey's Book of Naval Blunders.* Dulles, VA: Potomac Books, 2000.

Robertson, S. and Robertson, J.C. *Mastering the Requirements Process.* Reading, MA: Addison-Wesley Professional, 2006.

Romer, J. *The Great Pyramid: Ancient Egypt Revisited.* Cambridge, UK: Cambridge University Press, 2007.

Roth, L.M. *Understanding Architecture: Its Elements, History and Meaning,* 1st ed. Boulder, CO: Westview Press, 1993.

Smith, C.S. *A History of Metallography: The Development of Ideas on the Structure of Metals before 1890.* Cambridge, MA: MIT Press, 1988.

Standish Group. *CHAOS Report 1994.* Boston: Standish Group International, 1994.

Standish Group. *CHAOS Report 1996.* Boston: Standish Group International, 1996.

Standish Group. *CHAOS Report 1998.* Boston: Standish Group International, 1998.

Standish Group. *CHAOS Report 2000.* Boston: Standish Group International, 2000.

Standish Group. *CHAOS Report 2002.* Boston: Standish Group International, 2002.

Standish Group. *CHAOS Report 2004.* Boston: Standish Group International, 2004.

Standish Group. *CHAOS Report 2006*. Boston: Standish Group International, 2006.

Standish Group. *CHAOS Report 2009*. Boston: Standish Group International, 2009.

Suvorov, V. and Beattie, T. *Icebreaker: Who Started the Second World War?* New York: Viking Press, 1990.

Verner, M. *The Pyramids—Their Archaeology and History*. London: Atlantic Books, 2001.

Vladimirov, V. and Volny, O. *Yedinozhdy Prinyav Prisyagu*, Donetsk, USSR: Molodaya Gvardia, 1990.

von Hippel, E. *The Sources of Innovation*. Oxford, UK: Oxford University Press, 1985.

Walker, K.M. *Applied Mechanics for Engineering Technology*, 8th ed. Englewood Cliffs, NJ: Prentice-Hall, 2007.

Wiegers, K.E. *Software Requirements*, 2nd ed. Redmond, WA: Microsoft Press, 2003.

Young, R.R. *Effective Requirements Practices*. Reading, MA: Addison-Wesley Professional, 2001.

Index

Printed in the United States
by Baker & Taylor Publisher Services